Katharine and Isabel

Katharine and Isabel

Mother's Light, Daughter's Journey

Frances Wright Saunders

Consulting Psychologists Press, Inc.

PALO ALTO, CALIFORNIA

Project Director: Lee Langhammer Law
Associate Editor: Kathleen Hummel
Director Print Production: Laura Ackerman-Shaw
Production Artist: Francie Curtiss
Design: MaryEllen Podgorski
Manufacturing: Gloria Forbes

Library of Congress Cataloging-in-Publication Data
Saunders, Frances Wright, 1920-
    Katharine and Isabel: mother's light, daughter's journey /
Frances Wright Saunders.
        p.   cm.
    Includes bibliographical references and index.
    ISBN 0-89106-049-9
    1. Myers, Isabel Briggs. 2. Briggs, Katharine Cook. 3. Psychologists--
United States--Biography. 4. Myers-Briggs Type Indicator. I. Title.
BF109.M495S28 1991
155.2'83--dc20
[B]   91-18194
                                                                   CIP

Printed in the United States of America

To David, with appreciation,
and for Brett and Bradley, with hope

Contents

Part Four

Part Five

Preface

One day in the spring of 1957, when our sons were very young, my husband, David Saunders, then in the research division at Educational Testing Service, unexpectedly brought a guest home for lunch. Surprises of this sort from David (INTP) were not unusual, but on this particular occasion, near the end of the week, my cupboard was bare except for tuna fish, peanut butter, and graham crackers. The possibilities for a luncheon menu were not promising for the guest, a middle-aged woman with greying hair, plainly dressed, and reputed to be an intellectual giant. Her name was Isabel Briggs Myers, who with her mother, Katharine Cook Briggs, had developed a personality sorting instrument known then as the *Briggs-Myers Type Indicator,* in which Educational Testing Service was interested.

I remember my utter embarrassment at bringing out to the patio three plates loaded with tuna fish salad, some canned fruit, and triangles of cinnamon toast. I also remember how Isabel, as David called her, ate heartily while assuring me that this was her favorite food.

It may have been the next year when Isabel again visited in our home briefly, accompanied by Katharine Briggs, who I can still see as a petite, frail, white-haired woman wearing very thick glasses. I later learned that Katharine was eighty-four years old.

The memories faded, nearly thirty years passed, and in January of 1980, David and I were in Isabel's home at 321 Dickinson Avenue, in Swarthmore, Pennsylvania. No longer at Educational Testing Service, David had been invited to talk with Isabel and her son, Peter, about needed research on the (now) *Myers-Briggs Type Indicator.*® Not a psychologist, I was a silent presence as the discussion continued for several hours during which I observed with considerable awe the mental stamina of this woman, who was obviously in pain from the illness that would soon take her life. It certainly never occurred to me that one day I would be her biographer.

Two years later, I met Isabel's husband, Clarence Gates "Chief" Myers, who had come to Princeton with Peter. Then a man in his mid-eighties, Chief stood tall and straight and, despite his limited energy and deafness, was disarmingly charming.

These brief encounters with Isabel, Katherine, and Chief eased Peter Myers' task of persuading me to write about his mother and, inevitably, his grandmother and father. However, in June 1987, when Peter brought thirty-odd boxes of family papers to our home, my first reaction was to forget it. But unfailing curiosity led me on. I soon discovered rich contents that told the story of the loves, pains, successes, tragedies, restlessness, and determination of three generations of a remarkable family and their friends.

Katharine Cook Briggs and Isabel Briggs Myers preserved family correspondence, records, and miscellaneous writings that told most of their story. These materials spell out many events, some of which became intertwined with legend. Isabel Myers herself contributed to some of these legends in her later life, when her memory was less than impeccable. Were she given the opportunity, she would surely be the first to say, Tell the truth. This is what I have tried to do.

To all those persons who shared their thoughts and memories so willingly, I am most grateful. In particular, I would like to thank Isabel's grandchildren, Kathleen and Douglas Hughes and Jennifer and Jonathan Myers; her former son-in-law, Jim Hughes, always generous with his time and with his enriching memories, even when they surely caused him some pain; Betty Monk Myers Devlin; Katharine Downing Heisler Myers; and lastly, Peter Myers himself, without whose perceptive guidance and gentle candidness this biography could not have been written.

It was my pleasure and good fortune to be able to talk with four of Isabel's surviving classmates who were a part of that outstanding group at Swarthmore College known as "the Awful Ate"—Jane Brown Gemmill, Katherine Fahnestock Miller, Phyllis Komori Sellers, and Eleanor Atkinson Smith—all women now in their nineties and all with crystal clear minds. In 1986, Eleanor Smith wrote an invaluable 32-page memoir about Isabel Myers and the Swarthmore years. Another helpful Swarthmorean was Eleanor Stabler Clarke, a long-time member of the Board of Managers of Swarthmore College.

Mary McCaulley, director of the Center for Applications of Psychological Type (CAPT) in Gainesville, Florida, was heroic in providing memories and a lode of valuable material from her personal files. She and the staff at CAPT were unfailingly gracious in responding to frequent telephone queries at almost any time of the day or night. McCaulley also arranged interviews with the following persons who had known or worked with Isabel: Jamelyn DeLong, Brad Fisher, Ruth Lewis, L.J. McCaulley, Maggie Morgan, Bernard Murphy, Laura Newman, Margaret Thompson, Carol W. Walker, and Ruth Williams.

Others who have contributed in special ways are Scarvia Anderson, Miriam Bryan, Rae Carlson, Henry Chauncey, William Coffman, Lois Crooks, Junius Davis, Anna Dragositz, Henry Dyer, Alice and Thomas Hilton, Martin Katz, Fred Kling, Winton Manning, Donald Melville, John Ross, Robert Solomon, and Elizabeth Smith, all formerly or currently with Educational Testing Service; Alice Pennell Allen, Eleanor Barberousse, Carl Bereiter, Tom Carskaden, Richard Cordray, Kenneth Craik, Jacob Goering, M.D., Edward, Sally, and Scott Golden and the staff at Organizational Renewal Associates, Harrison Gough, Harold Grant, Ann and Arthur Hall, Wallace Hall, John Harker, Peter Jung, M.D., Gordon Lawrence, Lisa McGaw, William McGuire, Gerald Mendlesohn, George Moulthrop, Frances Murkse, Carl Rollyson, Eric, Jon, and Vivien Saunders, June Allman Thomas, Avril Thorne, and Cecil Williams. Two very small people, Brett and Bradley Saunders, deserve mention, for without them this biography might have been finished sooner, but not nearly so pleasantly.

No researcher can function without dedicated archivists who know where to lead and what to share. One of these, Gary Saretzky, archivist at Educational Testing Service, is due unending gratitude for the excellence of his archives and his graciousness in fulfilling numerous requests as I pieced together the story of Isabel Myers and her nineteen-year association with that organization. Carla Kemp, University Archivist, and Janice Atkinson generously allowed access to the professional papers of Isabel Myers while they were still being cataloged in the University of Florida Library.

Other libraries and their staffs that provided helpful information are American Association of Medical Colleges; Claremont College; the Labor, Management and Documentation Center, M.P. Catherwood Library, Cornell University; Cornell University alumni archives and the Cornell University Medical School; ETH-Bibliothek, Zurich, Switzerland; Harvard University and the Harvard Medical School; Health Sciences Library, the University of North Carolina; the Johns

Hopkins University; Michigan State University; Middlebury College; Oberlin College; Pomona College; Princeton University and Princeton University Press; Swarthmore College; and Temple University.

Consulting Psychologists Press (CPP) and its supportive staff have helped in numerous ways, and to Lee Langhammer Law, the editor with whom I have worked, goes an abundance of unique thanks that only long-suffering editors are due. Jack Black, the founder of CPP, shared its history, his own personal files, and his inimitable memories of Isabel Myers.

Takeshi Ohsawa, now president of the Human Resources Institute, Tokyo, who was one of the first professional users of the MBTI, provided an account of his meeting Isabel Myers and of the application of the Indicator by his company.

And finally, in this enlightened age when husbands no longer thank their patient wives for typing many drafts of a manuscript, I owe endless gratitude to my husband, David Saunders, who taught me to use a word processor and persevered even when I resisted. He provided invaluable information about the early years of Educational Testing Service, Isabel Myers, and the *Myers-Briggs Type Indicator,* and tutored me in the complexities of the Indicator itself. Although he has insisted that a woman's biography should not be dedicated to a man, his quiet professional counsel has surely transcended the "rules" of gender.

Frances W. Saunders
June 1991

Part One

CHAPTER ONE

*Advice
From Katharine*

*I*n early 1942, when the United States had, for a
month, been an active belligerent in World War II, Isabel Briggs Myers
sat down at her desk in Swarthmore, Pennsylvania, to write an
important letter. She was forty-four years old. A housewife and mother
of two children, both sophomores in high school, she wanted to do
something that would make a significant contribution to the war
effort—something more than she could do as an aircraft spotter for the
Civil Air Defense, or as a volunteer with the Red Cross blood donor
program or with the housing program for European refugee children.
She had worked with all these causes, which she considered generally
worthy, but none of them completely satisfied her, nor did they
challenge her intellectual capabilities.

The letter was to her mother, Katharine Cook Briggs, of Washington, D.C., with whom Isabel habitually shared her thoughts and
from whom she often sought advice. Dated January 8, 1942, the letter
marked a turning point in Isabel's life that would, in due course, affect
the lives of millions of people and make her name notable in the field
of psychological testing. An honors graduate from Swarthmore College, class of 1919, she had taken not a single course in psychology or
statistics. These academic omissions might deter someone who had had
a more orthodox education, or someone less excited than Isabel Myers
by a promising idea.

The idea, she wrote Katharine, came after reading in the latest
Reader's Digest (she would later remember it as from the *New Republic*)
an article entitled "Fitting the Worker to the Job," and it struck her as
"having extraordinarily interesting potentialities."[1] The article was about

the use of a "people sorting" instrument, the *Humm-Wadsworth Temperament Scale,* "a device to place the worker in the proper niche, keep him happy, and increase production."[2] If she could find a way to acquire some experience with the *Humm-Wadsworth,* this could enable her to be useful in the "enormous job of reallocating people" to suitable jobs, a move "in prospect" both then and after the war was over.

Isabel also wrote Katharine that she had already determined that three companies in Philadelphia used the instrument. At one of them, the Pennsylvania Company for Banking and Trusts, a large and highly reputable company founded in 1812, the personnel officer was Edward Northrup Hay, who lived in Swarthmore, and whose son, Steven, was a high school classmate of Isabel's children.[3]

Because she thought that Hay could provide her with the kind of creative work she wanted to do, Isabel Myers did not hesitate to approach him. She learned that for some time he had wanted to validate the *Humm-Wadsworth.* This meant that a competent person would examine the employees' on-the-job performance and compare this performance to the employees' scores on the scale. It was a task that Isabel knew she could handle, and she volunteered to do the work for Hay without pay. A man who appreciated an "idea person," Hay nevertheless advised Isabel "to think over her decision for a week." At the end of the week, Isabel was undeterred. She wrote Hay that her "interest in the *Humm-Wadsworth Temperament Scale* was undiminished," and she discovered "a growing fascination in other tests and other possibilities.... As to the problem of where I shall eventually work, I am content to leave that on the knees of the gods." Meanwhile, she would "greatly appreciate the privilege" of working under Hay's direction.[4]

Another important consideration was that her idea had the unqualified support not only of her mother, but of her husband, Clarence , an attorney (who, nevertheless, warned her that a training period was a long way from war work!) and her father, Lyman Briggs, a distinguished physicist who was head of the National Bureau of Standards. She was also certain that she could fit her schedule of work "inside the children's school hours."[5]

Hay took her on. He estimated that the project would require six months, working a thirty-hour week, and despite her willingness to contribute her time, he placed her on the payroll at forty dollars a week. She considered this an unexpected bonus, for money had never been and never would be her primary goal. The task, Isabel reasoned, would amount to "an unequaled cram course in personnel work, with unlimited material to work on"; moreover, she thought that she would make "a pretty competent personnel person at the end of it." Even so, she confessed a concern to Katharine Briggs that her acquired skills might not be marketable.[6]

Isabel began her studies at the Pennsylvania Company by rescoring all of the *Humm-Wadsworth* scales for several hundred employees. Hay had taught her how to score, and by July of 1942, considered her qualified to administer and interpret the test. But when she analyzed the collection of data, she found that the results were "not useful."[7]

Somewhat surprised, she talked the matter over with Katharine Briggs, who thought that there should be a test developed on *type,* that is, on particular kinds of personalities and how these variations affect the relations of people to the world about them.[8] An avid reader all her life, Katharine had long immersed herself in books and articles on character analysis, a skill she had intended to use in fiction writing. Instead, her studies eventually became the theoretical basis for the development of her ideas on type.

By late 1943, with confidence in the rightness and timeliness of developing an effective people-sorting instrument, Isabel had completed the first version of what would eventually be known as the *Myers-Briggs Type Indicator.* Over a period of three decades, the project would progress from Isabel's dining room table, to a cottage industry, to the auspices of Educational Testing Service, to Consulting Psychologists Press, its current publisher. In due course, the Indicator would become internationally known and would be translated into sixteen different languages.

Before 1942, Isabel's life, and to a large extent, her mother's, were years of preparation. Each woman had had a driving ambition to become a successful writer—and Isabel almost made it. Katharine, who worked longer and harder at authorship, finally gave up when she was surpassed by her daughter's achievements. After 1942, as Isabel focused more and more on the Indicator, she faced tragedies in her personal life that might have demoralized a less determined woman. At times, the fortunes of the Indicator were erratic and discouraging, yet she never gave up on the idea whose "time had come."[9]

However, the story of the *Myers-Briggs Type Indicator* did not begin in 1942 with Isabel's resolve to make an effective contribution to the war effort. More precisely, it begins with Katharine Cook and Lyman Briggs, two remarkable parents who rejected the Victorian belief that if a woman developed her mind, then her reproductive capacity would be irrevocably impaired. Devising their own unique system for educating their daughter, they were ahead of their time in this and in other ways of child rearing.

The atypical education of Isabel Briggs was made possible because her parents were themselves atypical of the norm in the late nineteenth century. Katharine Elizabeth Cook, born in East Lansing, Michigan, on January 3, 1875, was the daughter of Mary [Harris] Baldwin and Albert John Cook, professor of zoology and entomology at Michigan Agricultural College (now Michigan State University), and curator of the college's museum. Mary Baldwin came from a family among whom were physicians and distinguished educators, including four college presidents.[10]

Katharine's father, a graduate of Michigan Agricultural College, had also studied for a year at the Harvard Medical School.[11] As a professor of biology, he was immediately involved in the controversy on evolution that raged in academic circles in the last quarter of the nineteenth century. A strong and forthright person, he taught the theory of evolution to his students for some twenty years. Although he was not blind to the possible ill effects this might have on religiously orthodox students and friends, Professor Cook, nevertheless, was a scientific man who thought truth more beneficial than illusion. Since both religion and science sought for truths, he believed the two could progress without destroying the religious values in which he, too, believed.[12]

Along with other faculty children, Katharine began her education at home, where faculty parents, according to their training, taught different subjects. At age thirteen, Katharine began to take courses at the college, and in the fall of 1889, she was one of nine women in a freshman class that included ninety-three men, one of whom was Lyman James Briggs.

Born on May 7, 1874, on a farm near Battle Creek, Michigan, Lyman Briggs' roots went back to a settler of the Plymouth Colony. His grandfather, George Lyman Briggs, migrated from western New York to Michigan before the Civil War, and his father, Chauncey Lewis Briggs, attended Olivet College until military service in the Union army disrupted his education. Chauncey subsequently sent his son, at age fifteen, from the Briggs School, a public school that did not include high school, to the Michigan Agricultural College (MAC). Lyman was the first in his family to earn a college education.

In the 1880s, students entering MAC were offered a choice of two majors: agriculture and mechanical arts. Katharine and Lyman both enrolled in agriculture, a program that offered the same courses to female and male students. The men, however, worked on the college farm, while the women worked closer to the central buildings in the gardens of the horticulture department.[13]

Katharine's grades matched Lyman's point for point in most of their classes (both got 100 on their freshman geometry exams) until it came to mechanics, physics, and trigonometry, where he surged ahead with almost perfect scores. In their senior year, Katherine took geology, logic, and a new subject called "psychology," while Lyman enrolled in veterinary studies, chemical physics, and civil engineering. By modern standards, both were "A" students, he ranking first and she a close second, in the class of 1893.[14] Lyman then enrolled at the University of Michigan in Ann Arbor, where, in 1895, he took a master of science degree in physics. Now altogether committed to a career in physics that would eventually lead to his appointment as head of the National Bureau of Standards, he applied for admission to graduate school at the Johns Hopkins University in Baltimore. Just as he had largely done at MAC, Lyman planned to work his way through graduate school, but help came through his growing relationship with Katharine.

In the fall of 1893, several months after Katherine's graduation, Katharine and her parents had moved to Claremont, California, where Albert J. Cook became a professor of biology at Pomona College. The president of Pomona was Cyrus G. Baldwin, Katharine's maternal uncle.

No correspondence survives between Katharine and Lyman during the years of 1893 to 1895, two crucial years of separation; however, in the summer of 1895, Katharine took the train back to Michigan to visit her brother, Albert "Bert" Baldwin Cook and, for a more important reason, to see Lyman again. There is no record of when Katharine and Lyman became formally engaged, but it was surely at this time. By late July, Mary Cook wrote to her daughter: "Papa and I talked it over and concluded we could see our way to help Lyman to the means to go to Johns Hopkins. It seems the best thing for him to do [and]...he must have the best." And then follows a surprising statement for a parent of a daughter to make in 1895: "And if *you could* have done it, it would have been the same for you." But now, Mary Cook wrote to Katharine, they felt the same toward Lyman, and "in helping him, we can feel that we are doing for him and for you at the same time."[15] Later in the summer, she wrote to ask Katharine to be sure and tell them "when and where Lyman wants that first $200 sent."[16]

Judging from their letters, Katharine's parents were enlightened people who freely gave their love as well as provided cultural enrichment. According to family history, Katharine probably did not continue her education due to her inordinately poor eyesight, which made studying laborious.[17] The earliest known photographs of her show a young woman wearing "granny" glasses that made her look studious and serious. The glasses, however, did not discourage the handsome Lyman from his pursuit of her.

Although Mary Cook expected frequent letters when Katharine traveled, she urged her daughter to enjoy her time away from home. "I can't be thankful enough," Mary wrote, "that you have had this lovely summer and I am sure we shall never regret it. It has been a constant joy to me, and to Papa too, to know that you were having a good time. You are such a dear girl and are so much to us, that your pleasure gives a warmer glow to our hearts than pleasures purely our own."[18]

After a visit to relatives in Ohio (her uncle, James F. Baldwin, was a physician in Columbus, and her great-uncle, James Harris Fairchild, was president of Oberlin College), Katharine returned in late September to Claremont where, after a year of training in kindergarten work, she began to teach preschool children.[19] How long she taught is not known, but later in that academic year, she nursed her terminally ill mother, who died in April 1896.

It was not until December of that year that Katharine, age twenty-one, and Lyman, age twenty-two, were married quietly at her father's home in a ceremony performed by the Rev. William H. McDougal, pastor of the Claremont Congregational Church.[20] They left immediately for Washington, D.C., where Lyman had taken a job in the Bureau of Soils in the U.S. Department of Agriculture. After three semesters of study at Hopkins, where he had worked with Professor Henry A. Rowland on the newly discovered X rays (roentgen rays), Lyman completed his doctoral dissertation while employed at the Bureau of Soils. In 1900, Hopkins appointed him a "Fellow by Courtesy," which gave him access to the university facilities until he received his Ph.D. in June of 1901.[21]

On October 18, 1897, Isabel McKelvey Briggs was born and named after Lyman's mother, Susanna Isabella McKelvey Briggs; and on September 23, 1899, Isabel's brother, Albert Cook Briggs, named after Katharine's father, joined the family. Having a daughter made Katharine feel a spiritual closeness to her own mother, and she wondered whether she would mean as much to Isabel as Mary Cook had meant to her. To help ensure the bond, Katharine felt that keeping a record of their life together would remind Isabel of the "ideas and ideals, the methods and life, the home and the influences, that will have shaped her life and character." Such a picture would enable Isabel to determine whether the methods were "right or wrong." And if she, in turn, became a mother, Katharine wanted her to make use of what was good, improve the imperfect, and reject what was wrong.[22]

She began to keep a diary that recorded sketchy details of Isabel's early development. The diary was eventually superseded by a book-length, typed account of her children's lives entitled, "The Education of Suzanne [Isabel]." Written in ink that has long ago faded, in a fragile, leather-bound record book, the diary notes Isabel's birth and is followed by a poem copied from *Outlook* magazine. One line stands out as if it were Katharine's own prediction for her daughter: "Life's dreams seem to their full fruition born."

In an entry on October 18, 1898, Katharine noted that, although Isabel's mind was "busy all the day," she had not "spoken one word." By Isabel's third birthday, Katharine recorded: "She has a very good idea of number[s] and figures." One day she counted her fingers, and found she had ten; then, observing her bare feet, she counted her toes—and again there were ten. After a few minutes of thought, she announced, "Two tens make twenty!" At five years old, Isabel informed her Grandmother Briggs, in Washington to celebrate her fifty-fifth birthday, "Grandmother, you are just eleven times as old as I am."[23]

On May 10, 1901, Katharine wrote in "Suzanne" how proud she was of her babies and that her life was "so full of happiness and love that I don't see how it could hold any more of either." Lyman especially watched the boy "with ineffable pride." By the time of her next entry on July 19, Katharine wrote: "The radiance has gone from the world." Two weeks before, their small son had died from a cause she did not specify. She poured out her sorrow in words addressed to "Suzanne," only because she thought that a time might come when Suzanne would want to know what a mother thought in the midst of grief. "If a great sorrow comes to you, my little girl," Katharine wrote, "and I should not be there to help you bear it, remember this, the message from my grief to yours. Bereavement and sorrow are as much a part of life as birth and joy."[24] Seventy years later, these words would come as a poignant, painful message to Katharine's daughter.

CHAPTER TWO

"The Education of Suzanne"

Katharine actually began "The Education of Suzanne" in 1911 when Isabel was thirteen. Her opening chapter, with its touches of humor, begins:

> Ever since Suzanne was two or three years old, I have been variously told by friends, neighbors and teachers that she was wonderful – precocious – gifted – in danger of brain fever – a genius – a little Shakespeare – certain to go to pieces at the age of fourteen.... If I believed any of these things, I would not be telling this story of her education; there would be no point in telling it. That I do not believe them is my only excuse for writing what I am about to write. Suzanne is not wonderful; she has never been precocious, if to be precocious means to be unchildlike or abnormal; she is gifted only as every healthy child is gifted with an unknowable heritage of possibilities; she has never been nearer to brain fever than the measles; I can as yet see no indication of genius, and not the trace of a family resemblance to the Great Poet; before the year ends she will be fourteen, but as she just now bade me a brief farewell with eyes bright, and cheeks very red, and hand very purposefully grasping a tennis racquet, I was able to face the danger of nervous breakdown with perfect composure.[1]

When Isabel was an infant, she had a nurse—an overbearing disaster—who frightened Katharine by telling her that the baby's feet were "not alike." When Lyman came home from work, he assured the upset Katherine that Isabel had "perfectly good feet," but that one took after him, and the other after Katharine, which, of course, showed their daughter's impartiality. Although Lyman wanted to fire the nurse immediately, the woman stayed for another week, and left with the parting advice: "Don't never let her eat hog meat; it'll make her coarse."[2]

Before the end of Isabel's first year, Katharine knew that her small daughter was spoiled to the point of being "tyrannical," but Katharine "worshipped and adored her." One day, however, when Isabel, in her carriage near the dining room table, found the carving knife and was waving it in the air, Katharine's philosophy of permissive child rearing changed abruptly. She began to follow the ubiquitous "no, no" with a swat of the hand. A determined Isabel needed three increasingly vigorous swats to be convinced that when her mother said no it was to be taken seriously. From that moment on, Katharine "assumed the ruler's crown with confidence and authority." The lessons in obedience continued, with the penalty for each transgression a swat, or holding the disobedient hand firmly and with enough severity to make Isabel cry. The discipline had a cumulative effect that led to unfailing obedience to Katharine.[3]

At about this time, English philosopher Herbert Spencer's *Education, Intellectual, Moral, and Physical,* which advocated decisiveness and constancy in child rearing, reinforced Katharine's own newly conceived philosophy of "ousting the pretender, and secur[ing] for myself a firm seat upon the throne." Spencer's book, she said, "had no chaff, was nothing but wheat from beginning to end."[4]

When Isabel began to walk and investigate on her own, Katharine found that it was not difficult to teach her to come immediately when summoned because "much had already been accomplished." Katherine had two rules: first, never to give an unnecessary command, and second, when called, Isabel should give undivided attention by coming at once to her mother and looking directly into her face. When a neighbor accused Katharine of using corporal punishment, she replied that the "little spatings and spankings" were rather "corporal instruction."[5] By the time she was two, Isabel's "cooperative spirit" was clearly evident and inspired Albert J. Cook, after a visit to Washington, to comment on the child's "instinct of obedience." Katharine found this highly amusing.[6]

In addition to obedience, Katharine felt that she was teaching Isabel a "disciplined concentration" that could be focused on any subject and could readily and profitably "pass from one subject to another." Perhaps it was this power of concentration that made her appear to be a gifted child. Katharine believed that it was possible "to bring into the environment of the *obedient* [emphasis added] child every influence that is necessary for [her or] his healthy moral development" and that punishment after babyhood was demoralizing and ought to be unnecessary.[7]

From time to time, Lyman offered some philosophy of his own about child rearing. Early in Isabel's life, he made a statement that Katharine never forgot: "The people who keep the world moving are the people who think – and think – and think, and observe – and observe – and observe, and work – and work – and work." It would become her credo, and there is no doubt that it was passed on to Isabel. Lyman also said that no matter how many questions their daughter might ask, the parents must not only answer every one, but answer them at the time they were asked.[8]

In later years when Isabel reminisced about her childhood, she cited an example of her mother's doing just that. When the four-year-old tot was riding a Washington trolley car, she began to spell out words in a posted advertisement. The words "have you" were familiar, but the next word, "bugs," was not. In a loud voice she asked what was "bugs" [head lice] and what did it mean. She recalled that without hesitating, Katharine explained fully.[9]

In the summer of 1901, when Isabel was not quite four years old, she and her mother took a train trip to Michigan and California to visit Briggs relatives and Grandfather Cook. The journey, arranged not long after the death of little Albert Briggs, was in part a diversion for Katharine. In August, at "Uncle Bert's" in Owosso, Michigan, Isabel dictated a letter to "Papa,"a memento that Katharine carefully labeled and preserved for posterity. It reads:

> Papa, we made some maple sugar. Fannie helped me. Dear, all the horses but cept Johnnie...went away pulling up beans. We are going to take a little cake of sugar home. I feel so badly because you couldn't have some maple sugar up here.
>
> We went to Sunday school. I got a little card and paper.
> Your dear little Isabel.[10]

A year later, again in Michigan, and using her own children's stationary, Isabel wrote letters to her father in large, erratic printing.

"We saw some pretty hills that Mama called mountains with love Isabel," she wrote on May 13. The "3" is printed backwards.[11] She wrote three undated stories in her large, erratic printing that suggests they were composed when she was five.[12]

Katharine gave her daughter dolls, which were graciously accepted then laid aside in favor of "inventing imaginary animal playmates that she much preferred. She seemed to feel a sort of kinship for bears and dogs," whereas the "more feminine interests left her cold." Her play was, for the most part, with imaginary things.[13]

In 1903, Isabel and Katharine again took the train to California to visit Grandfather Cook. Reminiscing in 1979 about the journey, Isabel said that she was told later in life that she had entertained the passengers in various ways, one being to pretend she was a librarian. When a passenger asked her for a particular title, she disappeared, came back with an imaginary book, and said, "We don't have that one but this is a dictionary and it has all the same words in it."[14]

Lyman and Katharine, both lovers of books, read constantly to their child. From hearing Aesop's fables over and over, Isabel memorized many of them. When she was less than four years old, she began to recognize words from these stories on the printed page and would constantly ask about the words that were strange. Worried that this was taxing to a child so young, Lyman and Katharine stopped answering her questions—contrary to Lyman's earlier philosophy. Not to be so easily discouraged, Isabel would pounce with her questions on any unsuspecting source, such as the mail carrier, the milkman, or delivery persons. The parents gave in. By the time she was in kindergarten, she could read. At least one other mother informed Katharine that she would be "very sorry indeed" to have *her* child reading so young. Katharine was unimpressed.[15]

Isabel entered kindergarten in February 1903, and in April, after being quarantined with measles, she did not go back to school. "The Springtime is calling us," Katharine wrote in her diary in late April. "There is no kindergarten like Mother Nature's.... I want to carry out my own ideas without interference from anybody." She thought the children in kindergarten were much "too passive" and that the most successful day in education was the day when the most questions were asked and answered. She thought that "much could be accomplished" if teachers had the conviction that "it is not what a child knows that makes him clever; it is his attitude toward what he does not know."[16]

In the fall of 1903, Isabel entered first grade. She found out within a week that none of the other chidren could read, and though she thought this a bit odd, it did not deter her from devouring the supply of books available for six-year-olds. After two months, the teacher suggested that Isabel be put in second grade, but she told Katharine that Isabel was so advanced and well balanced that she belonged in third or fourth grade. By Christmas, history had repeated itself, and the somewhat flustered second-grade teacher then recommended that Isabel be put with the third graders. Katharine balked and took her home. There her studies proceeded "around the dining room table" and in the natural setting of a wooded area nearby. There was no set schedule, and no one stood over her to say, Today we will do this. Aside from arithmetic and writing, she did a "great deal of independent reading."[17] At age seven, Isabel believed that "the Bible is the most beautiful book...*Swiss Family Robinson* the most interesting, the *Life of Hernando Cortez* the most exciting, and [Washington] Irving's *Sketch Book* the stupidest."[18]

Katharine believed firmly that "it was all there in the books" and that no one needed to intercede between a seeker after knowledge and the knowledge itself. She abhorred the public school's way of disrupting a child's activities every half hour, and in some instances every ten minutes—a procedure she thought was "absolutely out of harmony with child nature." A child, she thought, if given a chance, would become "intensely interested in *just one line of thought*" and would enthusiastically become immersed in it until she was ready to drop it and go on to something else. The acquired knowledge would always be there to be drawn on unconsciously. Katharine called this her "natural method" of education.[19]

In November 1904, when Isabel was just past her seventh birthday, she kept a log of a month-long journey that she and her parents made to Costa Rica. She made duplicate copies—one for herself and one for her "dear Grandpa." Contained in a small bound book covered in red leather and with lined pages, the diary is not only remarkable for its descriptions, but for the bold, clear script in which it is written. Isabel showed a comfortable understanding of the geography involved, some of the perils of sea travel, and a ready acceptance of Christmas Day on board ship (the S.S. *Alleghany*), away from home and friends. Her spelling was not quite impeccable, but her diction and syntax were sophisticated.

She reported with good humor her father's trip on horseback and on foot to "the volcano," something that she and her mother avoided. (It was probably Irazu, one of six such peaks in Costa Rica over 11,000 feet and the one nearest San Jose where they were staying.) After climbing to the top, Lyman's companion suggested that they go down by a different route, and in Isabel's words: "But when they had got a little way...they had to climb over rocks and up steep places. Then beside that they had to go through bushes as there was no trail. Just as they got to some rather loose ground, Papa's footing gave way and he fell into some bushes [and] turned two summersaults.... Papa does not like path finding and thinks he will stick to the paths already found."[20]

Katharine continued to believe that teaching her daughter at home was preferable to public school. When Isabel was eight, Katharine introduced her to simple German through a beginning book, *Märchen Erzahlungen,* by Guerber. At about age "ten or eleven," Isabel began conversational German with a woman named Fräulein "Keut," and continued to read German at home. She would also study Latin, covering Caesar, Cicero, and part of Virgil, and by the time she was college age, she became competent in French.[21] During a part of her middle school years, other neighborhood children (at one time there were five) joined her "around the dining room table" under Katharine's tutelage. Although Isabel received most of her precollege education from her parents, she had brief periods in public school: a few months in third and fourth grades; and in fifth, two months, or just long enough to catch "hooping cough" from a boy she "never liked anyway" who sat in front of her.[22]

By the time Isabel was eight, she had an "intellectual intimacy" with Lyman that was remarkable. He talked to her about his work—topics related to mathematics, physics, and research in his laboratory. When she was ten, father and daughter discussed topics in his field that even Katharine could not follow, and which were, indeed, reminiscent of her husband's conversations with other physicists in which she could never take part. Later, Isabel's interest in a globe of the world led her to ask so many questions about the stars that Lyman presented her with Asaph Hall's *Starland*, thinking he would read it to her. She read it on her own, and then she and her father devised experiments in astronomy by tying strings to apple stems and, using a candle for the sun, bringing the apples into "eclipse."[23]

Students at that time typically spent eight years in elementary school before entering a four-year high school program. Isabel's unorthodox preparation stopped her momentarily at the door of the Western High School principal's office. After a painful interview during which she was tongue-tied, Isabel was eventually allowed to enroll in the ninth grade, where she took Latin, English, algebra, drawing, spelling, and gym. At the beginning of the spring semester, the math teacher invited her to audit the geometry class, a subject she would study more in depth at home. That year, her only full year in public school, "went nicely," despite Katharine's list of the Five Plagues of Public School Education: Rules, Definitions, Drill, Confusion, and Haste.[24]

However, for most of the next two years, she chose, except for a few weeks, to study again at home, continuing with languages, math, and, with the help of her father, physics. She read a physics text and visited Lyman's laboratory, where he guided her through experiments.[25] At this time, Katharine apparently had misgivings about Isabel's proficiency in Latin and had her evaluated by her ninth-grade teacher at Western High School. Emerson W. Matthews wrote Katharine that "Miss Isabel's...class work in Fourth Year Latin during the few weeks she was with me was uniformly excellent." He enclosed her last test, for which the average class grade was 51+; Isabel's grade was 98.[26] In the spring of what would have been her senior year of high school, she returned to Western High to study advanced Latin and German, English, algebra, and to her chagrin, trigonometry. In the preceding year, she had taken college boards and passed everything but trigonometry. Later when she was teased about her dazzling marks in college, she enjoyed being able to say, "But I once flunked trig!"[27]

Katharine, herself a music lover and competent musician, provided piano lessons for Isabel when she was seven. Isabel remembers this as a waste of time on someone with "no gift," but who could learn by rote. To the end of her life, she had no particular liking for music, but "no particular objection."[28] Dancing, however, was an activity that she enjoyed and participated in with enthusiasm throughout her college years.

As part of Isabel's education, Lyman and Katharine did not neglect her religious instruction. In his youth, Lyman was forced to attend a conservative church, an experience that made him anti–organized religion for the rest of his life.[29] However, both parents approved of Isabel's attending different churches with her friends in the Washington area, an exposure that would enable her eventually to make her own choices. In her girlhood diaries, Isabel frequently mentioned going to church and Sunday school, and she once lamented that she could not manage to read her daily chapter in the Bible. Her Grandfather Cook once offered her a dollar for every chapter in the Bible that she would memorize, but his delight in her competence moderated as dollar after dollar changed hands. When he lowered the price, Isabel lost interest.[30]

On Easter Sunday before her fourteenth birthday, she took her first communion at the Unitarian Church, a denomination that Lyman and Katharine felt was an acceptable compromise. Isabel took the sacrament "in memory of the women and children, old men and maidens, who in the world outside are drinking from the cup of life." and thought it "beautiful, beautiful, beautiful."[31] Later in the day, she went to an Episcopal church with a friend, who "slipped to her knees and said a little prayer to herself." Sometimes she got "heart-hungry for the little ceremonies of which they have so few at the Unitarian [Church]."[32]

It was not until Katharine was in her early sixties that she began to put in writing some of her own views about religion. She criticized the churches for being "a little too spiritual to be worldly in a big way, and a little too worldly to be spiritual in a big way." She observed that people who have "exhausted the possibilities of the world, and are fainting for some new manna seldom think of looking for it in a church. They are more likely to consult a psychiatrist."[33] Katharine considered herself one of those parents who "a generation or two ago would have prayed on their knees that their children might be good Christians, now moved heaven and earth to give them a good education."[34] By providing Isabel with the best in cultural and educational opportunities, Katharine felt that she provided the needed manna.

Katharine and Lyman gave their growing daughter considerably more than rigorous intellectual stimulation. There were the annual visits to Michigan, where Isabel enjoyed picnics, rowing, sailing, fishing, swimming, and dancing with her cousins; visits to the farm at Uncle Bert's (Katharine's brother), where she talks about feeding pigs that "got so absorbed in their eating that even when I pulled their tails with all my might I could not get them to turn around"; and horseback riding (her mount was Old Major). In Washington, when it snowed, both "Papa" and "Mama" went sledding with her. There were frequent excursions downtown for lunch and shopping, often for clothes in the latest fashion. As a result of one of those expeditions, Isabel began to get an allowance of five dollars a month, which her parents referred to as her "salary." Lyman introduced her to bookkeeping, instructed her to save some money each month, and gave her a bank book.[35] Once, on a shopping trip made after acquiring her advanced financial status, Isabel, with some chagrin, had to borrow "six dollars" from her mother to have enough money to buy a "lovely table-desk" for what was to be her own "den" on the second floor. Enhancing her money supply assumed importance. One entire summer, she worked diligently at swatting flies for ten cents per hundred. She relieved this tedium by composing a poem, left on yellowed paper and inserted in her diary on July 23, 1912:

Very
Wary
And contrary
Taking care extraordinary
Lest my swatter catch you napping
And you perish 'neath its slapping
Swat! *Swat!* Buzz! Bang!
Now I've kind of got the hang.
One, two, three, four,
Buzzing' round the kitchen door
Five, six, seven, eight,
Humming on the garden gate.
Very
Wary
And contrary
This is your obituary.

CHAPTER THREE

Aspiring Author

*I*n the summer of 1909, Lyman and Katharine moved from a rented house at 3451 Mount Pleasant Street, Washington, D.C., to 3208 Newark Street, where they had built the commodious new residence that would be their home for the rest of their lives. Resting on high wooded ground that was cooler and considered more healthful than the lower areas, the neighborhood, known as Cleveland Park, had once attracted prominent Washington families, including that of President Grover Cleveland, to have summer homes in the area. It would eventually become a favorite location for diplomats because of its proximity to the embassies on Massachusetts Avenue and—despite Katharine's contrary views—because of its proximity to excellent public and private schools.[1] A long-time resident, interviewed in 1958, recalled how "in those early days, many notable people lived in the area. Although it was about three miles from the White House, there was a country atmosphere about the place. The houses were not in blocks; the people were friendly and of more or less related occupations and interests. Scientists and builders, and architects and explorers, lawyers and teachers, a few bankers and a few politicians. It was said there were more brains to the square inch of territory than in any comparable area in the whole United States." Among the distinguished residents she mentioned was Lyman Briggs.[2]

Washington itself, with a population of less than three-hundred thousand, was slowly groaning into the twentieth century. The Library of Congress had opened in 1896, the District Public Library in 1903, the National Museum of Art in 1910, and the new and grand Union

Station (restored in 1988 to its early grandeur) was completed. There were theaters and the Lafayette Opera House (later renamed the Belasco Theater), and, by 1910, the excitement of moving pictures provided a large share of public entertainment. Although Washington considered itself a center of cultivated society, an anonymous English visitor declared that the city had "no influence over the arts and letters of the American people. The day is infinitely distant and in all probability will never come at all when every American artist, author, dramatist, and musician will turn instinctively toward Washington."[3]

Shortly after Isabel's parents arrived in Washington, President Grover Cleveland's term of office ended and William McKinley's began. McKinley's assassination in 1901 brought the young vice president, Theodore Roosevelt, into the White House. William Howard Taft followed in 1908, and the former Princeton professor, Woodrow Wilson, in 1912. In the surviving Briggs family correspondence, none of these historic changes are mentioned, nor are any of the events that piqued the curiosity of Washington society, such as the White House weddings of Alice Roosevelt in 1906 and of the two Wilson daughters in 1913 and 1914, or the remarriage of President Wilson in 1915, a scarce year after the death of his first wife, Ellen.

Immersed in his work, Lyman, the dedicated scientist, maintained a political neutrality. Katharine, who continued her involvment in reading and child rearing, now added to her priorities an activity that would occupy her for the next half century: writing. An old Michigan friend, Ray Stannard Baker, acted as her first unofficial literary agent.

Baker, who was from the class of 1889 at the Michigan Agricultural College, was now editor of the highly popular *American Magazine*, based in New York. After a visit to Katharine and Lyman in the spring of 1909, Baker sent her an article he had received on child training that reminded him of their "very interesting talk on that subject." He asked for Katharine's critique, adding that he thought perhaps she could give them some idea of her own methods in training Isabel."[4] Soon after that, Katharine began her opus, "The Education of Suzanne." However, the cumbersome proportions and, at times, florid and uneven style of Katherine's detailed account of Isabel's childhood and education clearly diminished Baker's interest. He accepted her critique of the article, however, as "exactly right," and although he thought her manuscript contained material for a "first-rate book," he wanted to make some suggestions after his editorial staff had read it.[5] In due course, Baker wrote Katharine what he had gently hinted at all along—that her manuscripts were "better adapted to a woman's journal." He urged her to "go ahead with it—and with others. Once you get the hang of it, you can go far." To help her more specifically, Baker got in touch with colleagues at the *Woman's Home Companion* and the *Ladies Home Journal* and sent them some of Katharine's work.[6] Thus began a fruitful relationship between Edward W. Bok, editor of the *Journal*, and Katharine Briggs, alias "Elizabeth Childe."

Bok thought "The Education of Suzanne" had good material in it, but it was not "in a form that lent itself to magazine publication, nor could it easily be thrown into such a form." However, Bok said, "it finally occurred to me to put...particular bits in the form of editorials for publication."[7] By the end of 1912, *The Ladies Home Journal* had published thirty-three 300-hundred word anonymous editorials that were taken largely from "The Education of Suzanne." The *Journal* also printed two of Katharine's feature articles, "Why I Believe the Home Is the Best School" and "Why I Find Children Slow in Their School Work."[8] The *Woman's Home Companion*, October 1912, published a clever short story, "Father's Library," and *Outlook* accepted three of her editorials. Her total earnings at the end of 1912 for that first burst of authorship were $1,130 (about $16,000 in current dollars).[9] Later, *Outlook* published two longer pieces, "Parents and Education" and "Teaching Concentration," the latter featured on the front cover under Katherine's pseudonym, Elizabeth Childe.[10] Not until a decade later would Katharine publish articles under her own name.

In the middle of Katharine's successes, Isabel, then fourteen years old, wrote her own editorial entitled "Window Teachers," which Katharine sent to Bok with one of her own pieces. In her diary on January 11, 1912, Isabel wrote: "We heard from my editorial today. Mr. Bok kept one and sent one back. It was mother's he sent back. Fifteen dollars in one morning is the easiest money I ever earned."[11] Isabel's first published work, "A Little Girl's Letter," appeared in the *Journal* in October 1912. Printed on the editorial page with an introduction by the editors, it reads:

> "Out of the Mouth of Babes" says the Bible, can we learn wisdom—and there is much wisdom in the little letter which we gladly print here for the benefit of every teacher:
>
> Dear Mr. Editor, I am only a High School girl, and a Freshman, which makes it worse; but there is a thing over at school

that bothers me, and I thought perhaps you could help if I wrote and told you about it.

In all the classrooms the desks are fixed on purpose so that nobody will have to sit facing the light. But some of the teachers stand by the windows all through class, so when I look at them I see their faces all blurry and funny against a patch of blinding sky. Of course they want me to pay attention, and if I don't look they think I am not; so I look. And when the class is over I go out into the hall with my eyes aching, a queer dizzy feeling in my head and a patch of pink swimming before my eyes.

There is one teacher, and she is the dearest thing that ever was. When I go to her class there she is, all dressed in white, standing against the nice plain blackness of the blackboard. And, oh, she is *so* good to look at! It's just plain fun to pay attention. But her class is over so soon, and I have to go back to the window teachers.

These teachers all read *The Ladies Home Journal;* I see them, and if you could just say something about it somewhere I would be so glad. I know they wouldn't do it if they only thought. They are really lovely teachers. Only they don't think.

A short time later, when Bok accepted another piece by Isabel on literary appreciation, she turned to writing instead of swatting flies to enhance her earnings. Again with the gracious help of Ray Stannard Baker, she sold several poems to *The Youth's Companion, Romance,* and *Woman's Home Companion.* The *Companion* published "When Multiplication Is Vexation," very much indeed like the Isabel who would forever fight deadlines and who abhorred schedules:

> The wind smells good. The little clouds
>   Are white against the blue.
> What difference does it make to me
>   That two times one is two?
>
> The woods are beckoning to me
>   And calling through the door.
> It's half an hour till three o'clock—
>   And two times two is four.

The brook is laughing 'cos we have
  To study 'rithmetics.
We might as well be wading there—
  But two times three is six.

It's washing down the dam we built
  Last night, but we must wait
Until the teacher's sure we know
  That two times four is eight.

And so we sit and watch the clock
  And wait and wonder when
The hands will get around to three—
  And two times five is ten.[12]

These literary successes would be followed a decade later by the publication elsewhere of poems and short stories, and, in due course, by a prize-winning mystery novel. The daughter-pupil was well on her way to surpassing the mother-teacher.

Were it not for Isabel's existing diaries, one might be inclined to think her a loner and bookworm. Yet her own detailed accounts of her life provide a broad picture that is not shown in "The Education of Suzanne." By the time she was in her early teens, Isabel socialized constantly with several girls in Cleveland Park. Among some of her best friends were Betty Pyle, Kathryn Drain, Marie Dowell, Priscilla Parsons, Polly Vorhees, Margaret Schoenfeld, Constance Brown, and Mildred Hawkshurst.[13]

Isabel was an avid tennis player. In Cleveland Park, when she and her girl friends began to play often, a crisis promptly developed over use of the "better" court alloted to men. Lyman went to a meeting about the matter, where the conflict was resolved in part by getting permission for Isabel and three of her friends to have use-cards. Katharine soon joined in the sport, and Isabel reported that, although she herself was improving, her mother was improving faster.

In the spring of 1912, the Cleveland Park Campfire Girls were organized with eleven members that included "Miss Isabel Briggs." By late September, four of the eleven had attained the high rank of "firemaker," which required twenty honors—comparable to merit badges in Scouts. Among the achievements required for the rank of firemaker, a girl had to swim a mile, cook, shop, and budget for her family. Although the requirements for the swimming honor called for a candidate, on six successive days, to swim distances that added up to a mile, the *Washington Times* reported that "Miss Isabel Briggs [achieved this] in one continuous swim. Miss Briggs, who is barely sixteen years old swam the Potomac several times this summer." The *Times* carried two photographs of the Cleveland Park group with Isabel, wearing beads, long braids, head band, and a "squaw"dress, smiling in the front row.[14]

Clearly, Isabel's schoolwork received first priority, but her diary in 1912 and 1913 records an impressive number of pleasant activities and hobbies. She was chosen as an alternate in rope climbing for the school meet in gymnastics, which led to "new tennis shoes and new bloomers"; the family went to see a performance of *Pinafore* that was "killingly funny"; she visited her father's office on a Saturday, at which time he gave her "a dear big geranium and a dear little maidenhair fern" from the [Department of Agriculture's] greenhouse; she took frequent drives with Betty Pyle and her parents in their new automobile; she heard a talk by Admiral Robert E. Peary (who had reached the North Pole on April 6, 1909); she met Helen Keller at a neighbor's house and took her for a walk in the woods (Keller was thirty-two, Isabel fourteen); and she learned to type on her mother's new machine.

On March 21, 1915, Isabel McKelvey Briggs wrote in her diary that "from now on, I am not going to waste my time." She was seventeen and had chosen where she would go to college. Her ideas about not wasting time, however, would eventually change to include men in her life.

CHAPTER FOUR

"In Numbers
There Is Safety"

In her precollege years, Isabel Briggs kept two overlapping diaries. The first, beginning in 1911 and ending on September 20, 1915, reveals a happy, busy adolescent student involved only with female friends. The second, a more intimate record kept largely in the spring of 1915, portrays a more sophisticated woman whose interests were focused on her relationships with men.

In Washington, D.C., where she grew up, she had enjoyed a relatively cosmopolitan social life. At seventeen, she juggled the attentions of five men, referred to in her diary as "A," "C," "F," "H," and "J." They took her to lectures, concerts, theater, opera, and out to dinner, and they were her partners at tennis. "In numbers there is safety," she said, "[but in the] right numbers, there is also much joy."[1]

One by one, she eliminated four of the five from her life before she left for college. "A," apparently an Englishman who worked at a laboratory in the city, was good for paying her compliments that she enjoyed. She postponed going to St. John's Episcopal Church with him until "I have my new spring suit and my new hat. Vanity!"[2] "F" appears to have been a religious type who often met her at church. Isabel decided that she was not yet ready to renounce "the vanities of this world," and, when all was over between them, she asserted that breaking up with him was "one of the thrills of my life."[3] She came to dislike "H," stating, "I can't believe what he says." She found him good for nothing "except to quarrel with" and she didn't enjoy quarreling with him. "La chose defendre has lost its savor!" (In her diary that spring, she recorded lengthy comments in French and German.) "J" appears to have faded away painlessly.[4]

By the end of the summer of 1915, Isabel and "C," who was older than she and had survived as her best beau, clearly enjoyed each other's company. He called her "the goddess of joy" and worried about what college would do to her. She confided to her diary that she couldn't "in this world (or the next) fall in love with the man," but she was not displeased that he might be writing to her. She had one final "gorgeous evening" with "A," who listened as she told him what women thought of men. He, in turn, told her what men thought of women. She savored this exchange, noting that this was the first time in her life that she had ever experienced "free speech" to a man of her own age. "Oh, the luxury of it!"[5]

His concern about what college would do to her may have been directed toward the "dangers" of the coeducational institution she had chosen—Swarthmore—where women and men attended classes and dined together. He may also have been concerned about Swarthmore's reputation for providing women the opportunity to develop ther minds and achieve scholarly distinction. This danger, however, was disregarded by the more liberal branch of the Society of Friends, known as Hicksites, who founded Swarthmore College in 1868. The first Board of Managers subsequently endorsed the radical concept of education stated by one of its founders:

> I see in this work the inception of a movement which is to prove what has never yet been fully proven, although tried to some extent, that it is feasible and desirable to give to woman equal educational facilities with man, not in the earlier stages of education merely, but to carry them together *pari passu,* to the heights of literature and science, and to prepare them alike to use to the best advantage…the talents with which they are endowed.[6]

For its first few decades, the College tried to accommodate both the views of liberals, who preferred to emphasize academic excellence, and the conservatives, who believed that Swarthmore's chief mission was to preserve Quaker beliefs. By the time Isabel enrolled in 1915, the emphasis had shifted irrevocably to the academic. A half century later, an alumnus from the class of 1915 said that Swarthmore then, as for many years before and after, "drew much more strength from women than from men." He also observed that because Swarthmore was one of the few high-caliber coeducational colleges, it attracted a great many applications from [talented] women.[7]

No evidence exists to explain Isabel's choice of Swarthmore, but circumstances strongly suggest that a coeducational school was important to her. However, when she was only thirteen, she wrote in a diary fragment that she was going to Swarthmore College, and "if you go to college you have to work, and I am going to work."[8] In the final sentence of "The Education of Suzanne," Katharine wrote, "Suzanne [Isabel] says she is going to Swarthmore, and since she says so, knowing her as I do, I have no doubt she will."

On September 21, 1915, Isabel took the train with some other women entering Swarthmore from Union Station, in Washington, to Philadelphia. From there they rode a local train to the small village made up largely of the college, with its student body of 445 and its faculty of 54. One of the women who met Isabel in Union Station by prearrangement was Jane Pancoast Brown, who was from an antebellum home in Loudoun County, Virginia.[9] Jane and Isabel and, in time, their Swarthmore alumni husbands would form a deep friendship that would end only with death many decades later.

In her room in Parrish Hall, on the evening of the 21st, Isabel wrote to her "Most Dearly Beloved Family" the first in a series of almost daily letters that would continue through her junior year. Their trunks had not been delivered, the bed in her room was so ugly that she wanted to replace it (her parents did so), and the unpalatable dessert that first night at dinner was "a sort of chocolate custard" which the juniors at their table called "New Jersey mud." She closed with "all the love in the world from your unhomesick Isabel."[10]

The next day, at registration, after some negotiation with the dean, she was allowed to take just what she wanted: English, English composition, algebra, astronomy, zoology (called biology), and Latin. Swarthmore women were also required to take physical education.[11]

In an undated entry in her diary about a month after her arrival at college, she wrote: "I wasn't having a very good time at the Junior-Fresh reception. And then, at the beginning of a dance marked Myers, I met the nicest part of the evening. I gave thanks first for his height (he's six feet four), then for his dancing and then for his realness. I can talk to him about real things, not kidding. We argued a lot of things, among them, I think, whether women are fickle. And we wanted another dance and took …[it] by strategy." Later, she wrote in her diary that she was to sit at a certain table in the dining room. "Myers, it seems, is already there. Selah!"[12]

Clarence Gates Myers was born on May 25, 1894, in the farming community of Marble Rock, Iowa. The youngest of the three children of Ella Gates and Wilson Crist Myers, Clarence was never close to his father or to his brother, Milton, a rolling stone, but there was a firm bond to his mother and to his sister Parcie, older by seven years. Wilson was an entrepreneur whose ventures never seemed to succeed; Ella, a schoolteacher at seventeen, had married Wilson a year later. Taking over his wife's paychecks, Wilson informed her, "In today's practice the husband carries the pocketbook." Instead of accepting his father's chauvinist views, Clarence rebelled at what he considered slavery. His mother, who was brought up as a Christian Scientist, accepted her situation while she hoped that her last and brightest child would have something better.[13]

Sloan Wallace, the principal of West Waterloo High School where Clarence was a student, helped Ella Myers fulfill her hopes. Wallace became interested in young Myers and encouraged him to apply for the prestigious Western Swarthmore Club Scholarship. A somewhat stunned winner, Clarence entered Swarthmore College in the fall of 1913, with board, room, and tuition paid for one year.[14] His mother and sister understood that his departure for college in the East meant that he would never again live in Iowa.[15]

When Myers first arrived on the Swarthmore campus, an upperclassman spotted him as a new kid and asked his name. At that time, there was a Native American and outstanding baseball player named Myers, who was known as "Chief." The upperclassman, sensing a chance for some fun, told the naive newcomer that he must be "Chief Myers." As the joke passed through college circles, the nickname stuck, and "Clarence" became "Chief" for the rest of his life.[16]

To supplement his scholarship, Chief worked in the dean's office, graded English papers, and peddled Christmas cards and calendars, while the more affluent students were "back home eating turkey."[17] When he could not afford to go home for school holidays, he stayed at the college and sneaked into his dormitory—officially closed—by way of the fire escape, while the housemother pretended not to notice.[18] He had left behind a girlfriend in Iowa, which restrained his dating during his first year at Swarthmore, but the romance ceased after his freshman year when the girl became interested in someone else. When he first saw Isabel McKelvey Briggs, however, he "never looked back."[19]

Legends vary as to when and how this first meeting took place, but Isabel's diary indicates that her earliest awareness of him was at the freshman-junior reception on November 6, 1915. This is confirmed by a list of significant dates entitled "Great Days" found in her papers. She identifies November 6, 1915, as "met." A college classmate believes that Chief, a junior, first became aware of her as the woman in the front row in Astronomy 262 who answered most of the questions.[20]

Although the letters Isabel wrote to her parents during her college years were preserved, few from her parents to her exist from this period. Her letters were typical of a happy college student whose studies were going extremely well; who attended ball games, receptions, and dances; who after an initial disappointment in getting a sorority bid was pledged to Kappa Kappa Gamma; who participated in intramural sports, such as field hockey, tennis, swimming, and diving (she needed to polish her back dive and would learn either the swan dive or jackknife); and who wrote of girlfriends, clothes, and men.[21]

Katharine visited Swarthmore on the weekend of October 16 and 17, 1915, staying in a guest room available for visitors and eating at the college with Isabel. The parents apparently visited again in November after the reception where Isabel and Chief met. At this time, they must have been introduced to Chief because Isabel began to mention him in letters home as if he were a known entity. Shortly thereafter, Katharine issued some caveats to her daughter about what to look for in a man. Isabel thanked her mother for "the summing up" and added, "He qualifies splendidly on strength and control and the moral code (I think). I'm not sure yet about the unselfish human interest of him."[22]

There is no doubt, judging from the photographs of a young Isabel Briggs, that she was both intelligent and beautiful—slim, dark-haired, well-proportioned, and self-assured, while Chief had qualities of control, independence, and self-sufficiency. By mid-December of her freshman year, Isabel wrote in her diary of her strong attraction to him. Soon afterward, she confided to both her diary and her mother that she had always wanted to meet a man "near my age who would seem to me to be bigger and stronger than myself, someone who wouldn't seem like a nice little boy all the time. And I think I've found him." But she was "nearly wild" to shake him, jar him, stir him up.[23]

Isabel learned that during the Christmas recess Chief was not going to Iowa, but planned to come to Washington to hear the Congressional debates. He would stay with a fraternity brother, who happened to be the brother of Isabel's roommate, Betty Pyle. When Isabel got home and found out that Congress had adjourned for the holidays, she wrote Chief and invited him to come see her at 3208

Newark Street. He arrived at the Pyles on Monday, the 27th of December, and remained in the city through New Year's Eve. That first afternoon, when he and Isabel were at Betty Pyle's house in Cleveland Park, Katharine dropped in; later, she told her daughter, "My dear, I've seen him again and I don't blame you a bit."[24]

During those few days in Washington, without the distraction of classes and fellow students, Chief and Isabel discussed love, marriage, and careers—all in the abstract, of course. He said that he approved of long engagements, but if "people couldn't be married before seven or eight years, they would be foolish to get engaged." Isabel did some fast mental arithmetic about his prospects—two more years in college, three in law school, two or three to get established—and decided such talk was "crazy."[25] He told her that the thing about her that appealed to him most was a "sort of strength, not stubbornness about little things." When he had first seen her at the dances, he had thought of her as "the ordinary girl," but as he knew her better he liked the "deeper thing."[26]

At spring break, when he came through Washington after a trip south with the debating team, he had dinner at the Briggs' home and probably spent the night. Although neither Isabel nor Chief were ready to admit it, they were already in love. Isabel's diary for the rest of her freshman year is full of "Chief, Chief, Chief."[27]

If Katharine was concerned that her eighteen-year-old daughter was in love, she considered this of less importance than Isabel's scholastic achievements. She prepared a memory book titled "A Promise Fulfilled," which covered Isabel's first semester at college and contained typed excerpts from letters and photographs and clippings from *The Phoenix,* the Swarthmore student newspaper. This memory book showed that Isabel had won the freshman Latin prize and finished the year with "A's" in all her courses. Meanwhile, in March of his junior year, Chief was elected to Phi Beta Kappa.

Chief was looking more and more interesting to Isabel's parents. In May, surely with Isabel's approval, Katharine invited him to stop in Washington on his way to Iowa for the summer. Chief's letter of acceptance contained some subtle caveats for Katharine and established that he, too, had a mind of his own. The subject of religious belief apparently had arisen, and Chief, whose childhood exposure to Christian Science had been ineffectual, recommended to Katherine, for its "comprehensiveness and fairness," William James' *The Varieties of Religious Experience*, a book he thought Isabel would like to own. He also wrote Katharine: "Your attempt to preserve the literary innocence of the precocious infant [Isabel] under discussion, reminds me of an attempt I once made to lock up my brother in our barn. I slammed the door, locked it, drove some nails into the casing and rolled a couple of barrels up against it, and when I went around the corner to find some more barricading material, I found him sitting on the ground making a kite, quite unconscious of all my efforts." Perhaps to allay Katharine's concern that his and Isabel's relationship was too serious too soon, Chief explained that he and Paul Gemmill, close friends since their freshman year, had picked up "a third one," which happened to be Isabel. Chief was content for the moment with the triumvirate, even if that meant Paul sometimes dated Isabel.[28]

The friends were separated during the summer of 1916, with Chief at home in Waterloo employed at odd jobs that included painting houses, construction work, and playing the bass fiddle in the Myers family orchestra,[29] while Paul was on the road assisting in magic shows—both trying to earn money—and Isabel was in Michigan and Washington with her family. Letters that flew back and forth between Iowa and the East were, on Chief's part, without sentiment.[30]

On the way back to college in the fall of 1916, Chief stopped for a day to "take advantage of the perpetual hospitality of the Briggs home." Katharine now wrote regularly, if not often, to Chief, but he did not always answer immediately.

Her letters to him are missing, but many of Chief's to her have been preserved. He sensed that Isabel's brilliant mother could be domineering, and he tactfully but firmly took her on. She had spoken of "restless conjecturing, play of doubts against convictions, idle imaginings and the like," suggesting that this might describe Chief's feelings about Isabel. He admitted that some of this might apply to him, but he wrote the following:

> Isabel seems to stand the test of all the uncomplimentary criticism I can mass, in my own mind, against her. She has character, personality, brains (imagination, exact, piercing, subtle—yet unromantic, and very real and practicable), attractiveness, enthusiasm, a naturally happy disposition.... She's not an ethereal dream creation, but a very real and useful person. It is impossible to give any adequate summary of my impression of her, except to say that I've weighed her in the most brutal of scales, applied the acid test so to speak—as far as it is possible in ordinary human relations—and find in her a most unusual and lovable girl.

He was concerned that Isabel be given the fairest of chances and admitted that he would be better satisfied if her experience with other men had been more extensive.[31]

Chief left Katharine mute, for he had described disarmingly the daughter that she had nurtured so successfully.

Part Two

CHAPTER FIVE

Swarthmore
and Chief

*C*hief stated his case to Katharine Briggs about her daughter, but this did not ease his own worries that Isabel's youth and inexperience might make her an inadequate judge of men. With the help of his best friend, Paul Gemmill, he drew up a written statement that directed her to broaden her invitations to dances and other college functions to include men other than Chief and Paul. They were seniors, would disappear at the end of the academic year, and for her own good, she must use her invitations to social events—consistent with her good judgment —"to her future advantage."[1] An indignant Isabel informed Paul and Chief that she did not use her invitations like a political boss dispensing patronage, and she was accustomed to doing as she saw fit in these matters. She decided nevertheless to play the game. On a campus such as Swarthmore's, with an enrollment of only 445, not to socialize with another student was possible, but the day-to-day contacts were unavoidable. Isabel and Chief not only ate at the same table in the dining room, but before the edict was sent to her, had enrolled in three of the same courses—Greek, philosophy, and history of ideas.[2]

During the fall semester, when their attempts at aloofness led to spats, tension was high for both of them. Isabel, however, appeared to be carrying it off more comfortably than Chief and enjoyed the company of a handsome, witty freshman named Jesse. Yet the result of the cooling period, painful to both of them, was to solidify their relationship.

Chief continued to write frankly to Katharine, who apparently continued to issue caveats to him. "I think I have lost a few odd tons of cynicism lately too; not that the supply is in any danger of running out," he wrote,

> but who could remain sarcastic and ill-humored before such an unprecedented example of patience and sympathy and sweet disposition?... It is almost unbelievable that you can find, in the same person, the girl who passed the College Entrance Board exams, and appropriated the [Anson Lapham] scholarship, etc., etc., and at the same time the girl who is...[so] tempting to squeeze![3]

At the same time Chief was writing those words to her mother, Isabel, uneasy lest by some unexpected occurrence Chief might never know how she really felt, poured out her heart to him in a letter sealed and placed in an envelope addressed to Katharine, and designated: " To be opened if anything happens to me."

Parrish [Hall]
January 22, [1917]

My dear—

You said once that I had never told you that I love you. I have wanted many times to tell you. But I have thought that I could wait—wait until I am older and you are surer that I am not a child. I can wait. But sometimes I am afraid that I may die and leave unsaid the things that are in my heart to tell you. So I want to write them and be sure.

I do love you. I love you with all my heart and body and soul. I think I have always loved you, even when I had no thought of it. I think sometimes that I have loved you since the beginning of the world.

I have tried to be wise and temperate. I have never said, " I love you." I have never touched you in caress. But I go to sleep with the thought of you held close to me. I dream of your arms around me and your kisses on my lips. I wake thinking of you and I carry you in my thoughts all day long. I love you always. And I am with all my heart and dearest love forever

Just yours,
Isabel[4]

Isabel and Chief became formally engaged at spring break on the train on their way back to school from Washington. That night, on campus, Chief said that the "old walls of Parrish east corridor were scandalized when they witnessed our parting."[5]

Isabel wrote with the news to her parents in separate letters. She explained to her " dear Daddy": You see, we just rather ignored all the national trouble during those ten days at home. But the day we went back and stopped at the capitol and caught the grave tension all through the place, we realized how close the war was coming to us. We had been taking our laughter in the shadow of the thing. And going back we knew that we didn' t know what was going to happen. So you see— And I am so happy.[6]

Isabel and Chief had been on the train back to Philadelphia on Monday, April 2, the day they were engaged—the same day that President Woodrow Wilson had gone before Congress to ask for a declaration of war on the German Empire. The war had been raging in Europe since August 1914, but until the United States formally entered the conflict, colleges were not dramatically affected. This was particularly true for a Quaker institution like Swarthmore, but, even there, tension was building between pacifists and the defendants of Western democracies. The board of managers, entirely Quaker, wanted the college to participate in a nonmilitary way by forming organizations to help the Allies. Chief and Paul Gemmill were among those Swarthmore men who turned out at 6:00 A.M., five days a week, for an hour of off-campus drill. By the summer of 1918, when the draft age was lowered to eighteen, Swarthmore's president, Joseph Swain, declared that if his institution did not accept a Student Army Training Corps, the college would be completely disrupted. Swarthmore, not without controversy, was the only Quaker college to accept such a unit.[7]

Meanwhile, in the late spring of 1917, with Chief's graduation imminent and his military status precarious, he and Isabel desired more time together than the college's rules would allow. There had been one long, illegal walk and an illegal street car ride.[8] However, if students went into Philadelphia, the college considered that its jurisdiction did not apply; but Chief's budget disallowed train rides, dinners, and entertainment in the city. Lyman and Katharine, remembering their own long separation after college, and aware that their children had little casual time left, sent them a book of rail tickets and a check to cover extra activities such as meals off campus. Isabel and Chief agreed that no other girl had such wonderful parents who appreciated and understood so completely.[9] After that the couple took frequent trips to Philadelphia and one to Atlantic City.

The generosity of Isabel's parents was offset by Katharine's wish to have the engagement announced immediately and properly. Neither Chief nor Isabel wanted to do this; Chief prepared a lengthly response to "Mother Briggs" describing his objections, while Isabel sent a loving, tactful explanation as to why they "just did not feel that way about it."[10] Katharine capitulated and sent a maxim for Isabel to " please memorize": *It is the PRIVILEGE of parents of grown up children to make suggestions; and it is the DUTY of the children to give serious consideration to those suggestions. It is the PRIVILEGE of grown up children to make their own decisions; and it is the DUTY of the parents to respect and acquiesce in these decisions.*[11]

Katharine was curious, however, as to how Isabel concealed the jeweled fraternity pin Chief had given her on May 10. Isabel told her mother that she wore it " on my undermost underthings, and when I undress—I pin it under the underside of my nighty."[12]

Chief now confessed to his "Rosebud" that there had been "hundreds of times when he had wanted to kiss her" and did not, because he was half afraid "they might not be as wonderful to you as they were to me." Now, he had discovered that she was *human*—had real human passions—and desired the same closeness that he did. Chief believed firmly that they loved each other with a love that "passeth all understanding." Indeed, it was a love that would last through the pleasures and pain of more than sixty years.[13]

Chief had now decided, were he not conscripted by fall, to enter the University of Pennsylvania law school. History repeated itself when Isabel's parents again offered to lend him money to further his education, but he declined with the proviso that he might take advantage of it later.[14] To start earning money immediately, he accepted a summer job with the Swarthmore Chautauqua, as did Paul Gemmill, a skillfull amateur magician. Although the Chautauqua had no formal connection with the college, it had been started in 1912 by Paul M. "Pop" Pearson, head of Swarthmore's public speaking department, and had attracted a number of students who wanted summer jobs.[15] Pearson was particularly pleased to have Myers, not only for his managerial abilities but because he was a skillful speaker who had just won first place for Swarthmore over six other colleges in the annual contest of the Pennsylvania Intercollegiate Oratorical Union.[16]

When Chief wrote his mother about his engagement and summer job, Ella Myers wrote enthusiatically about Isabel, but was unable to hide her disappointment that her son would not be coming home. Parcie was blunt: "I hope to Heaven you don't ever have to come back to Waterloo [Iowa] to get your start as a lawyer.[17] Parcie wrote Isabel that she had never seen a man she thought compared with her brother, "so no doubt you and I will have lots to talk about when we meet."[18]

Chief was able to have the week before commencement with Isabel, but he had to miss his own graduation.[19] Isabel finished her sophomore year with "A's" in the fall semester and rare "B's" in English and public speaking in the spring, with a "D" in physical education, a class that she shortchanged in lieu of excursions with Chief.[20]

———————

*W*hen the United States had entered the European War, leaders in Washington and most Americans believed their contributions would be largely naval cooperation, credit, and supplies to the Allies. Shortly after President Wilson's speech to Congress in early April, French and British representatives sent to Washington made it clear that their own manpower resources were exhausted and reinforcements were urgently needed.[21] Responding to this need, President Wilson had obtained quick approval from Congress for a selective draft that would deplete college enrollments. Most of the Swarthmore students tended to forget the beliefs of conscientious objectors in the fervent days of 1917 and 1918 when the world was being made safe for democracy. Swarthmore women, wanting to do their patriotic duty and stirred by the slogan, "Food will win the war," were hired in the summer as "farmerettes" at fifteen dollars a month.[22] However, after brushing up on her typing and shorthand, Isabel chose to make her contribution by taking a clerical job in Washington and living at home.

When Chief learned in late July that he had received a draft number that eliminated the risk of immediate military service (he had registered in Swarthmore rather than going home to Waterloo), he enrolled in classes, to begin September 28, at the University of Pennsylvania law school, where he had won a scholarship.[23] Katharine renewed the offer of financial aid, and this time, he accepted. He told her that he was already so much indebted to her for Isabel that she could hardly increase the debt. Chief added: "It is lovely, yes, but more than that—it is wonderful. I mean not just the things you have done and are doing for me, but the way you *feel* toward me. Next to Isabel's love, it makes the second wonder of the world for me."[24] To Isabel he wrote:

"You have brought me hope, faith, and charity—friends who are worthwhile, a return of self-esteem and confidence, inspiration for noble deeds—no matter how far beyond my power of accomplishment—but greatest and best, you have given me *yourself*. Is it surprising that I love you [?]"[25]

CHAPTER SIX

Marriage

*H*er engagement still secret, Isabel returned to her junior year at Swarthmore to become immediately involved with duties in her sorority and as an informal advisor to some of the freshman women. To become eligible for Phi Beta Kappa, her first choice of courses had to be altered to include physics and advanced French; she was also enrolled in two English courses (Chaucer and Shakespeare), history, political science, and international relations. Instead of stumbling in physics, as she feared, she found that with the background Lyman Briggs had given her, "all is as plain as daylight."[1]

When the excitement of sorority rushing was over, and with her own Kappa Kappa Gamma successful in luring its choice of freshmen women, Isabel soon realized that "it's going to be lonesome here." She had unpacked her trunk and put her clothes "all in order" the way Katharine had taught her to do. The results of her annual physical examination showed her to be in excellent health. Two seniors were competing with her for the same position (right half-back) on the women's hockey team, and she intended to "beat them to it." She was also involved in student government, athletics, the *Halcyon* (the college yearbook), and she showed her own patriotism by buying war bonds on the installment plan.[2]

She had left herself no time to reflect on Chief's absence, but her letters lacked the enthusiasm of her first two years at college. Her work during the summer in the "real world" had dampened her enthusiasm for coming back to school and had even tempted her not to return at all. Once on campus, however, she decided that Swarthmore meant more than it ever had before. She felt closer to her roommate, Elizabeth

(Betty) Neumann Frorer (later Mrs. Frank Dew), and to other women friends who told her she somehow seemed different. To Katharine, she confided: "I may be...very young and foolish but I feel very much older and more understanding about things—and people.... If growing up is ever a conscious process, it must feel a little like this. Anyway, I' m not sorry anymore that I'm going to be twenty this month."[3]

With academic demands heavy for both Isabel and Chief, they decided to "work like Sam Hill during the week and play like kids" on the weekends. By late October, that plan was moot. Chief had been called for his army physical, which he passed, and conscription was imminent.

After consultation with Lyman and the Swarthmore Conscription Board, Chief decided rather than to wait to be drafted, he would apply for transfer to the army aviation service. It was a risk he was prepared to take when he learned that being drafted offered no choices. He had reached a point in his life when he wanted to help in the war effort, without the urge, he said, of a "typical zealot" who waved his arms for his country, but rather because of concrete situations, such as "a flabby Russia, a LaFollette, or the German army crossing the Tagliamento."[4] His conversion to activism was a "desire to throw 180 pounds of bulk, personally, with as much force and skill as is in me...toward pushing back that eruption of half-human stuff [the German army] that apparently can flow anywhere it desires, with irresistible force."[5] He passed the more rigorous physical examination for the air service, was released by the local draft board to become registered in the aviation section of the Signal Officer Reserve Corps (SORC), and began the wait for orders to report for duty.

Facing what might be a long separation, he and Isabel chose to announce their engagement to their friends at Swarthmore. Isabel wrote notes to Parcie and to a number of family friends in Cleveland Park, only to learn that her mother had wanted to tell the news. Katharine had to accept her own philosophy about children's prerogatives and settle for Isabel's "sorry I wrote to those people if you wanted to."[6]

Chief came to Swarthmore on December 19 for a last day with Isabel before he took the train to Iowa to have a farewell Christmas with his family. Isabel went home for the holidays wondering when, if ever, she would see him again.

When Isabel returned to college in January, she was "up in arms about the comparative indifference of the student body" to the war effort. Several women who were also engaged to men in the service took steps toward putting Swarthmore "on a war basis." (One woman, although not formally engaged, was Jane Brown, who was deeply involved with Paul Gemmill, also in uniform.) The Committee of Ten was formed, and Isabel's group provided a "definite program" with which the college could begin. Isabel explained to her mother: "We are planning a campaign of advertising and talk and every possible means of influence to push the college into line, since it will not come to attention of its self." She was subsequently elected chairperson of the Committee.[7] She decided at this time to change her major from English literature to political science, in part, because "Dr. [Harold C.] Goddard [the renowned Shakespeare scholar] doesn' t seem to care a hang about his majors—and Dr.[Robert C.] Brooks [professor of political science] cares a lot." She dropped the Chaucer and Shakespeare and added another course in political science.[8]

Chief, meanwhile, still waiting for orders, came back to law school to try to take his end-of-semester examinations. Between cramming and writing, he still managed to spend time with Isabel— who neglected to write Katharine for four days. When she did manage to scribble a line, Chief added a note, "The fact that your precious has not been the dutiful child she usually is, that fact, I say is *me*."[9] He had received orders to report on February 2, 1918, to the United States School of Aeronautics, Princeton, New Jersey.

When the United States had entered the war in 1917, Princeton University had immediately placed its resources at the disposal of the government. Buildings, laboratories, and other facilities were made available to army, navy, and aviation training schools that were established on campus.[10] The United States had not faced total war since 1861, a period not known for the efficiency of the war effort. In the first few months after April 1917, the government had relied largely on voluntary and cooperative efforts, but this was superseded in early 1918 by a thoroughly organized mobilization of the country's resources. Herbert Hoover, in charge of Food Administration, was doing such an outstanding job that Isabel declared this as one area where no accusation of inefficiency could be brought. In March 1918, President Wilson gave sweeping powers to the War Industries Board, headed by Bernard Baruch. The American industrial machine was finally being organized for a victory effort.[11]

Isabel managed to maintain stability in her life, helped by almost daily letters from Chief. She planned to visit him the first weekend in March and, if she could find a chaperone, to stay at the Nassau Inn across the street from the Princeton campus. This plan was canceled, however, when she was elected to Phi Beta Kappa, and the initiation ceremonies were scheduled for Saturday, March 2. When her major professor, Harold Brooks, told her in confidence about the honor, he said her name led all the rest. Chief sent a wire of congratulations and said he would try to get a pass to be there for the banquet and ceremony. He got there, but late. Isabel went down to the "long hall...and here he was, coming along, and stopping to talk to people—oh, so many people—Jimmy! And oh my! You think that you know all about it, and then he comes back in khaki, and—"[12]

At the end of March, Chief finished ground school at Princeton, and after a brief leave spent in Swarthmore, left for flight training at Camp Dick, Dallas, Texas. This separation was painful to Isabel, for whom it was but a prelude to his leaving for overseas. She now began to talk with both Chief and her parents of marriage. Chief's first reaction was to sit down and compose his usual lawyer's brief, outlining side-by-side the reasons "for" and "against." He sent his brief to Katharine because he thought he and Isabel should have "the privilege of your mother's master-mind for such subjects."[13] Meanwhile, Isabel had her own ways of approaching Katharine. Earlier in the year, her mother had said to her, "I should be very sorry to see you married until you are several years older"; and when, at other times, Isabel touched on the subject of marriage, Katharine would counter with, "He may never be sent overseas." True, said Isabel, but this was merely dodging the question. She now wanted a specific answer from her parents.[14]

On May 6, Isabel wrote her mother:

> Three days ago I was reasonable. Now I am not. It's gone
> past reasoning. There are reasons *enough* so that it's not pre-
> posterous. People in general wouldn't be shocked. The chapter
> here [her sorority] wouldn't be shocked. Not all of the faculty
> would be shocked. It's perfectly respectable—perfectly
> possible. Well then—I want to be married. I think I have
> the right. We're doing enough, giving enough, if he goes to
> France. The world owes us that much. If he comes back, then
> spose it *does* make things harder afterwards—Chief & Izzy
> can afford to pay for it. They'll be happy. They'll have each
> other.... And if he doesn't come back...I don't think anything
> else matters very much in comparison.... You can't in the last
> analysis always settle a matter by logic.[15]

Meanwhile, Chief had chosen to train as a bomber pilot and was transferred to Park Field, Memphis, Tennessee. He completed his first solo flight there on June 1, which he called "one of the happiest days of my life."[16]

As events seemed to be lining up in favor of Isabel and Chief's being able to marry, Katharine offered one last caveat: It might injure Chief's happiness, or his chances for happiness. Isabel postponed further discussion with her mother until she could be home, which, because of Swarthmore's curtailed spring semester, would be in mid-May.

By the end of her junior year, she was associate editor of *The Halcyon* and vice president of the Women's Athletic Association, had a role in the class play, was elected to Phi Beta Kappa and Mortar Board, and had varsity letters in swimming and gymnastics. She carefully asked for and received permission from the dean of women to be allowed to live in the dormitory the following year, even if she were married. Her final grades were "A's" in everything, except for a "C" in physical education.

Once home, Isabel apparently had no trouble in persuading her parents to approve of her marriage to an air cadet, whose future was uncertain. Katharine finally wrote to Chief: "I hope that whether you go to France or not, that you and Isabel decide to marry. I am sure she is a very brilliant and dear girl, and I know she will be a wonderful help to you. I feel confident that we'll be able to help you a whole lot."

But it was her "reasoned enthusiasm" that counted most to Chief. "It's the difference between feeling that you're right," he wrote Isabel, "& *knowing* that you're right."[17] For Isabel, on the brink of marriage to the man she loved so deeply, she stood "at the Gates of Heaven" and trembled at "the thought of entering."[18] When Paul Gemmill (now engaged to Jane Brown) wrote Isabel that she was to marry "the best man in the world," it was something she already knew.[19]

The only matters left to settle were a date and permission for Chief to have leave from Park Field. After a lower-ranking officer promised Flying Cadet Myers that he could have a week's furlough, the commandant altered this to a weekend pass from June 15 through 17, with four days free time in Memphis to be granted later.[20] The wedding date was set for Monday, June 17.

The bridegroom-to-be had letters from Lyman, Parcie, his mother, and Katharine, each with a particular message. Lyman preceded his letter with a telegram that said simply, "It's all over but the shouting." Chief wrote Isabel, "Your dad is a peach! He's a whole lot nicer about letting me have you than *I'd* be, if I were in his place. Here you are just growing up and ripening into the apple of his eye,—and along comes a soldier cuss and takes you away—body and soul—doesn't even leave you with the *name* he gave you. But how nice it's going to be to have him for *my* dad too!"[21]

Although Parcie had a tussle with herself over losing her "best beloved kin," she and her mother, realizing it was wrong to idolize one in the family to such an extent, were proud of Clarence and prouder still "of daughter Isabel."[22]

Katharine, who now regarded Chief as one of her "grown-up children," exercised her privilege to make suggestions, and wrote a letter of counsel to him about sexual intercourse. Describing it as that "most intimate of all relations," she told him that she felt that the act made people "truly married." Furthermore, Katharine explained, intercourse was not a concession to anything, nor simply a means to an end, but that it was "worthwhile in itself,—even necessary to the happiest married relationship." Chief, who was more surprised than embarrassed to hear these words from his fiancée's mother, was confident that these were also Isabel's views.

In having the audacity to bring up the subject of sex, Katharine was far ahead of her times; she had also educated a daughter to believe her value as a woman was not solely determined by how physically desirable men found her. Isabel and Chief, despite the views of some prudish contemporaries to the contrary, agreed that they "ought to become man and wife" the very evening of the day they were married.[23]

The ceremony took place on June 17, 1918, in the presence of a few close friends in the parlor at 3208 Newark Street with the Rev. Dr. J. MacBride Sterrett, rector of the All Souls Memorial [Episcopal] Church, Washington, D.C., officiating. They left for Memphis late the same evening by train, traveling in a stateroom provided by Lyman and Katharine.[24]

War Bride

*I*sabel and Chief arrived in Memphis on Wednesday morning, June 19, with just enough time for her to be installed in their reserved room at the Chisca Hotel before he had to leave for Park Field, about twenty miles from the city. They would not be able to see each other again until the weekend. Meanwhile, Isabel began immediately to search for a job and for a suitable boarding house that would accommodate Chief's weekend visits.

A town with a population of about 160,000, Memphis was a thriving railway junction and an important trade and manufacturing center. Its location on a bluff overlooking the Mississippi River protected the town from flooding, while providing access to a major waterway. The business community, with personnel depleted by the needs of the war, had ample need for a person with Isabel's skills. They did, however, begrudge her her wish for temporary employment.

After unknowingly searching on the edge of the red light district where rooms were noticeably inexpensive, Isabel settled for a second floor front room at 1519 Madison Avenue, a tree-lined street in a pleasant part of town; board was offered two houses away. She estimated that she would need approximately twelve dollars a week to cover basic living expenses, and she would require a starting salary of at least seventeen dollars. Finding no suitable temporary employment through the classified ads or the United States Employment Agency, she turned to the Girl's Club, where the director sent her to an office training school. The school charged a ten percent commission to place her, but Isabel decided the cost was justifiable. By Saturday, she had a temporary job with an insurance company where she was to be paid eighteen dollars a week. Her new "boss" had had his patience tried by inaccuracy from her predecessors But, Isabel wrote her mother, "[This] isn't one of my sins."[1]

After two days at work, the boss was so impressed with Isabel's competence that he wanted her permanently or not at all. She declined the offer and once more was job hunting. After one day of unemployment, she was hired as a clerk/typist by the Fischer Lime and Cement Company at seventeen dollars and fifty cents per week.[2]

She wrote Katharine that she and Chief were very happy; in fact, she never "really believed there was such an extra special brand of happiness...I think I'd be quite content in Hades, if through some blunder of the authorities Chief was stationed there!" Isabel assured her mother that in the four days of her stay in Memphis, she was well established, sure of her room and work, and knew her way around downtown "quite thoroughly." She emphasized that she was not homesick and would not be as long as she kept busy.[3] She slowly but methodically worked her way through her thank-you notes, and the sale of a poem to *Life* for three dollars made her eager to get back "in the writing game."[4] She felt she should take over the correspondence with Chief's mother and sister because he didn't write often enough. Part of her job as Mrs. Clarence Myers would be to keep Ella Myers and Parcie happy.

As for her boarding house, it was run by an "iron-jawed lady with a gray pompadour and a silent disposition, and by her faded mouse of a sister." Meals were shared by the proprietors' "egg-shaped, bachelor brother," another bachelor who was "the very pattern of a decayed character actor," preoccupied with an unshaken belief that a diet of pickles had restored his health, a couple whose marriage was marred by his conceit and his constant belittling of his silent wife, and a "powdered little woman with a very tight string of very large pearls around her neck" and a brat of a little boy on her hands. "Oh, for a college table," she had said.[5]

Katharine worried about her daughter's being alone, and she asked Isabel if she were now glad that she went ahead and got married. Isabel's answer was a firm yes, "gladder—than I ever was of anything, except perhaps that Chief cared."[6] Katharine cautioned Isabel not to overdo it, to get to bed early, and not to skimp on her letters home. Isabel declined her mother's offer to do her laundry (as Katharine had done every week while Isabel was at Swarthmore) because she wanted to keep her own house in order without too much help from anyone else.[7] Katharine was sure that this meant that her daughter wanted to cut the "maternal cord," but Isabel explained that there was a big difference between wanting to be able to handle things alone and actually doing it—or else why would she still be asking "every day for advice?"[8]

Living in Memphis made Isabel appreciate things that she had taken for granted, such as the fine department stores in Washington and Philadelphia. She also had difficulty finding the degree of intellectual stimulation she had been used to in Swarthmore, and she did not understand the way the people in Memphis did their thinking. After talking to her new associates "just for companionship," she was always happy to retreat to her room.[9]

As she became better acquainted with women in the business world, she recognized that there were widening opportunities for women, which would remain open after the war. She thought that men and women should have equality of opportunity; however, she had some reservations.

> I think that under the spur of necessity a woman *can* do a man's work as well as *he* can, provided she is as capable for a woman as he is for a man. But I'm perfectly sure that it takes more out of her. And it's a waste of *life* to spend yourself on work that someone else can do at less cost. I'm sure that men and women are made differently, with different gifts and different kinds of strengths, and it ought to be that there is just as much woman work as there is man work. I don't mean that everybody ought to get married and divvy it up that way …but there ought to be some highly intelligent division of labor that can be worked out, so everybody works, but not at the wrong things.
>
> That leaves, though, a tremendous problem as to what are the right things. For instance, what are the right things for me? My instinctive answer to that is "being my man's helpmeet." But in his mind [Chief] doesn't think that is enough…. He thinks I ought to have some direct contact with the world's work—not just through him [and children]….Will it mix?[10]

She began to keep a record in a small notebook of thoughts about her role as a married woman. Three purposes would guide her: to have a "perfect marriage," to have "six perfect children," and to have a "writing career." To promote a perfect marriage, she would need "health and youth, comradeship and stimulus, good housekeeping practices, and respected achievement." She made a tentative schedule for the arrival of four children: Boy Peter, August 1924; Girl Nancy, April 10, 1926; Boy Roger, January 14, 1928; and Girl Katharine, October 19, 1929.[11]

Meanwhile, Chief was trying to survive and prevail as a flying cadet. He had progressed so well that he expected to receive his commission in two or three weeks. By mid-July, the only major requirement he had to pass before becoming a second lieutenant was cross-country flying. He and Isabel continued to have only weekends together, but she was finally allowed to visit Park Field on "Stunt Day." On Monday, July 23, after arranging to get time off from work, Isabel was invited to observe the pilots perform aerial acrobatics. To watch her husband dive, spiral, loop, and do wing-overs was more drama than she cared to experience again, but she was pleased—and secretly hopeful— at seeing the quarters for married officers.

Shortly after this visit, Isabel wrote a letter to Katharine confiding that she was almost sure she was pregnant. Anticipating a lament from her parents about her unfinished education, Isabel reasoned that anything more she needed could be had from books—an argument that Katharine could hardly refute. Both Lyman and Katharine responded with complete support, however, which abolished Isabel's worries.[12]

The pregnancy turned out to be a false alarm that faded quickly in light of Chief's big news: He received his lieutenant's commission on August 9. They celebrated with a weekend pass in Memphis, then, on the following Wednesday, spent a free day together at Park Field. They went rowing and picnicking on Lake McKellar, which was so deserted that they took off their clothes and went swimming. Later, Isabel asked Chief, "How many young married women of your acquaintance would do that, do you think?" The next week, Katharine sent Isabel a bathing suit.[13]

Plans for further temporary employment (the stenography job with Fischer terminated after three and a half weeks) or any thought of going back to college were discarded when a vacancy that came in the married officers quarters was awarded to the Myers'. Isabel was ecstatic.[14] After a month of domesticity, Chief informed Mother Briggs that, despite her worry over her daughter's probable inadequacies in the kitchen, Isabel could "make anything she sets out to make, and she sets out in new directions every day." He wished that Isabel did not have to struggle over an "infernal coal stove in preparing meals."[15]

Chief was flying only occasionally while waiting for his next orders. Finally, in late September, he was directed to proceed to the Air Service Depot, Camp Mills, Hempstead, Long Island, to await embarkation. He and Isabel left Park Field on Thursday, September 26, arrived in Washington on Saturday, and left for New York on Monday. Isabel found a boarding house in Hempstead and vowed to haunt the place until Chief was sent across. He had only daytime duties, which enabled them to spend the nights together. They made the most of their final few days in New York, thinking each hour was their last together. But, with his overseas equipment assembled, Chief waited.

Military personnel did not know, but probably suspected, that the Imperial German government had collapsed and the Germans had appealed to President Wilson for an armistice. While negotiations proceeded, the press, on November 7, made a premature announcement of peace, which set off wild excitement. The official signing took place on Monday, November 11, 1918, a day that Chief celebrated in New York with fellow officers. Isabel had left on November 8 to return to college and await Chief's discharge.[16]

Chief was able to get a five-day pass over the Thanksgiving weekend and spent his free time in Swarthmore and Washington. With the war over, his frustration increased at the continuing delay in his release, which kept him out of law school. It was imperative that he reenter before February 1 to take advantage of his tuition scholarship.[17] In December, his orders came, not for immediate discharge, but to report at Ellington Field, near Houston, Texas. With furloughs now easier to get, Chief decided to spend Christmas in Marble Rock, Iowa, with his family, whom he had not seen for a year. Isabel was in Washington.[18] To try to expedite her son-in-law's discharge, Katharine visited the Department of Military Affairs and was assured that it would come about that very day. Chief thanked his mother-in-law for her efforts—and sat at Ellington Field for nearly another month.[19] He finally arrived in Swarthmore on January 19, 1919.

The college had had no accommodations for married couples, but Isabel and Chief were assigned rooms on the third floor of the Benjamin West House, the first married student couple permitted to live on campus in the history of the college. Both of them were immediately immersed in school work —she trying to catch up in her fall classes, and he taking unfinished examinations and resuming course work at the

University of Pennsylvania law school. Chief commuted to Philadel-phia from Swarthmore.[20]

In addition to philosophy and two courses each in political science and economics, Isabel decided to try for the annual Lucretia Mott Fellowship award made to an outstanding senior woman who had submitted a thesis by March 1. Her paper, which also served as a requirement in the department of political science, was entitled, at the suggestion of Professor Brooks, "The Evolution of Congressional Personnel: A Study of the American People's Taste in Representa-tives." After her end–of–semester exams were over, she had exactly one month to do the research and writing. Chief helped, and Paul Gemmill, now a graduate student at the University of Pennsylvania in economics, did most of the final typing. Finished in the wee hours of March 1, the paper was deposited in Brooks' office by Chief and Paul, who entered through an unlocked window.

The award, presented on April 12, Somerville Day, an annual celebration for alumnae and women students, went to Gladys Reichard, a classics major.[21] Isabel was worried at "how disappointed Dad and Mother will be," but Chief was angry, and he was sure that the choice of Reichard was *"political."* Although no explicit evidence exists, the fact that Isabel was a married woman could have influenced the decision.[22] Before her graduation in June, Isabel became involved in an issue that was more important to her than winning an award, an issue that would have long-lasting ramifications.

The issue was the undemocratic, elitist practices of the sororities (called fraternities at Swarthmore), which marked too many worthy women as "unacceptable." Jane Brown and Katherine Fahnestock, seniors who spoke out at a Pi Beta Phi meeting, were to be expelled from the sorority if they did not recant; at a luncheon of alumnae, Jane was grilled for three hours, and in Isabel's words, "the sorority situation is growing thicker." Isabel published an article in the *Phoenix,* setting out the issues, and a questionnaire representing both sides was circulated before asking for a vote. The president of the Women's Student Government, Marguerite Drew, in an address to students and alumnae on Somerville Day, called for a reform of student government that would emphasize the existence of only those organizations "with a definite purpose" and "open in membership to all who fill certain published requirements."[23] Marguerite was careful not to mention "fraternities," and discussion of the issue was effectively silenced. However, this was not what Isabel had in mind. In an unprecedentd move, she mounted the platform and stated that the morning's discussion had resembled a performance of *Hamlet* with Hamlet missing from the cast. The fraternity question was "by far the most important one in the college at present," and she invited interested alumnae to remain to hear the matter aired more thoroughly. She presided while a "warm" but courteous and thorough discussion took place.[24] In due course, Jane, Katherine, and Isabel all quietly resigned from their sororities. Chief thought Isabel had "scored a hit" that compensated in some measure for the failure to win the Mott award, but he (and Paul Gemmill) did not take sides.[25]

Isabel thought the sorority experience (her "own private crusade") ranked "third biggest" in her life, next to Chief and the war. Katharine urged her to write a book about it that would be "to the abolition of fraternities what Uncle Tom's Cabin was to the abolition of slavery."[26]

Although a compromise was reached, and the sororities would not be abolished for more than twenty years, Isabel and the seven women who led this crusade would always remain close friends. All from the class of 1919, they poked fun at the Greek names and called their group the "Awful Ate." Four of them graduated Phi Beta Kappa: Eleanor W. Atkinson (Mrs. Erwin C.) Smith, who majored in German; Isabel Briggs Myers, political science; Phyllis M. Komori (Mrs. Maurice A.) Sellers, Latin; and Esther G. Taylor (Mrs. Frazier) O'Neil, English. The remaining four were: Jane P. Brown (Mrs. Paul) Gemmill, English major; Viola M. Conner (Mrs. Edward D.) Martin, history; Katherine F. Fahnestock (Mrs. Richard) Miller, public speaking; and Dorothy Fordyce Lucas, history.[27]

At the end of her senior year, Isabel had straight "A's" and graduated at the top of her class.[28] During her first three years, she had held, respectively, the Anson Lapham Scholarship, the Samuel J. Underhill Scholarship, and the Deborah Fisher Wharton Scholarship.[29] She was also the first woman to be allowed to return to college as a married student. The loss of the Mott award, despite her attempts to be brave about it, was, according to a classmate, a disappointment difficult to accept because, for Isabel, to lose was a rare experience.[30]

CHAPTER EIGHT

Lyman, Katharine, and Carl Jung

*W*hile their daughter was growing up, getting an education, and falling in love, Katharine and Lyman were following special interests of their own.

Up to the time of the United States entry in the war, Lyman's work had continued in the Department of Agriculture's Bureau of Soils. His studies in soil physics were pioneering and led to the development of a method of classifying soils according to their moisture content that was used for more than a half century.[1]

In 1914, he had made a research trip across the Pacific Ocean to Australia to measure the force of gravity at sea. Measurements were being made at points all around the world to try to determine the shape of the earth, but those made on board ships were especially difficult because of the pitching and rolling of the vessel. After several unsuccessful attempts, Lyman devised equipment that overcame this problem. During this journey, which lasted from June 26 through mid-October, he wrote every few days to Katherine and to Isabel, discussing with both women the trials and progress of the gravity apparatus. When he wrote Isabel from Riverside, California, where he had stopped to make some preliminary tests, he explained that the apparatus was at last tight.[2] From San Francisco, he took ship to Honolulu on the SS *Manoa*, on which the gravity apparatus was mounted. A brief stop in Hawaii enabled him to study the islands' soils and vegetation and to observe that the Hawaiians were a "fine looking race." He remounted the apparatus on the SS *Makuna*, and, on August 3, the ship arrived in Sidney, Australia.[3] Because of the outbreak of World War I in Europe, Lyman left Sidney for San Francisco a week earlier than planned; even so, in crossing the

Pacific, his ship ran most of the way with lights out to avoid being captured by the German navy. At sea, en route back to the States, he wrote Katharine: "We are due to arrive tomorrow morning. If you don't get this [letter], notify Mr. [William Jennings] Bryan [Secretary of State] that I have been 'captured.' I am almost the only American traveling 1st class and the other passengers [British] consider me very valuable in event of capture."[4] After a separation from his family of over three months, he arrived safely in San Francisco on October 7, eager to get back to Washington just in time for Isabel's seventeenth birthday."[5]

In April 1917, when the United States declared war on Germany, the Department of Commerce requested that the Department of Agriculture release Lyman Briggs to assist in organizing a division within the National Bureau of Standards to work on weapons specifications. Three years later, he was given a permanent appointment to the Bureau as head of the Mechanics and Sound Division. He constructed the first wind tunnel for aeronautical research, a project that was understandably of great interest to his new son-in-law. Lyman questioned Chief closely about how he looped an aircraft, made a half-wing, and came out of a loop. Chief trained in the "Jenny" and Lyman asked for, and got, a detailed description of the controls of the aircraft.[6] Without being intrusive, he was the kind of father Chief had always wanted. In his professional life, Lyman combined the rare talents of the inquisitive scientist with that of capable administrator.[7] In his personal life, he was gentle and never confrontational with Katharine, and he did not hesitate to stretch his daughter's mind as he shared scientific ideas and methods with her.[8]

Although Katharine was devoted to Lyman and took pride in his achievements, she did not accept the expectations of society that a wife find her identity through her husband. An early sign of this view appears in her story, "Father's Library," published in 1911 in *The Woman's Home Companion*. In this story, she anticipated by almost two decades Virginia Woolf's ringing feminist essay, "A Room of One's Own." In Katharine's piece, the father has a splendid large library, but he gradually takes over parts of the family room where the children work and play; meanwhile, the mother takes over a part of her husband's library and thus realizes a long-time ambition to have a "heavenly quiet place" all to herself in which she can work.[9]

In her early years as a parent, however, Katharine clung to the idea that nothing in marriage and child rearing should be in conflict with one's husband's career. She also ostensibly disapproved of mothers who hired nannies and worked outside the home.[10] Her avid interest in books and her preoccupation with ideas made her a misfit with most of the married women who were her contemporaries.[11] Her early work on children's education was pioneering, but it is not known whether she realized that the unusual methods she used in educating Isabel paralleled similar ideas that in the early 20th century made John Dewey famous.[12] In one of her unpublished manuscripts entitled "What Books Shall Mother Read?" Katharine wrote: "In my own early days I read everything about the care and training of children that I could beg or borrow. Some of it was true, some of it was not; much of it was sentimental foolishness.... I can't remember that even the best of all this reading matter gave me any very practical help, though it would not be safe to discredit it entirely. One can't always be sure where one gets one's best ideas."[13] She was incensed by a statement that appeared in an educational magazine: "Parents cannot be expected to understand the principles of Pedagogy, nor is it desirable that they should."[14] When Ray Stannard Baker concluded that Katharine's writing was more suitable for women's magazines, she settled for publication in the *Ladies Home Journal* and *Woman's Home Companion*.

Katherine's mind, a ferment of ideas, was not always focused on education. While Isabel was in college, she designed a tray for "traveling bags or satchels" that would provide separate compartments for clothing and for "various toilet articles, stationery, etc.," that was removable. A professional sketch shows the tray fitted into luggage known as a "Gladstone," which was then in vogue. In 1918, she applied for a patent, which was granted, "with improvements," a year later. After compiling a list of sixteen reputable manufacturers of leather goods, some located as far west as Chicago, and hiring an attorney to assist in negotiations (along with Chief), Katharine apparently gave up the project as impracticable.[15]

---

*F*rom the time the Briggs family moved into their home in Cleveland Park, Katharine had her own study, or workroom, on the first floor, with a bank of windows and a window seat that had a front exposure. Here were her files, her typewriter, her own comfortable chair, and her books, dozens of them. It was here, after she met Clarence Myers, that she began to ponder the idea of personality types. This idea would be the genesis for Isabel's development of the *Myers-Briggs Type Indicator.*[16]

Chief was different from any person who had crossed Katharine's path, and, as it became increasingly obvious that Isabel had fallen in love with him, Katharine wanted to "figure him out." Although she began by reading autobiographies and biographies, she found autobiographies to be more helpful because they did not introduce the biases of a second person.[17] Family legend has attributed Katharine's interest in type solely to "figuring out Chief," but the evidence strongly suggests otherwise. Learning to build characters for the fiction that she tried for many years to publish was a stronger motivation that sustained her interest long after Chief and Isabel were married.[18]

There is little information as to what specific books Katharine had in her library, nor of what she read, but in the decade beginning about 1917, many of the autobiographies available were memoirs of the Civil War and its aftermath.[19] Katharine is known to have read *The Autobiography of Benjamin Franklin* and Friedrich W. Nietzsche's *Ecce Homo.*[20] Other biographies available at that time were those of Ulysses S. Grant, Samuel Clemens *(Life on the Mississippi),* General William T. Sherman, Mary Boykin Chestnut (a diary), Frederick Douglas, Theodore Roosevelt, Henry Adams, Charles Francis Adams, II, and Edward W. Bok (the same editor with whom she had corresponded). Biographies of presidents and other statesmen were in print, and she was surely acquainted with the work of Lytton Strachey, in particular, his *The Eminent Victorians* (1918) and *Queen Victoria* (1921). Biographies by or about women were rare, although Lilian Whiting's *Kate Field,* about a pioneering woman journalist and editor, had appeared in 1899.

In an undated manuscript in Katharine's papers entitled "Notes on the Art of Creating Characters," she described her own theory for analyzing character based on the writings of Reymond Dubois, Alfred Jules Emile Fouillee, Karl Ernst Georges, Immanuel Kant, Georges Polti, and Theodule Armand Ribot. Fouillee and Kant were 19th century philosphers, Dubois, a physiologist, Georges, a lexicographer, and Ribot, a psychologist. Most relevant was the work of Polti, who, in 1922, had published *The Art of Inventing Characters.*[21]

None of this was light reading, nor is her proposed theory. As she read and pondered, Katharine was more interested in trying to understand the basic principles of behavior and personality than in application.

Then, in 1923, when Carl Gustav Jung's *Psychological Types* appeared in English translation, Katharine Briggs is alleged to have said, "This is it."[22]

Four years later, she wrote to Jung that his book had been her "Bible." In *Psychological Types,* Jung had a chapter called "The Type-Problem in Biography," which was one of Katharine's favorite texts in the book. She also confided to Jung that her own notes on the subject of home life and child training, based on his work, had been developed into a book-length manuscript that friends were urging her to publish. The material, she wrote, was "chiefly for the benefit of her children and grandchildren, who have been greatly helped by it…[but] every time I rewrite my understanding is so much more interesting and convincing to others that I wonder if I'd better not keep on doing it over and over for the rest of my life and leave its possible publication to the judgment of my descendents."[23]

Katharine corresponded sporadically with Jung until 1936. Now in the Jung Archives in Zurich, the letters between them show gaps in time that suggest some of them are missing. From a total of eight known letters, six are from Katharine to Jung, two from Jung to Katharine. According to Dr. Peter Jung, grandson of Carl, the letters deal with the "medical case history" of a person Katharine knew. That Jung bothered to reply to Katharine indicates that he must have taken both her and her "patient" seriously.[24] The question also arises as to how seriously Katharine Briggs thought of herself as a competent analyst.

When Carl Jung was in the United States in 1937 to give the Terry lectures at Yale, Katharine arranged to meet him in New York before he returned to Zurich. At that time, she told him of having worked out a type theory of her own before the publication of *Psychological Types,* but that when she recognized the completeness of Jung's formulation of what she had only partially devised, she burned her notes. Jung told her that she should not have destroyed her work, as she might have made a real contribution to type psychology. Later he had copies of his seminar notes sent to her.[25]

Katharine's relationship with her daughter appeared to be flawless up until the time Isabel and Chief became engaged. Each woman had been first in the heart of the other. Even during her busiest periods at Swarthmore, Isabel complied lovingly and faithfully to Katharine's request for daily letters, in which she expressed devotion to her mother in effusive language. Katharine responded with frequent boxes of food for dormitory snacks, new clothes, extra contributions of money to Isabel's bank account, and new furnishings to improve her dormitory room—in fact, no need or wish of Isabel's went unattended. But Clarence Gates Myers had now usurped Katharine's place in Isabel's affections. Isabel learned early in her marriage that dealing with both husband and mother would require finesse.[26]

Katharine's surviving letters to Chief indicate that letting go of her daughter to the extent that she did was not without a struggle, but she was intelligent enough to realize that the most promising course was to woo Chief. She went so far as to arrange for herself and a friend to take an airplane ride in a Curtiss Eagle that left a somewhat envious Isabel as the only one in her family who had not "been up."[27]

In the beginning, when Chief was dazzled by the contrast between Isabel's parents and his own, Katharine's approach worked well. He, in turn, tried to comply with her request for daily letters to "Mother Briggs," but after a few months in the air service, he found this burdensome. Later, when he and Isabel were establishing their home, Chief began to find Katharine's pronouncements and gratuitous advice not quite so compelling. Her "master-mind" and "reasoned enthusiasm" gradually began to lose their charm. He tolerated her and was never rude, but he always remained an independent person.[28]

A woman ahead of her time, Katharine was caught in a restraining net woven of sexism, cultural conditioning, and her own brilliance. Her parents, who had approved of her taking the same college courses as male students and who had ignored the pronouncements of medical authorities that to develop a woman's mind would jeopardize her reproductive functions, had not, however, reshaped her own expectations as to what she might do with her education.[29]

Part Three

CHAPTER NINE

Domesticity

*I*n the summer of 1919, both Isabel and Chief had jobs with the Swarthmore Chautauqua, he as a superintendent and she as cashier (ticket taker) and assistant group leader for morning children's events that required story-telling and teaching folk dances and songs. Educational lectures, in which Chief also participated, were scheduled for the afternoons, while family entertainment, usually drama and music, was offered in the evening.[1] Chief, who had begun Chautauqua with unfinished law exams facing him, was trying to study in the midst of his superintendent's duties. Isabel typed his Chautauqua speeches and read his law notes to him in "all the available minutes."[2]

Isabel thought the summer that exposed both Chief and herself to a wide variety of people was going to be one of the most valuable experiences either of them had ever had. They learned to smile at the local customs and accept the natives as they were. In those days of "dry" New England villages, a wagon loaded with "very unprohibition barrels" drove down the main street of this Massachusetts town. A puzzled inquiry about the local laws led a townsman to comment that yes, it was a dry town, but no one except the sheriff could make arrests, and the driver of that wagon just happened to be the sheriff.[3]

Lyman Briggs, on a business trip to a nearby town, surprised them with a visit, and was, in turn, treated to a full evening of Chautauqua activities. As Isabel said, "Our duties are always with us."[4] Several letters that Lyman had written to Katharine while he was away, she sent on to their daughter. Isabel responded: "I'm returning them as you would return to me a letter from *my* lover. You dear, dear father and mother of mine! I hope, when Chief and I have been married as long as you have, that he will feel that way about me.... I rather think that there's only one thing that would give you perfect content at the end of your life...if you had been all you could to the people who loved you most and needed you most."[5]

When Chautauqua summer duties ended, Chief and Isabel settled in Philadelphia in a private home at 6137 Washington Street, about thirty blocks from the law school. Not the most satisfactory location, it offered space and relative privacy for eight dollars a week. Chief had removed six "incompletes" accumulated in his course work by passing the examinations, getting three marks of "Distinguished" and three "Good." However, his appointment as teaching assistant in the Wharton School (at a thousand dollars per year) required so much time that he felt he was off to a "rotten start" in law school.[6]

He and Isabel were hardly settled when she was offered the position of assistant in the department of economics at Swarthmore, at a salary of eight hundred dollars for the remainder of the academic year, an offer she felt she could not turn down. Because she was "unaccustomed" to making her own decisions, however, she wanted Katharine's counsel about it. Katharine approved, and Chief and Isabel moved at once to Swarthmore to temporary rooms on the third floor of the Woolman School. Again, Chief commuted to the University of Pennsylvania.[7] To supplement their finances, they had taken jobs for the fall semester as Sunday-school teachers at eight dollars per Sunday at the Unitarian Church of Germantown.[8]

Aside from having to move four times during the year and to endure Katharine's open disappointment that Isabel's book on Swarthmore and the sororities would be shelved, the academic year 1919–1920 went well in other ways. As junior faculty, the couple participated in social events in Philadelphia and Swarthmore and were amused by their new roles as acceptable chaperones for college dances. They both acquired bicycles and savored long rides to quiet places away from the "madding crowd." Katharine continued to issue caveats about Isabel's health habits, and Isabel continued to assure her mother that she was in tip-top condition.[9]

As the presidential campaign of 1920 began to heat up, neither Isabel nor Chief was thrilled with the possible candidates. When she was a youngster, Isabel said she had the "greatest reverence for men in high places. It seemed that of *course* they were adequate, or they wouldn't have been in the high places. And now I'm appalled because I can't feel that *anybody* is adequate, barring my own family.... Professors, legislators, governors, and presidents —they all are such *mere people,* when their jobs call for something special."[10]

The presidential candidates to whom she implicitly referred were Attorney General Alexander M. Palmer, Governor James M. Cox of Ohio, and Woodrow Wilson's son-in-law, Treasury Secretary William G. McAdoo, competing for the Democratic nomination; and Governor Frank O. Lowden of Illinois and General Leonard Wood, evenly matched for the Republican nomination, with Senator Warren G. Harding of Ohio also contending. Cox was nominated, with Franklin D. Roosevelt as his running mate, while the Republicans were forced to settle for Harding as a compromise candidate, with a dour New Englander, Calvin Coolidge, in the vice-presidential slot. The winners would be Harding and Coolidge.

Despite the near hysterical Red Scare that swept the country in 1919 and early 1920, Chief freely expressed his somewhat "leftist" views to a horrified Katharine, who wondered whether she was getting senile or he had gone "batts." Neither, he said, but he was content to "arrive at the general principles that industry should be run primarily for service, not profit; that the social good is infinitely more desirable than this or that individual's desires or plans; that there should be something more than just equality of opportunity for the clever and the unclever— lest the clever succeed in hogging the whole earth. (His cleverness may be beyond question—but the unclever may have a wife and kids to feed). This 'something more' would take the form of a *minimum standard of decency* for every individual born into the world."[11]

Meanwhile, Chief, with Isabel's help, began to prepare his lectures for the 1920 Chautauqua circuit, still the best paying summer job available. His copies, some hand-written and some typed, which were preserved in Isabel's personal papers, carry the provocative titles of "Nationalized America," "Lincoln or Lenin," "Industrial Democracy," "Labor and the New Social Order," "The High Cost of Justice," and an amazing feminist tract, "Mrs. John Doe." This last lecture gave the historical background of woman's lack of rights from Biblical to current times, and closed with a timely challenge: "In the years to come the woman power of the nation will be added to its manpower for the solution of national problems and the realization of national ideals. Mrs. John Doe has the opportunity today to be man's equal and helpmate in the work of the world as well as the work of the home, in the duties of national citizenship as well as in personal life, and if she lives up to her opportunity, not only her own children, but whole future generations will 'rise up and call her blessed.'"[12]

Although this implicit defense of woman suffrage was, in fact, a combined statement from both Isabel and Chief, she was never involved in, nor apparently excited by, the crusade that had reached its peak in 1919. That year, the nineteenth amendment, which ensured women of the right to vote, became a part of the constitution.

Since Isabel seemed to have more free time than Chief, she typed his class notes, helped him grade his quiz papers, and crammed herself with "the principles of Chief's worst law subjects." She then "bombarded and quizzed" him at dinner and on the walk back to their rooms. In the middle of this hectic schedule, Isabel apologized to Katharine for "only weekly letters."[13] When spring vacation came, they took the time to attend the March 29th wedding of Paul Gemmill and Jane Brown at her home near Leesburg, Virginia.[14]

Chief's plans for his third year of law school were in temporary disarray when Joseph Willets, his boss at the Wharton school, urged him to choose economics over law as a profession and to begin full time teaching. After discussion with Isabel, Chief chose to stick with law.[15] His decision apparently displeased Willets and contributed to the loss of the assistantship for 1920–21, something Chief was not told about until June. In a letter of controlled outrage, Chief told Willets in typical Myers understatement that "the situation for me contains elements of seriousness."[16]

Isabel and Chief, after a careful analysis of their financial prospects for the coming year, and exceedingly weary of living like gypsies, had already made a deposit of $200 on a six-room bungalow in Morton, just outside the boro limits of Swarthmore. They would cover $1800 of the $5300 total cost by using their savings collected from Liberty Bonds, gifts, army pay, and Chautauqua income. To maintain mortage and up-keep, they would need a steady income of "from $130 to $150 per month" —no problem if both had jobs.[17] The planning and purchase, made solely by "the firm of Myers and Myers," left Katharine "duly and properly astonished."[18] However, she wrote Chief that she and Lyman were in accord that happiness for Isabel and Chief would consist in building their own future "without too much interference from the older generation."[19]

Three days later, his exams finished, Chief headed off for the Chautauqua trail and Isabel to Newark Street. Dean of the law school, William Ephraim Mikell, had given Chief permission to register six weeks late in the fall of 1920 to give him time to earn another month's wages with the Chautauqua group.[20] Determined that he and Isabel would not spend his last year in law school grubbing every minute and concerned about the lack of sufficient time to study as indicated by his final grades (three "Pass" and four "Good," the lowest marks he had ever received in his life), Chief successfully appealed to his family for a loan.[21]

The rigors of spending another summer "on Chautauqua" had little appeal for Isabel, even to be with Chief. She decided that by living at home and working in Washington, she could save more money and would have leisure time for writing. With the help of her father, she got a job at the Bureau of Standards, which led Chief to twit her about "rolling up money…all out of your long-suffering dad!" In fact, Isabel tried to dissuade Chief from skipping the first six weeks of the fall term to earn an extra few hundred dollars with Chautauqua.[22] Chief remained firm; he told Isabel that he would be glad to economize, "just so it doesn' t pinch," and he urged her to go ahead and select the needed furniture for their bungalow, to be paid for out of his summer salary.[23] Their separation, tolerated in the interest of establishing a home, came to an end on November 1. Savoring the year ahead, Chief wrote, "you …in my arms most of the time!! Won't it be great!!"[24]

Chief was awarded a $250 scholarship by Dean Mikell, which, along with their summer earnings, eased their financial needs. Swarthmore no longer needed a teaching assistant in elementary economics because the flood of enrollments brought on the year before by returning veterans had diminished. Isabel also recalled that the elementary course as taught in 1919–1920 was reputed to be a snap, but its reputation changed the year she assisted.[25] Rather than work at a secretarial job, Isabel chose to spend her new leisure time in decorating and improving the house.

She and Chief scrubbed, painted, varnished, and revamped the plumbing, wiring, and heating. She made curtains, linens, and tea towels. On five-by-seven cards, she filed menus and recipes and wrote down housekeeping goals that would make her "thoroughly proud" of herself:

House absolutely in order—except the cellar.
Clean enough for inspection.
Clothes in perfect repair.
Accounts in order.
All letters answered.

She began, but left incomplete, a "Diary of an Introvert Determined to Extrovert, Write & Have a Lot of Children"—and varied her list of goals to:

> Keep complete job list and do one every day.
> Housekeep till 10 A.M.
> Two hours writing.
> One hour outdoors.
> One hour self-development—music, study, friends.
> Wash face with soap every night.
> Never wear anything soiled.[26]

Her mind was too much on the needs of her house to be able to concentrate on writing, which she felt she could always do once she got settled. She wanted to do some "spring sewing, plan the outdoors planting around the house" (climbing roses and honeysuckle fences), and to make preparations to entertain the Awful Ate on Somerville Day.[27]

Except for Jane, the visiting members of the Ate were concerned about Isabel's preoccupation with housekeeping. (Jane and Paul, in an apartment in Philadelphia, were, like Chief and Isabel, struggling together through his graduate work.) In a round-robin letter to the Ate after Somerville Day, Isabel defended her position in rebuttal to Katherine Fahnestock's question, "What the dickens are you working for?" The whole purpose of creation, Isabel thought, was to work for a full life. "And that involves a certain amount of creature comforts, necessarily, I think. The rank and file of us don' t have energy or spirit to appreciate the subleties unless and until we are warmed and fed.... It's fine work when it's well done.... But there's a sort of categorical imperative upon us to do what we can do best, and that's what drives K. T. and Phil and Esther to minister to [their] particular ways of getting at life. Having the ability to serve Life in one special way, you' ve got to do it or feel that you've wasted yourself."[28]

At that stage in her life, Isabel had two immediate goals: helping her husband through law school and establishing a pleasant, smooth-functioning home. While Chief focused on his last semester's courses and looked for a permanent job, he had one more hurdle: studying for the Pennsylvania bar examinations scheduled for early July. He had planned to start the summer with the Swarthmore Chautauqua, but Lyman firmly intervened with a monetary "graduation present" that would leave Chief free to study and allow him to survive financially.[29]

Another worry, considerably more minor, was the intent of Chief's family to visit in June in the middle of his examinations. Katharine took care of that with a note to the Myerses that influenced them to postpone the visit for two weeks.[30]

Chief passed his final courses in law school with one "Distinguished," three "Good," and three "Pass." He took —and passed—the bar exams on July 5 and 6 and accepted a position to begin in September 1921 with Biddle, Paul & Jayne, one of the best law firms in Philadelphia. Their trials behind them, he and Isabel were ready to enjoy life to the fullest.[31]

CHAPTER TEN

Peter and Ann

After finishing the renovations on their house, Isabel and Chief's next priority was to begin their family. By late January 1923, Isabel knew she was pregnant. This one would be "little Peter." For the next several months, Isabel prepared the layette and knitted for her baby-to-be. Ella Myers rejoiced at the expected grandchild and that Isabel was in excellent health.[1]

Katharine had more detailed comments:

> I hope the housework is still going nicely. I'm sure you will enjoy a real spic and span house just as much as Chief. And if you really put your mind on the budgeting of your time, and conduct your work in a very logical way, I think you can get pretty good results without too great an outlay of time....
> You'll have to have more help when you are nursing a baby, for it's very unwise to get tired under those circumstances....
> Dad is very much concerned about it, and agrees with me that you should have daily help so long as you are in the baby business.... If Chief is as busy all the time as he seems always to be when I'm up there, I wonder if you two get as much out of each other as you have coming to you.[2]

The fact that Chief was "busy all the time" was due, in part, to his move to a new position with a larger Philadelphia law firm, Duane, Morris, and Heckscher, where he would remain until his retirement. Even Katharine conceded that Chief would now have "more things to think about...than he ever did before."[3]

71

The tone of Katharine's letters to her daughter during this time suggests that she was not entirely pleased about Isabel's pending motherhood. She had urged, coaxed, and desperately wanted her daughter to be a writer, and her hopes seemed to be dimmed. To encourage Isabel, Katharine had given her a year of tutoring by mail from the Palmer Photoplay Corporation, a correspondence school for writers in which Katharine was already enrolled as a student. Mother and daughter were to collaborate, but Isabel's heart was clearly not in the venture. Katharine implicitly acknowledged defeat—for the time being: "I wouldn't bother my head about writing this summer unless I felt very much like it," she wrote Isabel.[4] Katherine knew Isabel would be preoccupied by family life.

Isabel had had a series of rejections of both poetry and fiction from *Century, Atlantic, Good Housekeeping, Youth's Companion, Saturday Evening Post,* and *The Writer's Monthly.*[5] After her phenomenal successes as a teenage author and her outstanding record at Swarthmore in English composition, these failures were something of an aberration and suggest a preoccupation with her home and impending family.[6]

After those earlier years, when daughter outshone mother as a writer, Katharine finally sold a scenario, "The Ninth Name," to the editor of *Photodramatist* for $500.[7] In the wake of that success, she sold a second piece, "The Highbrow Kid," to *Photodramatist* to be "fictionalized" and published serially in *Story World* and to be considered for use in films. She began right away to work on a full-length novel titled "The Guesser."[8] No longer using the pseudonym of Elizabeth Childe, "Mrs. Katharine Cook Briggs" was the subject of a news feature in *The Washington Post.* "Quite a little romance forms a background for Mrs. Briggs' first success," the *Post* stated.

> She and her daughter, Isabel Briggs Myers, who is also a
> writer, strove for success in scenario writing jointly under
> a fictitious name—"Katherine McKelvey." They tried to
> collaborate in taking the Palmer Educational course...but
> Mrs. Briggs alone persisted despite repeated discouragement....
> She is now working on her first novel.

In closing, the *Post* identified both Katharine's husband, "Dr. Lyman Briggs," and her father, "Professor Albert Cook."[9]

When Katharine could not elicit much enthusiasm from Isabel about fiction, she turned to a discussion of personality types. Lyman's mother, who had just visited in Washington, was described in some detail. Mrs. Briggs grew up "in the wilds of Michigan," where she was not encouraged to "waste any time over books." Her schooling, which had ceased with the eighth grade, did not alter how the frontier judged her as an adult: by her "morals" and by "how hard she could work." Even so, Katharine thought Lyman's mother understood children and that she taught them obedience and "developed in them the intellectual curiosity that had been suppressed in herself."[10] (Katharine might have added that Mrs. Briggs' methods in child rearing seemed to echo her own.) In any event, Katharine concluded, "we may classify Grandma as Imaginative Temperament in which the craving for tranquility has dominated since infancy, with the subjective attitude taking second place, and the craving for understanding stunted by a life of manual labor very much overdone."[11] This elaborate summary was another precursor to the sophisticated personality sorting instrument that would later bring professional recognition to Isabel long after Katharine's death.

---

*I*f the Awful Ate had been concerned earlier with Isabel's nonintellectual activities, they now responded with pleasure to her pending motherhood. She would be the first in the group to make them "aunts." K. T and Phyllis shared an apartment in New York where they were enjoying to the fullest the world of art and drama. When they urged the rest of the Ate to come to New York for a fling and a reunion, Isabel and Jane declined.[12]

As the time drew closer for "little Peter's" arrival, Isabel and Chief went to her parents, where, after a needed vacation, he planned to return to Philadelphia and leave Isabel in Washington for the birth. The records are silent as to precisely what happened, but sometime in early September, a baby boy was stillborn. There are brave letters from the Awful Ate and a draft of one that Isabel wrote to a classmate, Verna (Mrs. Hugh) Denworth, who also lost her first baby. Isabel wrote: "Elizabeth and Peter aren't lost to us, they are just postponed. I know they are as disappointed as we are, and I know they are waiting somewhere, impatiently, for the next chance to come to earth and be our own babies. May it be next year for both of us."[13] The most courageous letter of all was to Jane Gemmill, now three months pregnant, for whom Isabel was "so happy." "I can't tell you how I love you for it," Jane replied. "You see my perfect world includes your happiness so completely." In anticipation of their enlarged family, Paul and Jane had bought a small house in Swarthmore at 316 Dickinson Avenue.[14]

One of Isabel's gifts for Christmas in 1923 was a leather-bound, five-year diary. For six months in 1924, she made entries almost daily, followed by a few scattered days in 1925. Most of the rest of the handsome book is empty. On January 1, 1924, she wrote that she was pregnant, probably with "Ann, due in August. Was a Xmas present."[15]

From late January through the rest of her pregnancy, Isabel fought recurring threats of miscarriage. Twice, when she had to stay in bed, Katharine came to take care of her; and on March 22, Chief accompanied her to Washington, obtaining a stateroom so she could lie down during the trip. Attended by a Washington obstetrician, Dr. Prentiss Willson, Isabel passed her sixth month safely. She decided to celebrate by having her hair bobbed.[16]

Lyman and Katharine were generous in providing suitable entertainment for their daughter. Katharine rented a piano (Isabel's had been sent to Morton), and Lyman brought Isabel a guitar that she had a lot of fun with until her fingers got sore. It was Lyman, however, who found the most lasting and unusual distraction—a "4-tube Radiola III radio"—just in time for the family to listen to the Democratic convention later in the month.[17] During one of the final days of political wrangling, Lyman, Katharine, and Isabel ate dinner "in front of the loudspeaker and stayed up until one [in the morning]."[18]

The deadlocked convention finally compromised by nominating lawyer John W. Davis, who had served as ambassador to Great Britain under Woodrow Wilson. The country had been shocked at the sudden death the year before of President Harding, and his successor and now the Republican incumbent, Calvin Coolidge, would easily win election to a full term as President of the United States. (The death in February 1924 of Chief's hero, Woodrow Wilson, did not rate a passing comment in Isabel's diary.)

Chief came to Washington for the Fourth of July weekend, returning to Philadelphia July 6. The next day, Isabel was rushed to the hospital, where a baby girl arrived prematurely. She wrote in her diary: "My little daughter was born at dawn this morning, and died in my arms. She was very sweet. I hope it won't be too long before she comes back."[19]

Chief wired her, "All my love remember third time is a charm."[20] In a letter that followed he wrote: "Poor dear sweet little Ann—just a flicker on this earth, then someone called out 'Wrong number!', and she had to go back to wait her turn with Peter." Next time, he said, they would make her healthy and strong so she would "grow up to be as lovely and adorable as her mother."[21]

Throughout her trials, Chief was supportive and loving. He did housework as best he could when Mother Briggs was not around, and on their sixth wedding anniversary, when Isabel was in Washington, he sent her red roses and "a big, fat letter" (It is missing). "Bless his heart!" Isabel wrote in her diary, "he's such a dear lover."[22]

In late August, when Isabel was finally at home again, Chief took her to see an unfinished house that he thought they should buy on Dickinson Avenue in Swarthmore, across the street from Jane and Paul Gemmill. Chief's increase in salary to $2100 per year, with a seventy-five dollar bonus added, now made larger quarters affordable. Isabel was pleased with the house and its "beautiful fireplace, lovely porch, and an attic for Ann and Peter."[23]

The next few weeks passed in a flurry of getting the Myrtle Avenue place ready to sell and working on the new one. On a Sunday, in late August, before they had moved in, Isabel and Chief "demonstrated to our prospective neighbors how we keep the Sabbath." She cleaned the front living room windows while he sanded the floors.[24]

Chief's plan to distract Isabel from dwelling on the loss of the baby appeared to be working well, but in her diary she wrote, "Very blue. Oh, little Ann."[25] When they painted each room in the Dickinson Avenue house, Isabel told herself that this one was for "Ann" and another would be "Peter's." They moved sometime before her twenty-seventh birthday on October 18. By then, she was pregnant again, with the baby due in April. Early in this pregnancy, probably at a little past two months, she miscarried. Her diary is silent for several weeks after she wrote, on November 18, "If I can just get safely through the next two months! My darling little Ann—but I reckon it'll be Peter that insisted."[26]

After three frustrated attempts to start a family, many women would have given up and turned to other interests—but Isabel merely decided to rest and regain her strength. While she waited for "Peter and Ann," she turned to writing poems and stories for a children's magazine, *Scattered Seeds*, published monthly by the Friends' General Conference in Philadelphia. Phyllis Komori, who wrote stories and did illustrations for the magazine, may have introduced Isabel to the editors. Her writing, by no means great literature, was clever and, not unexpectedly for a religious publication, usually carried a moral lesson. One poem,

"The Toy Balloon," suggests that Isabel may have had some doubts about her own expectations:

> We went to the circus the week before last,
> And they bought me a toy balloon.
> Twas just like a bubble,
> (But that was the trouble),
> And round as a full red moon.
>
> It drifted and floated and bobbed round my head,
> And danced at the end of the string.
> I was glad that instead
> Of the popcorn I'd said
> That I wanted that beautiful thing.
>
> But it hit Mother's hatpin and quick as a wink
> My beautiful bubble was dead.
> The next time we go
> To the circus I know
> I'll have peanuts and popcorn instead.[27]

———————

*I*n the spring of 1925, Katharine Briggs was diagnosed as having a uterine fibroid tumor. Instead of following the recommendation of her doctor in Washington, who advised radium treatments, she went to Columbus, Ohio, where her uncle, James F. Baldwin, a gynecologist and eminent surgeon, removed the tumor. Dr. Baldwin also discovered that Katharine had gall stones that he removed in a second operation. Lyman, in Ohio with his wife, kept Isabel and Chief informed by telegram and letter. Before leaving Washington, Katharine had written Chief her plans and asked him not to tell Isabel until it was all over to "spare her the emotional strain and worry of suspense."[28] The surgery went smoothly and, later, Isabel took the train to Columbus to accompany her mother home. Before they left for Washington, Katharine wanted Dr. Baldwin to examine Isabel to try to determine why she had suffered three miscarriages.[29] The medical records have not been found, but when Isabel returned to Swarthmore, she lost no time in starting another pregnancy. On April 24, 1926, her diary entry says: "WE HAVE A SON. And he is perfect & so is the whole world, since

4 P.M. Ten lbs. 12 oz. of darling, blessed, sturdy Peter-baby. 'Ask—it shall be given unto you'—in the end.''[30] When friends and relatives heard of the safe arrival of Peter, there was much joy. The Awful Ate breathed a loving, collective sigh of relief. Jane Gemmill, whose son, Robert, was now a year old, "wanted to hug the whole world" *after* she stopped crying.[31] Chief was proud of his son, proud of his wife, and a touch chauvinistic about the size of this male child, who had to have a special crib because he was too large to fit in the infant's bed provided by the hospital.[32] Later, when Isabel and Peter were back in Washington visiting the grandparents, Chief wrote to his son, on a sheet of small children's stationery, decorated in color with a small boy flying a kite:

Dear Little Peter,

Hello there little fellow! Your daddy misses you …and all your dear little tricks sumpin' fierce!… Your daddy loves you wee man. He thinks you are absolutely the nicest little thing he ever saw or felt or hugged, and he knows you're growing up so fast, alas, he'll have to stop saying these things to or about you in your presence.[33]

For Peter's first year, the parents were wholly absorbed in him and his well-being. When he appeared to have a touch of rickets, Isabel would sit in the sun for long periods of time holding Peter in her lap.[34] In her five-year diary, she made a single entry on April 24, 1927: "Peter is one year old—26.5 lbs. of sturdy preciousness with *such* a good start in life…[but] the biggest thrill is, have we or have we not given Peter a little sister for his birthday?"[35] The answer turned out to be yes. On December 29, Isabel Ann Myers was born, as had been Peter, at the Columbia Hospital for Women in Washington, with Dr. Prentiss Willson the attending physician.[36]

Now thirty years old, and with a surviving son and daughter from five pregnancies, Isabel was willing to settle for two children instead of the six she had originally wanted. She had her Peter and Ann.

CHAPTER ELEVEN

The Mystery Novel

*D*uring Peter and Ann's first years, Isabel was immersed in their care and development. At Katharine's urging, Isabel had become more stringent with Peter's discipline. Isabel reported to her mother:

> I've spanked him twice for infringements of the rule about talking after being put to bed, but that was all that was necessary. We are also shutting him up a great deal at the dinner table while Chief gives me the day's news. He stays very still for a while, then breaks out with a very polite, "Can I sing now?", when Chief has paused. We usually let him, then, though just singing is not allowed. It has to be conversation, and Peter digs up the greatest lot of ancient history to relate in a cheerful hodgepodge so as to be allowed to keep the floor![1]

Ann, at ten months, whose every act was a joy to her mother, walked before her first birthday and amazed her parents with her verbal precocity.[2]

Isabel's favorite book on child psychology was *Inner Life of Childhood* by Frances G. Wickes (with an introduction by Carl Jung), but she soundly criticized the writings of Bertrand Russell, which her mother recommended.[3] In addition to recommending books, Katharine constantly advised her daughter on Peter's and Ann's rearing and development.

When Peter was not yet two, Isabel wrote Katharine after returning from a visit to Washington that she had immediately started

a very astringent jacking-up of discipline…. The thing
you said which most IMPRESSED ME IN OUR LAST
DISCUSSION WAS THAT IF PETER didn't take me
seriously there was *nothing* he was taking seriously…. I spank
occasionally for things that I am not even perfectly sure he
remembers are on the forbidden list, on the general principle
that it is good for him to be a little concerned lest he make a
mistake. The deliberate inculcation of the tense attitude is a
very interesting experiment, and I am sure, as you say, that it
can't possibly do Peter any harm.[4]

Katharine, who was convinced that this was the right thing
for Peter, praised Isabel's careful attention to the "obedience pro-
position."[5]

———————

*I*f Katharine had some sense of satisfaction in helping
to rear her grandchildren, her attempts at fiction had been totally
frustrating. She had sent her novel, "The Guesser," to ten publishers and
two film producers, all of whom turned her down. In the plot of "The
Guesser," she had tried to interweave a love story with Carl Jung's
theories of personality, and the emphasis had turned out to be more on
Jung than on love. The letters of rejection were courteous, but an editor
from Thomas Y. Crowell stated frankly: "My impression is that the
extraneous matter weighs down the story to such an extent that the
book will not prove profitable."[6] Even after Katharine had revised the
novel, D. Appleton & Company was less tactful: "In its revised form it
is…still too deeply permeated with surgery and discussion of Freud, so
full of hospital life that we have not any confidence in its success with
the fiction-reading public."[7] When Crowell publishers found the novel
unsuitable after Katherine's revisions, they suggested she use a professional literary critic, J. Walter McSpadden. In McSpadden's five-page
intelligent critique he pointed out, among other things, that, although
the discussion of Jung would be over most reader's heads, "it gives the
story a certain solidity."[8] Katharine dismissed him and enclosed a check
for his fee of twenty-five dollars. A bewildered McSpadden responded
that he had carefully read her second letter and was at a loss as to how
to advise her further with her story.[9] The yellowed manuscript of "The
Guesser," with its several revisions, survives in the family archives as a

monument to Katharine's unfailing belief in Jung's theory of personality types.

Katharine's disappointment with her lack of success in writing fiction was somewhat assuaged when, on December 22, 1926, *The New Republic* published her pioneering article about personality type, "Meet Yourself." This essay is still cited as the first significant discussion about type in an American periodical, and the first statement to summarize in print the basic ideas on which the *Myers-Briggs Type Indicator* would be based. At the time, the *New Republic* stated on its editorial page that the article by Katharine Briggs should not be interpreted as having the blanket endorsement of the magazine, but it represented a point of view held by "an important school of thought" that could be employed "profitably and perhaps pleasurably by anyone."[10] On its editorial page, *The New York Times* recommended the article as a pleasant diversion for those who liked "to answer questionnaires in company, or who delight in fortune-telling with cards or by palmistry, or who enjoy discussions of their own and their friends' characters—not reputations." The *Times* continued: "She has compiled certain details from Jung's theory of types which enable you to classify yourself and your friends."[11] Such flippant remarks in a distinguished newspaper like the *Times* were more proof to Katharine that a woman's mind was not to be taken too seriously by the public.

She turned again to one of her favorite subjects, educating children, in an essay, "Up From Barbarism," published in the *New Republic* in December 1928. The theme: "In so far as interest and attention are controlled and directed, we may regard ourselves as civilized—educated. But in so far as interest and attention are merely reactions to environment, we must acknowledge ourselves childish and primitive."[12] Weaving into the discussion some of her Jungian concepts about type, she gave examples of children with four different personality types whose interest needed to be captured in different ways. To train these children in the same way, Katharine admonished, was like "sending the goldfish to school with the canary."[13]

While her writing continued, Katharine found time to learn how to drive the automobile that Lyman had bought. On April 29, 1927, at age fifty-two, again the maverick among her peers, she passed her driver's test and was awarded her license.

Shortly after that, Katharine wrote Isabel, "Dad has been appointed Assistant Director of the Bureau of Standards." This put him at government grade six where his salary could go as high as $7500 and placed him in charge of all research and testing. Katharine pointed out that her husband was "already acting director" when Dr. George K. Burgess was out of town, and at other times, was Burgess'"right-hand man."[14]

While Lyman progressed steadily in his profession and Katharine struggled with her novel, Isabel read an announcement in the August 1928 *New McClure's* magazine that would almost overnight bring recognition to the name of Isabel Briggs Myers in the world of fiction. *New McClure's* and the publishing house of Frederick A. Stokes Company were jointly sponsoring a contest for the best mystery detective novel, the winner to receive a cash prize of seventy-five hundred dollars and serial publication during the spring and summer of 1929 in *New McClure's*. The literary agents of Curtis Brown, Limited would select the finalists, from whom the winner would be chosen by a panel of judges. Isabel decided to enter.

By October, with only two chapters completed, she was uneasy about meeting the deadline of January first. However, the more she wrote, the more enthusiastic she became about both the tale and the competition. By mid-December, with the advice and help of Chief, Paul, and Jane, she had finished what she called the "fourth installment," or sixteen chapters, with four or five more chapters to go.

A major problem she faced during the months of intensive writing was how to stay awake. At nine o'clock in the evening, when she was too sleepy to think, she would nap for two hours and then work from eleven to three. "In case you have never tried it," she wrote to Curtis Brown, "it's quite an undertaking to write a detective novel in five months with little One-year-old and little Two-and-a-half hanging on to the typewriter half the time!"[15]

The day before Christmas, when she had two more chapters to write, Ann was mildly ill and fretful. Christmas morning, Ann was diagnosed as having the flu. Two days later, Peter came down with the flu as well. With Isabel's troubles mounting, Paul Gemmill, now on the faculty at the University of Pennsylvania, volunteered his stenographer's services on Friday and Saturday. Isabel wired Curtis Brown to determine whether the manuscript was due on Monday, December 31, since January 1 was a holiday. When they wired back that she could bring it in on January 2, the reprieve looked to Isabel "like an extra month." On Saturday, when Chief came down with the children's illness, Paul volunteered to proofread the entire manuscript.

Isabel wrote Katharine about the final frantic hours:

New Year's Eve, we were all three working on it. I wrote
about six pages that day…[and] while I was writing, Chief
was reading and revising…and Paul was sitting with his little
portable on his lap, following close on Chief's revision and
my O.K.…. Well, and so at last we came to Jerningham's final
speech in which he justifies my main title of "Murder Yet
To Come"…. And then I was done. Emptied. Finished. Not
another idea in my head…. The last word of the book was
written about half past eleven on the day for the closing of
the contest. How's that for coming out even?[16]

Paul finished typing the last chapter a little after midnight, Isabel
rewrote a scene in chapter 8, corrected typing errors, and finally got to
bed at 3:30 A.M. Ann woke at 6:00 A.M. The part-time nursemaid, Mary,
stayed with the children while Isabel took her opus to Curtis Brown on
Wednesday. Once in New York, she remembered to get return postage
at a post office before she left the manuscript at West 39th Street with
an unimpressed secretary.

"And so it was finished," she wrote Katharine. "I walked slowly
back to the station through the New York streets, feeling exactly like
every hopeful youth who has tried to storm the metropolis with the
product of his or her brain. New York! New York! There's my best!
Will it make a dint [*sic*] in you, or will it not?"[17]

Isabel had wondered whether it was within the bounds of
possibility to write a novel in a five-month period. She felt strongly that
accomplishing this was a crucial test of whether she would ever do
anything significant in her life that could lead to "some sort of a
career."[18]

All of her efforts, and those of Chief, Paul, and Jane, were
rewarded when, on February 26, Edwin G. Rich, general manager at
Curtis Brown, wired her: "You win stakes McClure prize contest
congratulations."[19]

Isabel and Edwin Rich immediately began a steady correspondence. He made suggestions for revisions to be finished in a month; he
had sold the English rights for an additional five hundred dollars and he
asked Isabel to "sit down and tell me all about yourself" for urgently
needed publicity.[20] When Isabel seemed perplexed by the request,
Katharine wrote Edwin Rich twenty-two typed pages about her
daughter, a veritable condensation of "The Education of Suzanne." In

her closing sentence, Katharine said: "I don't suppose much of what I have written will be just what you want for publicity material…and if you care to ask questions…I shall be glad to tell you what I can. It has been lots of fun to be her mother, and I have enjoyed telling you about it."[21]

If Rich acknowledged Katharine's gratuitous contribution, his letter was not preserved, but he graciously thanked Isabel for her "entertaining story" about how she came to write. Isabel's version, accompanied by a new 3-by-5 photograph of herself, appeared in *Smart Set* (a magazine that had merged with *New McClure's*) in a full-page spread in the August 1929 issue. This same issue published the first of six installments of the serialized version of *Murder Yet to Come*. The book itself would not be published until January 1930, when the last of the six installments would have appeared in *Smart Set*.

Isabel wrote a witty, crisp account of herself for the magazine:

> You want to hear about me? Well—I am thirty-one, and I am married, and I have two babies, and that in itself is such a blissful state of affairs that I sometimes have difficulty in believing it.

> You see, I know my luck. In June 1918, at the end of my junior year, I married an army flier and went back with him to his post to be as near him as I could. That is, I worked in Memphis while he flew at Park Field, and all that summer, I only saw him about twenty-four hours a week. At last, for a few weeks in September, we were able to get officer's quarters on the field, where all day long the planes rose and circled and stunted and slanted down to earth across our roof, so close with their motors hushed we could hear the hoarse whisper of their propellers and the sigh of the wind through their wires. And to this day, the drone of a plane overhead catches at my breath—until I remember that it can't be "Chief" at the controls.

> But this, of course, is 1929. Lt. Clarence Myers has become Clarence G. Myers, Esq., practicing law in Philadelphia. And four tiny bare rooms under a flat, hot roof, on a flat, hot flying field, have been replaced by a beloved little ivy-covered colonial house in Swarthmore. And there is Peter, not quite three, and Ann, just past one…and that was everything in the

world that I wanted, I thought, until on the first of last August I came across the announcement of a contest in the pages of a magazine and…then I knew I wanted something else. I wanted to try a detective novel, myself!

Even at the start, which is always my most optimistic time, I knew it was a preposterous thing to undertake. Five months to do it in…and I had two babies on my hands!… But I did so want to do this novel—worse than I ever wanted to do any other writing. I had to do it! So I girded up my resolution, as Arnold Bennett says you must, and went to work.

The only solution seemed to be to work at night. I did a good deal in the daytime, but with Ann and Peter climbing over my chair and punching the shift keys so that capitals ran riot on the page, I couldn't make much progress. (Even thE most feaRsome paSSage lacks impresSiveness WHen wRitten like thiS.) In the evenings, though, between nine and three, stretched six heavenly, uninterrupted hours—if I could stay awake to use them. Mostly I stayed awake, though many a time my head bumped the typewriter in the middle of a sentence.[22]

Although Isabel had asked for her mother's help in "criticizing and improving characters," Katharine had not contributed significantly to the novel. When she had criticized the style of Isabel's book, her comments were not welcomed. Later, Isabel apologized for "any coolness in my original reception of your criticisms."[23] *Murder Yet to Come* was dedicated to "Clarence G. Myers, in grateful appreciation of the keenly critical judgment and unfailing resourcefulness which were invaluable to me in the concoction of this tale." Katharine never again tried to write fiction.

Isabel received many letters of congratulations from friends and family. Chief called her his "phenomenon," his "celebrity," and one who deserved all the fame. "Go to it," he wrote, "from your worshipping servant." Paul Gemmill, with his "mask of bored certainty," was not surprised because he *knew* it was a good story."[24] Pricilla Griffin, Isabel's favorite English teacher at Swarthmore, wrote that Isabel had the kind of analytical mind to make a "Sherlock Holmes System "of her own, and "loving hard, working hard, and thinking hard" had made a dream come true.[25]

No one was more thrilled than the Awful Ate. Now married to Maurice Sellers and living in upstate New York, Phyllis (Komori) wanted more details about the "distinguished authoress"; Katherine (Fahnestock), now married to Richard Miller and the mother of two small sons, was no longer concerned about Isabel's talents being squandered in domesticity. Dorothy Lucas had come to Swarthmore in mid–March to talk over with Isabel a disappointing love affair, and Isabel took time to listen and counsel in the middle of her revisions for Edwin Rich. Viola Conner Martin, now in Cambridge, Massachusetts, had a two-week-old son, her first, and wrote a congratulatory letter to Isabel from bed.[26]

When the check from *Smart Set* arrived in May, Isabel had two immediate uses for it: to buy a Studebaker sedan and to repay two thousand dollars borrowed from her parents to help with the purchase of the Dickinson Avenue house. With more than half of her money left, she began to study the stock market for promising investments. She lost no time in inviting Katharine and Lyman to drive to Swarthmore for the weekend of May 11, and she wanted Katharine to stay on a few days with the car to teach Isabel how to drive. "I'd rather get my start from you than from anybody else in the world," Isabel wrote her mother. By May 21, she had her driver's license.[27]

Earlier in May, Isabel had sent the last installment to *Smart Set* and the final manuscript for the book to Stokes. After Chief had carefully examined her contract for the English rights, and for American rights with Stokes, who had the right of first refusal for her next two books, Isabel signed and returned them. Curtis Brown did not take a percentage of her prize money, but no royalties would be forthcoming from Stokes until their share of the prize ($2500) had been recovered from sales of *Murder Yet to Come*.

Edwin Rich was avidly interested in her next novel, but Isabel's attention was focused on the details of editing, proofing galleys, and last-minute changes about which her publisher was patient and courteous. When she wanted to get her hands on the page proofs, however, Stokes wrote that they had been "carefully read by our reader and returned to the printer several days ago."[28]

While Isabel allowed a new plot to simmer in her mind, it occurred to her "quite forcibly" one day that she had "all the rest of my life to write books," but only "just now for bringing up my little people. So that comes first."[29] In establishing her credentials as a writer, she felt that she had not kept pace in maintaining her credentials as a mother.

CHAPTER TWELVE

Acclaimed Writer

*T*he nationwide publicity that followed the appearance in January 1930 of *Murder Yet to Come* identified Isabel Myers as a promising young writer. From New York's *Herald Tribune, Times, Daily Mirror* and *World,* the *Philadelphia Record* and the *Inquirer,* the *Washington Star* and the *Post,* and the *Boston Globe,* to papers in the Midwest and Far West (including the *Honolulu Advertiser*), reviews were favorable to lavish. The *Saturday Review of Literature* ended its review by urging people to "read it by all means—the style is clear and direct, the story rapid, the plot ingenious. You will be a little disappointed in not having more details, at the end, of the criminal's procedure, a fault of most mystery stories, but the explanation is satisfactory and the chances are odds on that you will be fooled."[1]

The Michigan State College *Record* commented: "Friends of the family will be able to detect in her novel traces of the enthusiastic nature of Prof. Cook, her grandfather, the studious thoroughness of her mother [Katy Cook], and the mechanical intuition of her father [Lyman J. Briggs], directed toward a plot-invention instead of physics."[2]

However, a reviewer in the *Philadelphia Inquirer* had some negative criticisms that Isabel wrote to "fight about" with. After a page of rebuttal, Isabel asked why the reviewer thought the method of the murder was "perfectly impossible?…Couldn't you kill a person with a marble statue by whanging them over the back of the neck? I know I could—given sufficient provocation."[3]

The London *Daily News* gave the book faint praise: "This story is ingeniously told, even though it possesses no very original features."[4]

But the Birmingham and Manchester papers, the *Irish Statesman,* and *Country Life* gave her rave reviews.[5]

A syndicated columnist noted that the "three best mystery stories written recently—in the opinion of this addict...[are by] three women writers." The other two novels were Mignon Eberhart's *While the Patient Slept* and Mary Plum's *The Killing of Judge MacFarlane.*[6] Surely the most succinct acknowledgment came from the Waterloo, Iowa, *Daily Courier,* which stated, "Ex-Waterloo man's wife wins $7,500 for mystery novel."[7]

As a result of the widespread publicity, Isabel was asked by a writer, Frank Carstarphen, who had adapted other works, if he might coauthor with her the dramatization of *Murder Yet to Come.* Uncomfortable about the thought of working with another writer, she asked Edwin Rich for advice. Rich discouraged her from that kind of involvement and suggested that Carstarphen get in touch with Curtis Brown.[8] Unfortunately for Isabel's publisher, however, Carstarphen had planted the seed of an idea in her mind that was irresistible. Without the needed experience, but with unshakeable confidence, she began work on a mystery drama in three acts. Both Curtis Brown and Stokes regarded this as a digression from their request for a second book, which could take advantage of the extensive publicity accorded *Murder Yet to Come.*

In September, Isabel wrote Stokes:

> I have been trying to push the work on my next book, in the hope of being able to submit it to you in time for the spring list, as you so kindly suggest. But I have come to the reluctant conclusion that it cannot be done. The work goes far more slowly than I had hoped, and it is impossible at this point to promise when it will be done. The children take more and more of my time, and the story in its development has undergone many fundamental changes which will, I think, make it much better in the end, but which certainly have delayed its progress. Even the original title is no longer applicable. The present working title [changed from "The Unwilling Suicide"] is "Death Signs the Check."[9]

Two months later, after more queries from Stokes, Isabel promised that there would be another book, and she had now changed its title to "Death Calls for Margin."[10]

Before the year was out, *Murder Yet to Come,* in its seventh printing, was a best-seller. Translation rights had been sold to French, German, Hungarian, Danish, and Norwegian publishers.[11] This stimulated Isabel to write," Long ago, I read the saying of a certain wise man, 'Beware of what you allow yourself to want. Some day you may get it!'" When she had written the last line of her mystery novel, she thought she was through. "But I'm not [because]…my publishers want to know when the 'next' one will be ready! So beware of what you want. Some day you will get it. And it will get you!"[12]

She was still confident that she could make her next mystery even better than *Murder Yet to Come;* but, contrary to her publisher's wishes, she continued to "take time out" to "attempt a dramatization" by herself.[13] In March 1931, Isabel wrote Katharine that two acts were finished of a three-act play, *Death Calls for Margin,* and it was already in rehearsal by the Swarthmore Players Club, a competent amateur group.

As she did in writing *Murder Yet to Come,* Isabel had largely worked at night on *Death Calls for Margin,* while Peter and Ann were in bed. Even then, she had disruptions. "You write a little something on a piece of paper, preferably the question to which you want an answer," she wrote Katharine, "and you look at it and look and look and look, and after a while if you're lucky you get it. If you aren't lucky, somebody calls, 'Mother, *Mother!*' And that's *that.*"[14]

She continued to change lines while *Death Calls for Margin* was in rehearsal—until the cast threatened to lynch her if she altered another syllable.[15] She took care to send copies of the play to Curtis Brown in hopes the agency could sell her manuscript to a New York producer.

On four evenings, May 4 through May 8, 1931, the Players Club presented *Death Calls for Margin,* a drama set in Philadelphia shortly after the stock market crash in October 1929 and based on Isabel's unfinished novel of that name that "just wouldn't novelize." In a cast comprised of local people, Chief portrayed a detective on the homicide squad, and Isabel took the leading female role of Mary Landreth, a divorcee.[16]

The small suburban Philadelphia newspapers liked *Death Calls for Margin,* but Isabel was incensed when Arthur B. Waters, drama critic of the *Philadelphia Ledger,* wrote "not too favorably" about it. On May 6, she "bought a new hat, took the next train into town," and planted herself in Waters' outer office until he could see her—an hour and a half later. Waters agreed to give her five minutes, but her approach caught his attention, and over an hour later, Isabel had convinced him to be an advocate for her play. Waters told her that he was a friend of New York theater moguls Lee and J. J. Shubert and that he was going to call them and their nephew, Lawrence Shubert Lawrence, who managed the family's Philadelphia interests. Waters kept his word and brought Lawrence to the Friday evening, May 8, production in Swarthmore.[17]

On May 15, while Curtis Brown still had copies of the play out for consideration, Isabel signed a contract with Lawrence Shubert Lawrence, who planned to produce the drama in Philadelphia in the fall, thus inaugurating a series of plays to be offered locally, "previous to Broadway presentations." After reading more than a hundred manuscripts, Lawrence selected Isabel's work to be the one he wanted to stage first.[18]

Lawrence suggested substantial revisions, which Isabel finished in one sleepless burst of activity in preparation for a production in June at the Buck Hill Falls Inn, a summer resort in the Pocono Mountains of northeastern Pennsylvania. The play, presented on Saturday evening, June 20, again featured Chief in the detective's role, but at Isabel's urging, Barbara Pearson, daughter of Chief's former Chautauqua boss, Paul Pearson, played Mary Landreth. After two years at Swarthmore College, Barbara had just finished two years of study at the Yale School of Drama as an outstanding student of George Pierce Baker.[19] Her credentials sufficiently impressed Lawrence that he chose her without a try-out. Present for the performance at Buck Hill Falls were Lee J. Shubert, Lawrence Shubert Lawrence, and prominent Broadway director, Harry Gribbell.

In the midst of her excitement, Isabel wrote few letters to Katharine, but mother and daughter were able to communicate by telephone.[20] Isabel's activities had reached a point, however, when Katharine thought that some solid counsel was overdue. Isabel's play promised to achieve immediate professional recognition. This pleased her parents, who were not surprised, but Katharine was concerned about Isabel's health.

> *You must eat, and you must sleep,* and you must put these things into your religion. You have already taken risks by letting yourself get so thin.

> And I have some psychological advice as important as the physical. Watch out for ego inflation. It can take possession of you from many directions and very subtly—not as egotism at all, but as excitement.... If you exalt your ego at all by

thinking you are [writing another play] you insult just to that degree the greater intelligence which really is handling your life…. This is a critical time right now…but I won't preach to you any more.[21]

Katharine assured her daughter, however, that she and Isabel's father certainly loved to have Isabel write.[22]

Katharine's counsel was more relevant than she could imagine. Intoxicated with her success in writing drama, Isabel had neglected to keep Frederick Stokes fully informed. In early October, he wrote her that he had just returned from a two-month vacation, and he had been wondering why he had not had the pleasure of hearing from her since last March. After reminding her that he had hoped to limit publication of mystery stories to her work and that of Ellery Queen, Stokes wrote, "If, however, our hopes for new manuscripts from you are not to be realized we shall, with extreme regret, have to make efforts that we have not thus far made to fill your place." He hoped that her silence during the last six months indicated that her manuscript was nearing completion.[23]

In her reply, Isabel broke the news about her contract with Lawrence Shubert Lawrence. She explained that Lawrence had inserted a clause in the contract forbidding the publication of the play in novel form for a period of six months after its production, and, "of course we don't know at present whether it will run for two days or two years. Neither do I know, having been so engrossed with the task of learning the craft of the theater, just how long it will take to recast it in the mold of a novel, but it does not seem that it should take very long, and I am working on it now."[24]

Trying to salvage the situation, Stokes replied promptly and courteously, sending congratulations on her success, even as he hoped soon to have the manuscript so the book would be ready for "prompt publication when this is permitted by the producers of the play."[25]

While Stokes continued to wait, Isabel enjoyed some of the fruits of fame. She was honored in New York at a Theatre, Arts, and Letters Luncheon in the company of a distinguished group of guests that included cartoonist Peter Arno, now with a new magazine, *The New Yorker;* poets Vachel Lindsay and James Weldon Johnson; and writers Hendrik Van Loon, Robert Nathan, and Joseph Wood Crutch. She was in demand as a speaker, usually at women's clubs, and the *Philadelphia Ledger,* in their Sunday edition, published a long interview with her, accompanied by a photograph.[26]

In the interview, "this thoroughly modern yet intrinsically old-fashioned young woman" declared that success in marriage was to be valued "above all else." Speaking as a wife and mother, and not as an author or playwright, Isabel said that she viewed marriage as a joint undertaking, but she thought it was more the job of the woman than the man to work at achieving a happy relationship. A strong believer in Jung's theory of types, Isabel explained that a woman was more likely to be an expert in personal relationships than a man, and it was "only by cherishing the 'feeling relationship' between two persons that you get a very happy marriage."[27]

Isabel neglected to say that, irrespective of Jung's theories, Chief had contributed his share to their "joint undertaking." He had supported and participated in her authorship every step of the way, he had served as her legal counsel, and unperturbed by the subtle disapproval of some of the neighbors, he helped (and did so for most of their married life) with household work. If Isabel was a woman ahead of her time, Chief's views kept pace with hers.[28]

Isabel was no longer optimistic about the professional debut of *Death Calls for Margin.* By the spring of 1932, almost a year after Lawrence had bought her play, she received an inquiry about its status from a puzzled Frederick Stokes. She wrote Stokes that the Shuberts had repeatedly postponed its production, due in part to the "inclemencies of the theatrical season, and because of their own private calamities." The earliest date, she thought, that the play would be staged was sometime in 1933.[29]

The Shubert brothers had been temporarily able to ignore the national economic stagnation known as the Great Depression and the resulting "inclemencies of the theatrical season" when, in 1929, they staged a thriller, *Death Takes A Holiday,* adapted by playwright Walter Ferris from a work by Alberto Casella, an Italian writer. Named one of the ten best plays of the year and a Broadway blockbuster, it set a receptive mood for the Shuberts to take an option on Isabel's murder story. But in April of 1933, the assets of the Shubert Theater Corporation were sold at public auction, and J. J. Shubert was involved in a costly divorce. Although the Shubert brothers would eventually re-establish their theatrical empire, their economic recovery did not occur soon enough to salvage Isabel's aspirations to become a bona fide dramatist.[30]

Death Calls for Margin, which began with such promise, came to nothing. Activities in the theater were severely curtailed in the financial crises of the Great Depression, and the Shuberts' problems were very real indeed, but Isabel's failure to capitalize immediately on the literary success of *Murder Yet to Come* caused her to lose an established, expectant readership. Her aspirations to conquer yet another literary genre rather than to repeat her success in fiction had had its price.

Meanwhile, in the wake of still more inquiries from Stokes, she sent a short story about a child's kidnapping to her agent. After a futile effort to place the piece with popular magazines, Curtis Brown explained that this was not a propitious time to write about such a topic. The baby son of Charles A. Lindberg had just been kidnapped in March 1932, and the public was in no mood to read a fictional account when the real life drama filled the newspapers. While editors considered her story, Isabel sent a manuscript of children's poetry entitled "Little Things Are Nicest" to Stokes. This, too, was rejected.[31] Exasperated but still courteous, Frederick Stokes wrote: "If you have decided definitely that you are not going to do any more work of the sort that you have done so admirably, please let me have word to that effect and I shall take the hint. At present, however, I can only repeat what I wrote you [a year ago]...that it seems very unfortunate for you not to do a book a year."[32]

Katharine supported Stokes in believing that Isabel should and could write a novel a year and that neglecting such an "opportunity that most people would jump at" was "preposterous contrariness." Her daughter, Katharine thought, exaggerated the difficulty, and any woman with an "orderly brain" should be able to organize her life so as to run a house and a career.[33] While the children were babies, Isabel had had a helper named "Mary," who was soon dismissed for unknown reasons, but Isabel may well have been trying to prove to Katharine that she did have a sufficiently orderly brain.[34]

In any event, three years after indicating to Stokes that this second book would soon be available, Isabel sent him the manuscript for *Give Me Death,* another mystery novel. Published by Stokes in October 1934 and in a British edition in 1935, it received a brief, noncommittal review in *The New York Times* and a few favorable reviews in England. Publication rights were sold to Denmark, the Netherlands, and Sweden.[35]

Before the novel faded into oblivion, New York playwright Stuart Miles wanted to dramatize it, but Isabel would consent only to a collaboration. "The world has suddenly grown very exciting again," she wrote Katharine.[36]

While working on *Give Me Death,* Isabel had finished a second play, *Hostage to Fortune,* which interested Arthur J. Beckhard, a Broadway producer of two highly successful plays. Enthusiastically, Isabel worked with him throughout the summer of 1933 in high hopes of having "the career I've dreamed of."[37] By September, when Beckhard had not found a financial backer, Isabel's expectations declined. After Beckhard finally produced *Hostage to Fortune* on August 8, 9, 10, and 11, 1934, at the Peterboro, New Hampshire, drama festival, his relationship with Isabel ended.[38]

    Give Me Death and *Hostage to Fortune* were notable primarily because they were the culmination of the literary career of Isabel Briggs Myers. She summed up her frustrations in a letter to a Swarthmore classmate:

> I want to write books. I want to write plays. I'd like to be Chief's wife in a thorough and artistic fashion, not just with what is left of me after a long day spent wrestling with a recalcitrant scene or chapter. And I'd like to have my time— and thoughts—for Ann and Peter.... There are so many things I always meant to do. I like living in a small house, and I value my privacy so highly that I'm doing my own work rather than let a servant invade our peace.... But at the same time—I'm a lazy person with a passion for leisure that can be overshadowed by taller desires but never rooted out.[39]

CHAPTER THIRTEEN

Family Matters
and a Crusade

*I*n August 1928, when Isabel had first read in *McClure's Magazine* the announcement of the mystery novel contest, the national press was focused on the coming presidential election in November. Calvin Coolidge, with his now famous statement, "I do not choose to run," had, in effect, passed the Republican mantle to the incumbent Secretary of Commerce, Herbert Clark Hoover, a Quaker from Iowa. Hoover's record in directing war relief in Europe and in serving as United States food administrator had established his reputation for vigor and progressivism. He won the election over Democratic candidate, Alfred E. Smith, a New Yorker and a Catholic, by carrying forty out of forty-eight states. Never had the nation as a whole been more sanguine about its present or more confident about its future than in the months preceding the presidential election of 1928.[1]

Less than a year later, on October 29, 1929, the stock market crashed. Values on the New York Stock Exchange had fallen by $26 billion in less than a month. By 1931, the United States was in the depths of the Great Depression, with unemployment figures high and bread lines long. In spite of President Hoover's cautious but unsuccessful efforts toward economic recovery, by the summer of 1932 "a vast apathy, born of confusion and despair, settled over the nation."[2] That fall, Hoover was succeeded by the Democratic governor of New York, Franklin Delano Roosevelt, who would be elected to the presidency for an unprecedented four terms.

The member of Isabel's family on whom these political changes had the most impact was Lyman Briggs. In July 1932, Dr. George K.

Burgess, director of the Bureau of Standards, died of a stroke while working at his desk. Lyman, who had been assistant director of research and testing for five years, was immediately named acting director. On the recommendation of the Secretary of Commerce, under whose aegis the Bureau operated, Hoover proposed Lyman's name to the Senate for approval as the new head. In view of the certain change of administration that would take place in November, the appointment was tabled until after the presidential election. Pressed to name a Democrat to the position, Franklin Roosevelt is said to have replied, "I haven't the slightest idea whether Dr. Briggs is a Republican or a Democrat; all I know is that he is the best qualified man for the job." In March 1933, Roosevelt nominated Lyman Briggs as director of the National Bureau of Standards, and in June, the Senate confirmed the appointment.[3] Later, the family watched with pride as George Washington University conferred on Lyman the honorary degree of Doctor of Science.[4]

As acting director, Lyman had already confronted the task of trying to hold the Bureau intact in the face of cutbacks in the budget that reduced salaries, staff, and programs. The job called for someone "ruthless and rugged," but Lyman faced his duties with patience and dedication. He proposed a series of week-long leaves for all employees and a program of part-time employment that enabled him to keep about two-thirds of the staff on the payroll.[5] Asked in an interview to describe his feelings about the budget cuts, Lyman told a story about a historical pageant that was produced in London to help take the minds of the unemployed off their troubles. Marching in procession down the street, the players in the pageant came to a halt in front of two Americans. One of them commented that a certain character looked like the Roman, Appius Claudius. To settle the matter, the other American said, "Pardon me, but are you Appius Claudius?" The man replied, "No, I'm un'appy as 'ell."[6]

Lyman's unhappiness grew out of concern for the welfare of his staff and preservation of the Bureau's ongoing research. A colleague, who observed that Lyman's "serenity of temper" was his most outstanding characteristic, described his laboratory as a "tangle of piping and tubing and ticking instruments, but it was comfortable, and a tranquil spirit filled it."[7] His combination of talents served him well in managing the Bureau during the Depression years and would do so during a second world war less than a decade away.

It is not surprising, then, that Lyman, preoccupied with the Bureau's problems, was willing to hear about, and sometimes accepted,

Isabel's detailed advice about how to earn money on the stock market. She not only involved her parents, but in August 1929, convinced Paul and Jane Gemmill that she had found the proverbial pot of gold in a promising stock in a company called American Founders Corporation (AFC), an investing conglomerate later called United Founders. The Gemmills, with profound thanks to Isabel for getting them in on the deal, decided, in Paul's words, "if the water's fine, why not go a little deeper?"[8] They borrowed on Paul's insurance policies, from Jane's mother, and from their bank to buy more than a hundred shares of AFC. But, almost immediately, Isabel warned the Gemmills that she and Chief had decided to cut their "marginal operations [that is, buying shares with only a twenty percent down payment] to a minimum.... Better to own 40% as much stock, own it outright, and sleep serene." Marginal buying was unsound, her broker had said, for people who did not have an abundance of money to deliver on demand.[9]

By October 12, 1929, Isabel wrote her parents that she and Chief had "170 shares of United Founders, 45 of Public Utility Holding Corporation, 32 U.S. Electric Power, and 200 Manufacturers Investment," worth $15,277. This was all paid for, Isabel wrote Katharine, except for $6400 she and Chief owed their banks.[10] Precisely what happened to the paper profits of the Myerses and Gemmills is not recorded, but the historical knowledge of the market's decline after October 29 strongly indicates that Isabel and Chief and Jane and Paul all lost heavily. (In an interview in 1988, Jane Gemmill confirmed this.) Isabel thanked her father on October 29 for the check he had sent her and the "sudden sense of safety" that it provided.[11]

The stock market debacle was hardly a blip in the friendship of the Gemmills and the Myerses. Paul was well on the way to a full professorship in economics at the University of Pennsylvania, where he would remain on the faculty until his retirement.

Complete success in authorship and investments had eluded Isabel, but her joy in her family remained intact. When Lyman and Katharine had sent her a generous birthday check, she spent it on "the project at present nearest my heart—namely, the transformation of the nursery...into a playroom that shall be a real kingdom for Ann and Peter."[12]

Both children, aside from chicken pox (which Isabel contracted at the same time), tonsilectomies, and mild cases of whooping cough, had been healthy. Ann, at four and a half years, continued her "phenomenal progress" in learning to read and spell and, indeed, Isabel thought, spelled better than Peter.[13] Even so, it seemed that Peter was well qualified to skip kindergarten and, in the fall of 1931, to begin public school in first grade. With that purpose in mind, Isabel took Peter to the principal's office for an interview and to present her case. While the discussions proceeded, the bored, ignored five-year-old found an interesting red button on the wall, pushed it, and set off a fire alarm that caused an immediate evacuation of the building. The principal was amused, but Isabel was horrified at the likelihood that Peter had destroyed his chance for entering first grade. Fortunately, he had not.

The next September, when Ann entered kindergarten, she was not a happy pupil. Most of the time she sat alone and refused to participate in what the other children were doing. Ann would not be five years old until December, but Isabel was sure her small daughter's behavior in school was due to boredom.[14] Not only could Ann read, but she had become a budding poet, asking her mother to take dictation on the typewriter. Isabel arranged for Ann to have a series of tests at the Philadelphia Child Guidance Clinic to measure her intelligence and comprehension and her competence in reading and arithmetic. The results, as dazzling as Isabel had expected, gave Ann a "mental age of eight" and a reading level well into second grade. The clinic observed that she appeared "both physically and mentally more mature than her chronological age would indicate."[15] Fortified with this information, Isabel was determined to have Ann moved to second grade—Peter's room. Moreover, Isabel convinced the supervising principal of the Swarthmore school district that she genuinely desired to have Ann in second grade with her brother. The principal granted Isabel's request, but with the understanding that it was an "educational experiment and in some measure against our conservative judgment."[16] Isabel thanked the principal for allowing the "educational experiment," even as she reassured him with more evidence of Ann's achievements. By spring, Isabel reported to her mother that Ann was getting on nicely, but her "youthfulness showed up most conspicuously in a sort of irresponsibility" that Isabel was sure would improve with time. Socially, she thought Ann was blossoming.[17]

Katharine was not surprised at Ann's scores, but she disapproved of Isabel's writing down Ann's poems. "It makes her too important for her own good," Katharine said.[18] With Ann now in the same grade as he, Peter had "perked up decidedly," with a dramatic improvement in his reading and a "star" in arithmetic.[19] Isabel decided that, for psychological reasons, Peter should now have a room of his own at home—

no more nursery—with a desk and study lamp, a comfortable chair, book shelves, space for his "electrical possessions," and his erector set.[20] Years later, Peter acknowledged that his life was never as happy after Ann was in his same grade at school. It seemed to him that she overshadowed everything he did until they were both adults.[21]

———————

*I*n the spring of 1933, with family matters presenting no unusual challenges (but with her novel for Stokes still unfinished), Isabel launched an intensive campaign to abolish sororities permanently from the campus at Swarthmore. The Women's Student Government, in calling for abolition by a vote of 160 to 108, had suddenly raised the touchy issue again. Aware of Isabel's commitment to this in 1919, the dean of women, Frances Blanshard, asked her to marshall the alumnae who were in favor of abolition. Isabel sent out six hundred letters, wrote a letter to the *Phoenix,* and prepared a "brief" for abolition, which she presented with immense satisfaction to the faculty committee appointed to consider the matter. The committee would probably like to find a compromise, Isabel said, but in her mind, there was no compromise. Katharine, who agreed with Isabel's position, praised the brief as not giving the committee "a logical leg to stand on."[22] After carefully laying the groundwork (supported by the Awful Ate) to have sororities removed from campus, Isabel had to wait for a thorough airing of the question until December, when a vote did abolish sororities at Swarthmore College.[23] Jane Gemmill commented that this vote ended an era when "sororities hurt people cruelly."[24] For Isabel, the decision was a triumph that she and her friends had waited almost fifteen years to achieve.

———————

*D*uring the next eight years, Isabel's life, though uneventful, was one of happiness with Chief and the children—no creative bursts, such as writing novels, plays, and poetry or instigating needed reforms, distracted her from homemaking. Evidence of her state of mind at this time shows in an incident that involved Carl Jung and Katharine Briggs.

When Jung had given the Terry Lectures at Yale University in 1937, and Katharine arranged to meet him in New York, Isabel went with her. When asked several years later what Jung and her mother talked about, Isabel commented, "I don't know. I didn't listen."[25] Fifteen years later, she would feel quite differently about Jung.

Chief, now a partner in the law firm of Duane, Morris, and Heckscher, had also been appointed Solicitor of the Borough of Swarthmore.[26] Although other wives tried to promote their husband's careers by appropriate entertaining, Isabel would have no part in such maneuvering. Chief apparently approved of her stand.[27]

While Isabel focused on the children's educational progress, Chief involved himself in activities with them. He built a basketball backboard on the garage for Peter and his gang of friends; he found two baby owls in the hollow of a cherry tree, brought them home, and made a large cage to accommodate the birds that soon became pets for the children; he built a tree house in the backyard that was solid enough to be used years later by the grandchildren.[28]

Chief had also become, in practice, the family correspondent, taking responsibility for writing to friends and relatives. Outspoken when principle or good thinking were threatened, Chief not infrequently wrote issue-oriented letters to the editor of the local paper. A few months before December 1941, when the United States entered World War II, he wrote to the editor of *The Swarthmorean* in reply to a published letter critical of Roosevelt:

> I am less concerned with the "treasonable implications" of the proposed union with Great Britain than I am with the treasonable implications of pressure groups which are seeking to hamstring the administration in the present crisis. Prating about the fundamental documents when a hurricane is all about us strikes me as slightly irrelevant, incompetent, and immaterial. We can't protect ourselves against Panzer Divisions by quoting the Declaration of Independence, or even Washington's Farewell Address....Whatever his peacetime sins, this man Roosevelt has shown that he does not intend to fight Hitler with an umbrella....Your implied suggestion that he should be impeached would apply to a majority of the Congress of the United States, for it was they who enacted the Lend Lease Bill into law.[29]

From time to time, Isabel received inquiries from Curtis Brown, but these ceased after a brief note from a new manager who complained that it took "two years to get an answer before. Maybe it will be another two this time."[30] The sustained courtesy of Frank Rich and Frederick Stokes was no longer the rule.

Instead of trying to write dramas, Isabel now helped to stage them by joining the Swarthmore Players. She served on the Junior Plays committee, and from time to time, performed minor roles. Peter and Ann were also involved with the Swarthmore Players and in Scouting. Peter as a sound effects person and later as electrician, and Ann in minor roles and sometimes as a member of the stage crew. Just as Isabel had enjoyed her experiences with the Campfire Girls, her children became active in scouting.

While the children participated in these extracurricular activities, Isabel kept careful watch on their schoolwork. She listed their grades, their various test scores, and their standings in class, all reported regularly to the grandparents. Once, when Isabel appeared to be bursting with pride over Ann's exceptional abilities, Katharine wrote back that she wanted to "hear about Peter also. I love him, too."[31] Isabel's letters show an unmistakable rapport with Ann, just as Katharine had been close to her daughter. When Peter was past ten years old, Isabel described him to Katharine as "a shy, remote, bookish child," a highly interesting observation in the light of her later conclusion that her son was an extroverted feeling type.[32]

The family began to take long car trips, combining sightseeing with visits to relatives. In August 1932, Chief and Isabel drove to Iowa to introduce the children to his side of the family. Chief's sister, Parcie, raved about Ann ("she's beautiful—she's something rare and special.") Both children, who were showered with love by "*all* their relatives," took to it "like ducks." From Iowa, the family motored to Michigan where they visited with Bert, Katharine's brother, and Grandma Briggs, Lyman's mother.[33]

A few years later, they took another auto trip, by way of Iowa, to California, stopping en route at Colorado Springs and the Grand Canyon. They visited Yosemite, the redwood forests, and San Francisco and came home by way of Yellowstone Park and Salt Lake City. Both Peter and Isabel started a travel log, but each gave up a short distance west of the Mississippi.[34] The family also spent several summers vacationing on Lake Saranac, in the Adirondacks, in a cabin large enough to accomodate a friend for each child.

At age fifteen, Peter had his first summer job as a helper to a local electrical contractor. The next summer, he and a high school classmate, Richard Cordray, had student internships for two months at the Bureau of Standards and lived with the Briggs family.[35]

Near the end of that same summer, Peter took the train from Washington to Springfield, Massachusetts, where he set off on a bicycle tour of New England. In early September, when he had arrived at Saranac Lake on his return route, he paused there for a brief change of pace. Leaving his bicycle with the familiar boatman, he borrowed a canoe and paddled to a small island he remembered from previous family visits. On his way back, the sky began to darken, the wind rose, and the water surface became choppy. At some distance ahead, he saw a small sailboat with a single occupant in considerable trouble; the man was moving from the tiller at the forward end of the boat to the mast at the stern, trying desperately to lower sail. Peter paddled harder until he came alongside the rocking vessel and could hold the tiller while the man lowered the sail. When the man turned around, Peter realized that he had "rescued" Albert Einstein. With Einstein holding to the bow of the canoe, Peter paddled both of them to shore in a wind that was just short of gale force. Einstein's physician and his stepdaughter, who had been wildly waving their arms on shore, were furious at Einstien for risking life and limb. Grateful to Peter, however, they invited him into their cottage to dry out. Peter spent the rest of the afternoon talking with his distinguished host, who happened to know of another distinguished physicist named Lyman Briggs.[36] Einstein, an escapee from Nazi Germany, was then on the faculty at the Institute for Advanced Study in Princeton, New Jersey.

Isabel later reported to Katharine that Peter was home, safe and sound, but the trip was "quite a saga" of which they had heard "only parts."[37] Unknown to either Peter or Isabel, of course, was one connection through which Albert Einstein knew Lyman Briggs. The United States had entered the war on December 1941, after the Japanese bombing of Pearl Harbor. Even before the declaration of war, Lyman Briggs, who had become scientific advisor to President Roosevelt, had been called to the White House to discuss a startling communication that the President had received from three leading physicists, one of whom was Albert Einstein. The physicists informed the President that recent significant experiments with uranium indicated "the probability of achieving a chain reaction" in which atomic fission occurred to release enormous quantities of energy. Further research was imperative before the full resources of German science would make use of the same discovery that could lead to a powerfully destructive weapon.[38]

Roosevelt appointed an Advisory Committee on Uranium, with Lyman Briggs as chair, which eventually became the Uranium (or S-1) Section of the National Defense Research Committee to "mobilize science for war." An offshoot of this was the Manhatten Project, which developed the atomic bomb. It was an "awesome responsibility" that the President of the United States had placed on the sixty-six year old Lyman, whose Bureau of Standards had barely recovered from the Depression.[39]

By the end of the fall semester of his senior year in high school, Peter would be able to observe and to share vicariously his grandfather's profession. Having completed the necessary requirements for high school graduation one semester early, Peter enrolled at George Washington University and, for the next year, lived with Lyman and Katharine Briggs. His rigorous courses—chemistry, German, mathematics, mechanical engineering, and physics—were enhanced by frequent evening discussions (and games of billards) with his grandfather, whom Peter remembers as profoundly affecting his life. His grandfather's influence, along with the excitement of college work, inspired him to get the straight A's that, in high school, had been Ann's sole prerogative.[40]

When Swarthmore High School graduation ceremonies were held on June 3, 1943, Peter returned to share in the event. Ann finished first in her class, received the Hermann Myer Memorial Award in German, the Phi Beta Kappa prize, and "a year's subscription to *Reader's Digest* for being valedictorian." But it was Peter and a classmate, Katharine Downing, a friend of the Myers family, whom the National Honor Society elected to membership.[41] Ann, accepted at Middlebury College in Vermont, deferred entrance for a year while she worked at the Pennsylvania Company in Philadelphia. Peter was beginning to become interested in Kathy Downing, winner of two scholarships at Vassar College, as more than just a friend. He continued at George Washington University until he reached eighteen and could, he hoped, enlist in the United States Naval Air Corps.

With his own children no longer at Swarthmore High School, Chief anonymously established two five-hundred dollar scholarships to be awarded to senior boys who, "in the judgment of the School District, are possessed of character, qualities of leadership or initiative, and either high general scholarship or technical aptitude ... [and] who might not, for financial reasons, be able to attend college immediately upon leaving high school." One of these was awarded to Howard Pennell, a beau of Ann's who, after a year at Swarthmore College, enlisted in the Army's 83rd Airborne Division.[42]

---

*B*arely a generation earlier, Isabel and Chief had been involved in the Great War fought "to make the world safe for democracy." Now they were witnessing another global conflict, which would draw in Peter and other young friends of the family. The United States had troops both on the Pacific front and in Europe, and peace would not come for two more years. Chief, now forty-nine, could best make his contribution to the war effort by volunteer civic services—and by helping Isabel, who, after her stint as a volunteer, had now found her own unique niche.

By the time her children had finished high school, Isabel was well along in developing her "people sorting instrument." There is no doubt that her initial idea was an altruistic one, meant to help the war effort and the demobilization process. However, it is also clear that she needed something significant to challenge the second half of her life. The two priorities she had established for her young womanhood—writing and nurturing a family (though not the six children she had originally planned for)—had met with some success.

The important letter that she sat down at her desk to write to Katharine Briggs in January 1942 implied a restlessness, even boredom. At that time, when Isabel had read the article in the *Reader's Digest* about the *Humm-Wadsworth Scale,* she had begun her apprenticeship with Edward Hay at the Pennsylvania Company. The student had now leaped rapidly ahead with her own idea of a "people sorting test." On May 5, 1943, Chief had applied through his law firm to the United States Register of Copyrights for a copyright on Isabel's "eighteen pages," an action that marked the formal beginning of what would become the *Myers-Briggs Type Indicator.*[43] The idea for the Indicator, which evolved at a propitious time for both Isabel Myers and for the field of psychological testing, would be a consuming interest for the rest of her life. The transition from focusing on home and children to developing a psychological test was made easier by the intrusions of war. "It is a very good thing for me to have the Type Indicator to think about and work on," Isabel wrote her mother in late 1943.[44]

Part Four

CHAPTER FOURTEEN

The "People-sorting" Test

The purpose of the Indicator, Isabel said, was to implement Carl Jung's theory of type. In his book, *Psychological Types,* Jung had set forth four basic psychological functions—sensing, intuition, thinking, and feeling. Sensing and intuition are two modes of perceiving—becoming aware of or learning about things (people, events, or ideas). Thinking and feeling are two methods of judging, or reaching conclusions about things. The sensing person collects information through the five senses, while for the intuitive person outside stimuli act as springboards for unconscious associations. The thinking person is logical and impersonal, while the feeling person's way of coming to conclusions is subjective and personal. Finally, there are two "directions" in which any of these functions may be expressed: as an introvert or extravert. The introverted person's main interests are in the inner world of ideas and concepts; the extravert's main interests are in the outer world of people and things.

The Indicator reports an individual's personality profile in terms of a four-letter type, one letter from each of the four pairs or dimensions—sensing (S) versus intuition (N), thinking (T) versus feeling (F), judging (J) versus perceiving (P), and introversion (I) versus extraversion (E). This produces sixteen possible types: ISTJ, ISFJ, INFJ, INTJ, ISTP, ISFP, INFP, INTP, ESTP, ESFP, ENFP, ENTP, ESTJ, ESFJ, ENFJ, and ENTJ.[1]

Isabel also believed in another facet of Jung's theory, in which he referred to *dominant* and *auxiliary* processes. She explained these processes by comparing them to one's right and left hand: One is dominant, but the other is always a "helper." Both processes are important. For example, the extremely perceiving person with no capacity to come to conclusions, or without the judging function, is "all sail and no rudder"; the extravert, whose dominant process is focused on the outside world, needs to develop an inner life, without which he or she is likely to be "superficial."[2] The judging type will need to learn to be more accepting. Thinking types, to be well balanced, will need to develop and appropriately use their feelings—and vice versa.

Some specific illustrations will help to explain these various aspects of type. In the early years of their marriage, for example, Franklin and Eleanor Roosevelt represented an extraverted and introverted pair. Franklin, the extravert, was the socializer and the joiner, while Eleanor, the introvert, was considered the wallflower. An extravert married to an intovert will not infrequently complain that when a party is just getting good and lively, the spouse usually thinks it is time to go home. Or the introvert may not want to go to the party at all.

A famous and celebrated sensing type is surely seen in the great Italian master, Michelangelo, whose palpable figures seem to speak. A classic example of the intuitive person is Albert Einstein, who probably barely knew one color from another, but "saw" the invisible interior of a tiny atom.

Queen Elizabeth I of England, who used her head, some would say even brutally, to survive from early girlhood to the end of her forty-four year reign, exemplifies a thinking type. Albert Schweitzer, whose life as a missionary-physician was devoted to helping the poor, was very likely a feeling type.

Two teenagers from the twentieth century provide an example of judging and perceiving types—Boy (J) was talking on the telephone to Girl (P):

Boy: What time do you want me to pick you up?

Girl: Well, I'm working on my report right now.

Boy: But what time do you want me to pick you up?

Girl: I have to call Michelle before we go. I may need to borrow her skirt.

Boy: Louise, *what time* do you want me to pick you up?

Girl: I was thinking that maybe we could stop by the mall while we're out. Is that okay?"

Boy: Yes, but *what time do you want me to pick you up?*

Girl: I've got all these things to think about. You decide.
Just come over any time you want.

Boy: Okay (hangs up).

Thirty minutes later, the boy appeared—much to the girl's
surprise. As she explained later to her mother, of course she wasn't ready
because he never told her what time he was coming. Now he was mad
at her, and she couldn't figure out why.[3]

To identify these differing profiles, Isabel devised questions that
she tried out on members of her family or on friends whom she believed
showed characteristics that fit some of the types. Isabel phrased her
questions in the form of two or three choices, such as: "Do you prefer
to (a) eat to live, or (b) live to eat." To collect her first data, she wrote
the questions on 3-by-5 cards so that she could make tabulations on the
back that enabled her to see patterns developing. She asked these
questions only of people whose preferences she was "pretty sure about,"
and if they did not answer according to their perceived type at least sixty
percent of the time, she discarded that question.[4]

Chief, who had been an early focus of Katharine's observations,
was thought to be an introverted, sensing person. The responses that he
gave became a base from which to begin. As Isabel later built a
description of this type (ISTJ), it clearly portrayed a person like her
husband. The ISTJ she said, was

> super-dependable, with a complete, realistic, practical respect
> for the facts.... He does not enter into things impulsively,
> but once in, he is very hard to distract, discourage, or stop....
> If necessary, he will do jobs himself rather than leave them
> undone. He will go to any amount of trouble if he "can see
> the need of it," but he does hate to be saddled with a policy
> that "doesn't make sense." It is hard for him to see any sense
> in needs that differ widely from his own...but in a specific
> case, where he sees something mattering a lot to somebody
> right before his eyes, he may come to sympathize pretty
> generously with the desire.[5]

Isabel concluded that she herself was an INFP. Her introverted
feeling type, she said, had a "great faithfulness to duty and obligations"
and chose "final values without reference to the judgment of outsiders,"
sticking to them "with passionate conviction." Persons who were

INFPs wanted their work to contribute to "something that mattered to them, perhaps to human understanding or happiness or health," and they were perfectionists, "happiest at some individual work involving personal values." Their intuition would help solve any difficulties encountered.[6]

Despite her firm belief that she was a feeling type, Isabel still heard friends and former teachers praise her "analytical mind" and her outstanding ability as a thinker. Phyllis Sellers, something of a talented amateur psychologist, wrote to Isabel that she believed that Isabel "could be in conflict between cold intellect and emotional moodiness... I think you have used the former to master the latter. But you need both to be the complex person you are."[7]

Much later in life, Isabel would say that Jung's theory and Katharine's bringing it "down to everyday life" preserved the happy marriage of an ISTJ (Chief) and an INFP (Isabel), who had only their introversion in common. A close friend of the family commented that Chief and Isabel, the two introverts, were not aware of "what people thought," and even if they were aware, they cared not a whit![8] Isabel and Chief learned that their own different approaches to life were not only "forgiveable, but interesting." The Indicator became "the corner-stone" of their relationship. After a period of not being so sanguine about Isabel's casual housekeeping, Chief was able to say that she was doing other things that were more important to her. She fervently agreed.[9] She confessed to Jane Gemmill, also deeply involved in helping to construct questions for the Indicator, that had she known about type before she met Chief, she probably would never have married him.[10]

In addition to Jane Gemmill, she enlisted Peter (and to a lesser extent, Ann, who was not as outgoing) to try the "game" out on high school friends. When Peter was eleven, Isabel had "a nice discussion [with him] of the [Jungian] functions, and judging and perception," to which the young Peter had a serious response: "This is important."[11] His progressive understanding of what his mother was trying to do helped to pave the way for Isabel's first large group to be tested: Peter's senior class at Swarthmore High School. Isabel then collected data from a V–12 unit at Swarthmore College, as well as from Haverford and Bryn Mawr.[12] In the summer of 1942, when Peter and Richard Cordray were living with the Briggs family in Washington, they tried the questions on practically everyone they knew.[13] Later, Cordray gathered data for Isabel from his fellow servicemen at Fort Benning, Georgia, Ann collected profiles at Middlebury, and Peter did the same with two successive years of Rhodes scholars and their spouses.[14] Servicemen who had taken the Indicator also rated their peers as to leadership ability and how they might act in an emergency.[15] Slowly, Isabel built a storehouse of profiles.

When Form A of the Indicator came into being, it was made up of 172 questions, printed on both sides of nine 8 1/2-by-11 mimeographed sheets and stapled together. The answers, or choices, were to be marked on a separate sheet, from which the scoring was done by hand. Various answers were assigned numerical values that placed a person closer to one side or the other of the four letter pairs. Isabel encouraged subjects to make a choice, even if they did not feel strongly about it; however, if a choice were impossible, that question could be omitted.

Isabel classified Ann, like herself, as an INFP, while she considered Peter to be an ENFP—that "shy, remote, bookish child" who would become a Rhodes scholar and a research physicist. (Cordray once observed that the Myerses were a "proper Victorian family," and Peter, who seemed to feel that he was a misfit, once said that he wondered if "they brought the wrong baby home from the hospital.")[16]

In any event, Isabel described the ENFP type, in part, as "an enthusiastic innovator, always seeing new possibilities...and [going] all out in pursuit of them.... Being a perceptive type, he aims to understand people rather than to judge them.... He hates uninspired routine [and] is happiest and most effective in jobs that permit one project after another, with somebody taking over as soon as the situation is well in hand."[17]

Form A—the eighteen pages completed in the spring of 1943—had been superseded by Form B, a more polished version of Form A with fewer questions. Using Form B, Isabel collected her first large group data from Peter and Ann's graduating class at Swarthmore High School.[18] She continued to refine the instrument and, in 1944, upon the completion of Form C, she persuaded Edward Hay to let her give the Indicator to every applicant for employment at the Pennsylvania Company, where he was personnel director.

Hay had made his contribution to the war effort in the Office of Price Administration, where he was involved in solving management and operation problems. As the end of the war approached, and concurrent with a half-time position at the Pennsylvania Company, Hay began to spend time as a consultant in management and personnel work. In 1945, he founded his own management consulting company,

Edward N. Hay and Associates.[19] That year, Hay signed a five-year contract with Isabel to use and distribute the Indicator with "business, industrial and/or commercial clients." Isabel reserved the right to veto any client that she considered "unsuitable" or one who might use the Indicator inappropriately.[20]

In introducing the Indicator to a skeptical client, Hay wrote:

> I don't blame you for being reserved about the Briggs-Myers Type Indicator. However, it is going to make a tremendous mark on industry, the schools, and vocational guidance, and I hope you will be interested to work with it.... The importance of the test is not merely that it has a good theoretical rationale but that it actually does work as it should. The limits of errors seem to be smaller than for most questionnaire types of tests. Her statistical work has been fabulous in extent and quality and I think you will be impressed when the manual, now in preparation, is available.[21]

Hay's support, and, in a sense, his daring, launched the Indicator professionally, but Isabel still coveted research data from a much wider ranging clientele. Two other people helped to bring this about: Donald W. MacKinnon and Lyman Briggs.

MacKinnon, who met Isabel and learned about the Indicator when he was professor of psychology at Bryn Mawr College, moved, in 1947, to the University of California, Berkeley. There he presented Jungian concepts and Isabel's own formulation of Jung's types to his students, who also took the Indicator.[22] With a grant from the Rockefeller Foundation, the Institute of Personality Assessment (IPAR) was founded in 1949 at Berkeley with MacKinnon as its first head. For the rest of his active life, MacKinnon used the Indicator, together with other tests, in his studies of highly creative people. Among his subjects were student playwrights, writers and poets, architects, mathematicians, honor students in engineering, research scientists, and some California medical students. Isabel scored about one third of these answer sheets for IPAR out of a total of 614 subjects.[23]

At about the same time that Isabel met MacKinnon, her father attended a meeting of George Washington University's board of trustees, of which he was a member. Lyman Briggs talked with Dr. Leland W. Parr, head of the Department of Bacteriology, Hygiene, and Preventive Medicine, about the personality sorting instrument that his daughter had developed. Parr, who had enormous respect for Briggs and was interested in the "wide differences in motivation and interest that could be expected from the difference in types," obtained the approval of Dr. John Parks, dean of the medical school, for the Indicator to be given to entering classes for the next seven years.[24]

When Isabel had begun to construct the Indicator, there were in use, besides the *Humm-Wadsworth* (1940), at least three other instruments that measured personality through self-report. One was primarily a research instrument, while the others were oriented toward use by clinical psychologists.[25]

Isabel reviewed what was available and began to study statistics. Richard Cordray, who was an honors graduate from Swarthmore in electrical engineering and mathematics, "kept her honest" in regard to her statistics. According to Cordray, however, she soon surpassed him in statistics through her own private study of the subject in college texts.[26] But learning statistics was not quite as simple for her as Cordray had thought, as Isabel relates in one humorous account where she refers to a confusing statistical concept as a "nice stubborn little hybrid, [a] cross-bred mule—a son-of-a statistic," and called the world of statistics "a [very] suspicious world" in which every time "you turn around you have to square yourself."[27]

Financial support for all of these undertakings was furnished completely by Chief and Katherine and Lyman. On Isabel's fifty-second birthday she wrote to her father: "My birthday letter came yesterday, with the wonderful checks...for the Indicator. A thousand Thanks!... It seems to me like a thing in itself, with a future and rights of its own to growth and fame and fulfillment, with me in something like the role of its general manager—much more than it seems like something Mother and I deliberately decided to do and did.... You and Mother have been so wonderful in backing it up."[28] Birthday checks from her parents regularly went to Isabel "lest the Indicator should become financially embarrassed."[29]

Once when Lyman and Katharine had given her a generous check, she bought five "of the most beautiful solid walnut file drawers...good looking enough to live with us in the living room." Altogether, the drawers would house "five thousand cases—and some day," she said, "I am going to *have* five thousand cases."[30] Her prediction came true.

As she established and refined the text for the Indicator and relentlessly continued to collect data, she worked with tools no more sophisticated than pencil and paper. Later, she would buy a desk-top hand calculator—but the age of computers was well into the future. In due course, through his Philadelphia law firm, Chief registered the "Briggs-Myers Type Research" with the Commonwealth of Pennsylvania as a business located at 321 Dickinson Avenue, Swarthmore, Pennsylvania. He was always careful to keep Isabel protected and her endeavors legal.[31]

Peter Myers has observed that his mother was truly a scientist, trained early in her life by Lyman Briggs (INTP) who had taught her to ask questions, search for answers, and use thinking to arrive at what she wanted. She grew up having a respect and appreciation for, and a facility with, "cause and effect" in the scientific method. It was Lyman's joy to see the dawning of his daughter's understanding. In fact, Isabel's father may have been more of an influence than her mother in her understanding of the world and how it works. He was the role model without whose example Isabel's capacity to develop the Indicator would have been far less effective.[32]

If Lyman were the role model, Katharine (whom Isabel had classified as INFJ) was the persistent seeker who devised the theoretical foundations on which Isabel could build. When she was in her eighties, Katharine told a friend that she didn't have much to do with "making up the Indicator" and had asked why not leave her name out of the title. Isabel refused. By the time Isabel had developed Form C and its scoring process, Katharine wrote, sadly,"I realize what a back number I am getting to be about your work, for I don't understand how to interpret the figures."[33] During the years that Isabel pursued her literary career, Katharine was the one who kept type alive, both with her historic article, "Meet Yourself," first published in *New Republic* in 1926, and by continuing to bring the topic up in conversations and correspondence.[34] Isabel herself said that the Indicator project was the "result of four pieces of tremendous good luck" that she had had in her life. These were her father, a research physicist; her mother, a college-trained, creative woman; her unusual husband, Clarence Myers; and Carl Jung, whose *Psychological Types* was published in English at precisely the critical time when Katharine Briggs had begun to devise a similar theory.[35]

After working on the Indicator for scarcely three years, Isabel wrote a friend that she considered her original aim in undertaking the Indicator to be "satisfyingly fulfilled, even if I should walk in front of a truck tomorrow and never do any more."[36]

*Katharine Cook, 1893, a college student
at Michigan Agricultural College*

*Lyman J. Briggs, 1893, about the time
he and Katharine Cook became engaged*

Katharine Cook Briggs holding her baby, Isabel, 1898

Katharine and Isabel, c. 1905–1906

Albert J. Cook, c. 1905, father of
Katharine Cook Briggs

Katharine C. Briggs about the time
Isabel entered Swarthmore College

Lyman and Katharine's home at 3208 Newark Street, Washington, D.C., where
they moved in 1909

Isabel Briggs,
posing with a new doll, c. 1907

Dec. 2, 1904.

This morning we went to see the Sabana, which, they say, used to be where they had their bull fights. But it was too far out from the city "Sabana" in English means "grassy plain"

Journal entry from Isabel's "The Diary of
a Girl Going Traveling," 1904

Isabel Briggs, a young lady of 13

Thursday   Sept. 15, 1910.

Betty and I are going to Swarthmore College. If you go to College you have to work, and I am going to work. I started today on As You Like It. I read it in Lamb's Tales from Shakespeare and as soon as my book, which we have ordered from Lowdermilk's comes, I shall read it in the original. When I spoke of the passage, "Tongues in trees, books in the running brooks, sermons in stones, and good in everything," Mama suggested that I should memorize it. I was startled. It is not a thing that I would think of memorizing. It just is. It's a part of the English language. It seems to have been adopted. I guess it is what people call classic.

A page from Isabel's diary, "The Book of Me," 1910

Cleveland Park Campfire girls, Washington Times, September 24, 1912. *"Miss Briggs, who is barely sixteen years old, swam the Potomac several times this summer"* (Isabel, first row, far left)

Isabel McKelvey Briggs at Swarthmore College, 1916

Isabel at the time of her engagement to Clarence Gates Myers, 1917

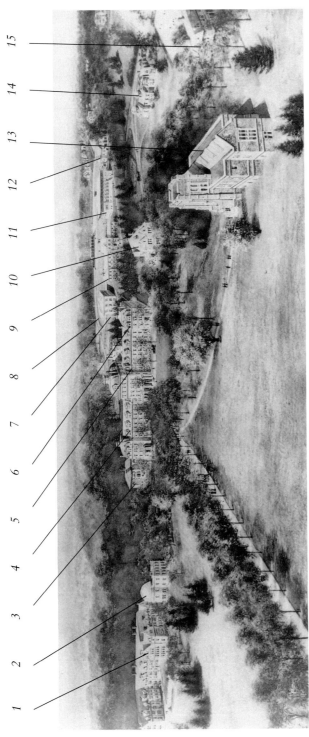

Swarthmore College campus at the time Isabel and Chief were students there: 1 Wharton Hall (dormitories); 2 Sproul Observatory, 1875 as President's house, converted 1911; 3 Hall Gym, 1912 (boys); 4 Parrish Hall, 1881 (dormitory rooms and dining hall); 5 Parrish Hall Annex, before 1897; 6 East end of Parrish Hall; 7 Beardsley; 8 Swarthmore Field, sports field; 9 Science Hall, later called Trotter, 1881, West Wing 1895; 10 Somerville Gym, 1893 (girls); 11 Hall of Chemistry, 1904 (called Pearson after 1961); 12 Friends Meeting House, 1879; 13 Carnegie Library, 1906; 14 Cunningham House and Student Observatory, 1888 (converted to Scott Foundation Offices 1970); 15 West House, 1724, restored 1875

*Clarence Gates ("Chief") Myers
as a U.S. Air Cadet in 1918*

*Isabel and her classmates, known as
"The Awful Ate" at Swarthmore.
L to R: Dorothy Lucas, Esther O'Neill
Taylor, Elinor Atkinson Smith, Vida
Connor Martin, Jane Brown Gemmill,
Katherine Fahnestock Miller, Isabel
Briggs Myers, Phyllis Komori Sellers*

*Swarthmore table party, c. 1917. Isabel, top row, third from right and Chief, top
row, fourth from left, in cap*

Isabel and Chief after their garden wedding at her parents' home in Washington, D.C., June 17, 1918

Chief and Isabel in front of their first house on Myrtle Avenue, Morton, Pennsylvania

Mr. and Mrs. Clarence G. Myers, Swarthmore, c. 1919

Isabel with baby Peter in the summer of 1926

Isabel with Chief holding two-year-old Ann

Isabel with Peter, Ann, and her typewriter when she was working on her mystery novel, fall of 1928

*Isabel Briggs Myers,
acclaimed author, c. 1929*

WESTERN UNION

Received at

26P F 7

UW NEWYORK NY 1124A FEB 26 1929

MRS CLARENCE G MYERS

321 DICKINSON AVE SWARTHMORE PENN

YOU WIN STAKES MCCLURE PRIZE CONTEST CONGRATULATIONS

E G RICH

1139A

```
        Dear Chief:

                We opened this, not knowing when you would get home.
        We have telephoned Isabel, and she wanted us to leave this for you.
                                                P.F.G.
```

Telegram to Isabel announcing her the winner of the mystery novel contest, February 1929. Typed memo is from Paul Gemmill

Yet to COME

This Was the Mysterious Fate That Threatened a Lovely Lady. And Then Three Modern Musketeers Came Riding to Her Aid

By ISABEL BRIGGS MYERS

Illustrations by DELOS PALMER

"WAS I asleep?" questioned Linda. "I don't see how I could have slept—haven't slept for days! And yet," her hand trembled in Ryker's clasp, "it must have dreamed that crash. Maybe—I'm still dreaming——"

IF YOU frequent the theater at all, you have watched the curtain rise on at least one play from the pen of Peter Jerningham. If you missed "Butter Side Down," you certainly saw "Shorn." And if you haven't already seen "Challenge," you will before the year is out. The critics agree that "Challenge" is the best thing he has done.

I know nothing, being his secretary—and more than that, his friend—I have good reason to know better. The finest proof of Jerningham's genius is something the critics never heard of—his solution of the murder of Malachi Trent.

It was Jerningham's wish that no one should ever hear of it. And it was he who had shared with him those three perilous days and nights at Carmichael House, recognized his right to dictate. We agreed that no one but Jerningham himself should ever lift the curtain of secrecy behind which the grim drama had taken place. And having so agreed, we fled thankfully from that house where Death had made himself at home.

Jerningham and I, too weary for speech, came back together through the November dusk to that peaceful sanctuary of his bachelor apartment in New York. We had been expected. There was a roaring blaze of hickory logs awaiting us in the great fireplace. Without a word, made for the two huge chairs on either side of the hearth, and stretched out at ease, to let the warmth and the security and the blessed sanity of the place soak into the chilled marrow of our bones.

I WATCHED Jerningham's face in the glow of the fire. One by one the lines etched there by the last three days softened. The tiny muscles around his eyes began to relax. His mouth lost some of its grimness. But even his favorite pipe could not banish the Carmichael House look. I recognized him, nor the bandage that crossed his forehead, nor the black silk sling which took the weight of his right arm from his broken collar bone.

"Mac," he said at last, with a deep breath of satisfaction, "there's nothing like a roaring blaze to exorcise the powers of darkness. No wonder Carmichael House is being so badly—in three weeks I shall doubt if it ever existed."

"Then I'll hire you a stenographer tomorrow morning," I declared, "so you can record what happened while it's still fresh in your mind. If we wait till my hand is fit to run a typewriter, you'll have forgotten a lot of the fine points."

Jerningham frowned.

"And why," he inquired, "do I want a record of this horrible business?"

"Because some day you'll need it badly!" I prophesied.

"The story will come out sooner or later, and if it doesn't come out exactly straight there'll be the devil to pay. In your shoes, I'd publish it immediately and be done with it."

All the grimness had returned to Jerningham's face.

"I'll take my chances," he said. "If we publish, we'll never hear the last of the Carmichael House. We'll see it on the front page of every paper, meet it on the lips of every acquaintance, eat it at every dinner table, hear it in the intermissions of every play, and dream it every night! No, thanks! I've had all I can stand now."

"You're taking it too hard," I protested. "There's no need to feel like that."

"Perhaps I won't," after a month or two," he half apologized. "I'm going to do a lot of intensive forgetting. Pretend to myself I never watched the blood running from my own fingertips, or staked other people's lives on my own hunches, or heard a scream in the night!"

In spite of the fire, he shivered.

"It's lucky "Challenge" has two more weeks of rehearsal," he said. "I'll be as busy as I haven't have time to think. Perhaps I'll come out of Jordan cleansed of my foolishness and ready to follow your advice. But in the meantime—" he half grinned at me, but there was an undertone of appeal in his voice—"in the meantime, if you don't want to see me in the psychopathic ward, don't mention Carmichael House in my hearing."

"All right, old man," I promised.

But in that agreement we reckoned without the gentlemen of the press.

IT WAS three days later that we returned through the early dusk from a rehearsal, to find a young man awaiting us in Jerningham's apartment. He introduced himself as Collins, of the Associated Press. Jerningham's face stiffened, and I saw the two men taking each other's measure.

"Mr. Jerningham," Collins said without preamble, "I want to know who murdered Malachi Trent."

"Who murdered him?" Jerningham parried. "How do you make a murder out of an old man's fall from his library ladder?"

"I have strong reasons to believe he was murdered," the young man persisted. "You were there. You must know all about it. And I want the straight of it from you before I stir things up."

Jerningham laughed and shook his head.

"I know those strong reasons," he returned. "You compound

First installment of Murder Yet to Come *in Smart Set, August 1929*

Peter Briggs Myers and Isabel Ann Myers, spring of 1930

Peter Myers,
Naval Officer, 1944

Ann Myers, graduation
from Swarthmore High
School, 1943

July 1st 1950.

Mrs.Clarence G.Myers,
Hotel Beau Rivage,
Geneva.

Dear Mrs.Myers,

Thank you very much for kindly sending me your interesting questionnaire and the equally interesting descriptions of your results. As you have given the matter a great deal of thought I think you have done so much in this direction that I'm hardly capable of criticising it or even knowing it better. For quite a long time I haven't done any work along that line at all, because other things have taken the foreground of my interests. But I should say that for any future development of the Type-Theory your Type-Indicator will prove to be of great help.

I should have liked very much to see you, but I'm only just recovering from a tedious illness and shall leave presently for a long and much-needed holiday from which I shall not return until the fall.

Hoping you have a nice time in Europe,
I remain
yours sincerely

C. G. Jung.

Professor Dr. C. G. Jung's response to Isabel's inquiry letter for a meeting, 1950

Isabel with grandchildren, Douglas and Kathleen Hughes, sleeping in the family car, c. 1960

Four generations of Briggs-Myers women: Isabel, Katharine, infant Kathleen Hughes, and Ann Myers Hughes, summer of 1956

Isabel Briggs Myers surrounded by family: Katharine, Lyman, Peter, Ann, and grandchildren Jonathan Myers and Kathleen Hughes, c. 1957

CHAPTER FIFTEEN

Peter and Ann
Grow Up

*I*n 1945, historic events occured in rapid succession: Franklin D. Roosevelt died in April, and Vice President Harry S. Truman, former Missouri senator, became president. By May, the war in Europe ended. In early August, the United States dropped two powerful atomic bombs on Hiroshima and Nagasaki and, on August 14, the Japanese nation surrendered.

Isabel left no comment about these moments in history, yet she and Chief were inherently grateful that their own son was unharmed and that their other young Swarthmore friends, especially Richrad Cordray and Howard Pennell, could now return from military duty.

During the war years, when the Indicator consumed much of Isabel's time, she wrote Katherine that she thought that to have this project "to think about and work on" was "a very good thing."[1] She now realized that the Indicator had implications far beyond her initial hope to use it in easing the problems of demobilization. Isabel told Ned Hay, who continued to encourage her and to follow her progress, that she wished her research went faster. When Hay accused her, "You want it to be easy, don't you?" Isabel insisted not easy, but "useful—*soon*."[2]

For a few weeks in the mid–1940s, she kept a diary that showed her preoccupation with the Indicator. Isabel's focus on her work prompted Chief to tell her that he thought her interests were "limited— but most of them are out of this world." Isabel countered by reading to him her "brand-new introverted feeling sketch, in which she described IF's, such as herself, with their "warm side being inside like a fur-lined coat." An amused Chief agreed that it was foolish "to put the warmth outside for show."[3]

Those early years when the children were away were nevertheless "golden" for Isabel and Chief. This period marked the first time in months that they had had any real leisure, she wrote Katharine, and "just about the first time in our lives that we have had any substantial time alone together. Time enough to talk and philosophize and exchange confidences about what makes men and women tick."[4]

Isabel faithfully corresponded with Peter and Ann, and she regularly sent boxes of hard-to-come-by food and supplies to both children. Peter, a trainee in the Navy's V–12 program for engineers at Worcester Polytechnic Institute, Worcester, Massachusetts, was, Isabel thought, "the salt of the earth…there is no one like him." She and Chief agreed that the year Peter had spent in Washington with his grandparents had brought rich returns. "Mentally, there is the grasp and perspective," which he had learned from Lyman Briggs (who finally retired as head of the Bureau in 1945 when he was seventy-one), as well as "growth in his powers of expression…and learning how to use time," Isabel wrote Katharine. When she confided to her son that she felt closer to him than she ever had, he had told her that maybe it was because he "very much wanted" what she had to give him.[5]

Peter was trying to understand religion in a search for an acceptable personal belief. Isabel wrote to him that for a member of one sect to say, or even to think in his most secret heart, "I have the only truth; the rest of the world is damned," was not only "arrogant but downright dangerous." In fact, she thought it to be one of the "Seven Deadly Sins" called "pride." Continuing her homily entitled "The Lord, *Thy* God," to Peter, she explained:

> I don't think you need to be confused, or to alter your conceptions much—just extend them some. Your own unconscious is, you say, synonymous to you with "God." It is no less intimately and personally yours, for being itself part of a greater thing.

> There are two aspects of God involved here, and many people have unnecessary difficulty in harmonizing them [the personal and the universal]…. What I mean by the personal is the God within you, of whom you have actual knowledge by contact and experience…. What the Church calls "revelation," we call intuitive perception—what the scientist is likely to call inductive reasoning, proceeding from the particular to the general.

When Isabel tried to explain the Universal to Peter, she resorted to a drawing from his geometry book. "Then let God be symbolized," she said, as "a column, a shaft, running through the center of all creation. And let each of us be a plane intersecting the shaft. Then our 'intersection with God' is the center and core of our being, our unconscious, our share of God. Our 'God' is always there, always in relationship with us and our problems, always personal to us—but also always [connected] with that Whole which...'guides all animate energy.'"[6] Peter wrote in his diary that he had trouble understanding his mother's "weighty stuff" and that the "shaft and plane explained beautifully the relation of God to us as individuals, but it still leaves me up in the air about "what *is* God.""[7] After a month, he was disappointed when her "little writings about the Bible...and religion" stopped. He was afraid they would, however, because they were "a project which faded when it lost its novelty."[8]

For Isabel, the novelty of the Indicator never diminished, even when another chance at fiction writing might have tempted her. A friend had sent Isabel and Katharine a clipping from the *New York Herald Tribune* announcing a Harper Prize Novel competition that would end on July 1, 1943. Isabel was not interested. Katharine, who had decided long since that fiction was not for her, had continued, however, to write and polish philosophical and religious essays. When she sent her manuscripts to Harper & Brothers to be considered for a book, an old friend from Cleveland Park, Tina Skeer, a sometime poet living in New York, reassured Katharine that her writing "would light a candle for people groping in unhappy dark[ness]" and that Harper's would be feting and honoring her when the book came out. Despite Tina's optimism, Harper's rejected Katharine's work.[9]

When Katharine sent some of her psychological and religious essays to Peter, he was more sanguine than Harper's. Indeed, he found her definition of God (as a fourth dimensional concept in contact with three Jungian "dimensions") easier to understand than his mother's "little sermons."[10]

By the end of the summer of 1945, Peter had completed all of the course requirements to graduate in engineering and, for his senior research project (the term "thesis" was prohibited by the military), was allowed to do supplementary work in the fall at the Bureau of Standards.[11] When he finished writing his senior paper, Isabel was avidly interested in seeing it published in an appropriate scientific journal. In response to Peter's lack of interest in this kind of recognition, Isabel told him that that was a state of mind he would have to contend with all his life (because of his type), but if he did not write up his contributions, they would "never get into the record." She then sent a copy of Peter's paper to Katharine and Lyman for their "judgment" and emendations after she had done her own editing.[12] There is no record, however, of Peter's grandparents actually becoming involved in it.

His research done and Navy commission in hand, Peter entrained in November for Seattle, where he was assigned to sea duty for seven months on the USS *Sanborn*. Before he left Massachusetts, at the urging of Worcester Professor Francis J. Adams, Peter had applied for a Rhodes Scholarship.[13] Discharged from the Navy in August 1946, he returned to Swarthmore and lived at home while waiting to hear from Oxford. That fall, he took two seminars at the college, one in political theory and one in philosophy, and audited a third in economics at the University of Pennsylvania. In December, he learned that he had won a coveted Rhodes that was to begin in September 1947.

In the spring, Peter moved to Washington with his grandparents and again worked at the Bureau of Standards. Meanwhile, at Swarthmore he had met a young woman, Elizabeth (Betty) Monk, who was a fellow student in one of his college seminars; at Easter, she and Peter became engaged.[14] Isabel and Chief were pleased with this match.

*A*nn, majoring in German at Middlebury, continued to get superior grades. She often took time, however, to correspond with two Swarthmore friends, Dick Cordray and Howard Pennell, who were overseas. Howard and Ann's relationship became serious enough during their separation for her to wear his "wings" during her freshman year at Middlebury.[15] That summer, in 1945, Ann attended an exclusive German "Summerschule" in Bristol, Vermont, run by Middlebury College for promising young scholars. By the time Howard Pennell returned from overseas, Ann was infatuated with a fellow student at Middlebury named John Secord, a man she would eventually marry.[16]

In the Army Air Corps for five years, Secord, from Watertown, Massachusetts, had enrolled at Middlebury College in March 1945 after a medical (psychological) discharge the previous December. He and Ann probably met that same spring. They studied together and completed a joint senior research project using the Indicator, and in the summer of 1947, Secord did some clerical work for Isabel.[17] When Ann graduated Phi Beta Kappa from Middlebury in June 1948, her fiance still needed one semester of college work for his degree.

From the beginning of Ann's infatuation, Chief and Peter were apprehensive about John Secord, but Isabel tried valiantly to believe in him for Ann's sake. She wrote a memorable letter of encouragement to him that became a treatise on life's needs and challenges to which she hoped he, a psychology major, would respond.[18] He did not. As a last resort, Isabel pleaded with Jane Gemmill to talk with Ann because she was afraid of doing anything that might alienate her daughter. With great caution, Jane tried to learn Ann's reasons for wanting to marry John Secord. Ann's only response was that she felt that he would be "utterly loyal."[19]

Following their marriage on June 26, 1948, on the lawn at 321 Dickinson Avenue, and after a brief honeymoon in the Poconos, Ann and John left for Berkeley, California. Both were enrolled at the University of California in psychology, she as a graduate student and he an undergraduate. By fall, Chief and Isabel were outraged at hearing from Ann that she and John had decided to drop out of school and become dairy farmers. Both parents wrote sizzling, albeit well-reasoned, letters against the idea. Isabel's letter, ten pages long, was written after she had visited local dairy farms and interviewed the owners.

Convinced by the irrefutable reasoning of Chief and Isabel, John and Ann returned to Middlebury College where he received his Bachelor's degree in February 1949. Since jobs and living quarters were hard to come by, Ann had, for the spring semester, accepted a housekeeping arrangement in a local physician's home with part-time baby-sitting responsibilities, while John enrolled in graduate studies at the college.[20] For months, while overworked with her domestic duties, Ann tried to help her husband with his course work. When he became increasingly critical and languid, their relationship deteriorated steadily until Ann, to the utter relief of her parents, opted for divorce. Opposed to divorce in principle, Chief and Isabel were nevertheless "profoundly thankful" that the marriage was coming to an end before Ann was "any more scarred by her attempts at the impossible."[21]

The decree became final in November 1949 in Reno, Nevada.[22] Ann returned to Swarthmore to try to recover from the year's ordeal before beginning graduate work in German. She said many years later that, although she knew Secord had problems, she thought he was brilliant and that she could "salvage" him.[23]

If Ann's brief marriage was a disaster, Peter's choice of a spouse "in the best Swarthmore tradition" pleased Isabel and Chief.[24] Well-bred, beautiful, and intelligent, she would always have a special place in Isabel's heart. Peter, who had arrived in New York on the SS *Washington* just in time for Ann's wedding, and Betty Monk were married on July 28 at her parents' home in Maplewood, New Jersey. After a month's honeymoon in Maine, Peter and Betty sailed on the *Queen Mary* to England where, for the next two years, he continued to study at Oxford University for his doctorate in physics.

Isabel, whose life for so many years had revolved around her home and family, still experienced tension between her roles of homemaker and professional woman. As the one diminished, the other steadily evolved. She once commented that the Indicator, "unlike children who grow up and leave home," would keep her busy for the rest of her life. More and more, the Indicator proved to her the importance of type in "education, vocational choice, marriage, and human relations." It was, she said, "proof that your type affects nearly everything you do and the way you do it and the satisfaction you do or don't get out of it."[25]

---

*F*or several months before Peter's graduation from Oxford University on June 21, 1950, Isabel took time from her research to make plans with Chief and Ann for a trip to England and a five-week tour of Europe.[26] Isabel was excited about her first trip abroad. She also eagerly awaited an answer to a letter she had written Carl Jung, asking if she might visit him in Zurich. "You have no reason to remember me," she wrote Jung, "but I met you once in New York before the war at an interview you granted my mother, Katharine C. Briggs." Briefly reviewing that meeting, Isabel then wrote a three-page description of the "Briggs-Myers Type Indicator" for which the "psychological insight has been my mother's, the labor and validation of proof has been mine." She enclosed a sample of Form C. What she most wanted to discuss with Jung, she said, was what "*makes* the deficits in type development."[27]

Acknowledging the receipt of Isabel's letter and materials, Jung's secretary wrote that "both Dr. and Mrs. Jung are down with a rather bad kind of gastric flu" and an appointment with him would depend upon his health.[28] The seventy-five-year-old Jung himself replied on July 1:

Thank you very much for kindly sending me your interesting questionnaire and the equally interesting descriptions of your results. As you have given the matter a great deal of thought I think you have done so much in this direction that I'm hardly capable of criticising it or even knowing it better. For quite a long time I haven't done any work along that line at all, because other things have taken the foreground of my interests. But I should say that for any future development of the Type-Theory your Type-Indicator will prove to be of great help.

I should have liked very much to see you, but I'm only just recovering from a tedious illness and shall leave presently for a long and much-needed holiday from which I shall not return until the fall.

Hoping you have a nice time in Europe, I remain

yours sincerely,
C.G. Jung[29]

Isabel had told Katharine that she hoped to see Jung, and the letter that awaited her when she arrived at the hotel in Geneva was disappointing to both mother and daughter. However, Isabel, who disliked dwelling on the negative, put the disappointment aside to enjoy touring the continent with Ann, Betty, Peter, Chief, and Chief's sister, Parcie Myers. After visiting England and Scotland, they toured France, Belgium, the Netherlands, Italy, and Switzerland. Ann left the family in England on August 4 to return to Switzerland to do graduate study in German at the University of Basel.[30] The next day, Isabel, Chief, and Parcie sailed from Liverpool for New York.

Peter and Betty did not arrive in the United States until late fall, when he began work as a physicist on transistors and semiconductor devices in the Switching Research Department of the Bell Telephone Laboratories in Murray Hill, New Jersey.

After a year of study in Switzerland, Ann came home to enroll in graduate school at the University of Pennsylvania. Isabel and Chief welcomed the move, and for Isabel in particular, to have Ann nearby was a delight. She dearly loved her daughter and saw in her so much of herself; she had hoped that Ann would eventually carry on her work with the Indicator, something that Ann, although supportive and interested, had obviously elected not to do. Nothing would have made

Isabel happier than for the mantle to be passed from Katharine to Isabel to Ann, a succession recognized in later generations as "the Matriarchy."[31]

In any event, Ann was on the verge of yet another choice in life, one that would bring enormous joy to Chief and Isabel—her marriage to James A. Hughes, Jr.

CHAPTER SIXTEEN

The Indicator
Comes of Age

In many ways, the 1950s marked ten of the most gratifying years, personally and professionally, in the life of Isabel Myers. The decade had begun with Peter's finishing his doctorate at Oxford, followed by the family's European tour. But the two events that brought her the greatest satisfaction were Ann's supremely suitable second marriage, followed by the arrival of four grandchildren, two to each of Isabel's children.

In the spring of 1952, Ann's last semester before completing her Master's degree in German, she met James A. Hughes, Jr., a senior majoring in labor relations at the Wharton School. From Glenside, Pennsylvania, with a background similar to Ann's, he was intelligent, outgoing, ambitious, and responsible. Jim and Ann were not engaged until the end of the summer, but he still remembers vividly his first encounter with Ann's mother.

Arriving at Swarthmore to pick up Ann for their first date and finding her not ready, he was greeted by Isabel. She sat down in the living room with Jim and, looking at him intently, asked him "lots of questions." She was interested in him as a person, his goals and interests, not what might have been expected—his pedigree. As he answered her questions, she looked into his eyes and gave him her total attention. When she spoke, Jim recalled, "there was no waste of words; there was something awesomely admirable about the precision with which she thought and the precision with which she spoke." At first, he was impatient with how slowly she spoke, often with her eyes closed while she thought about what she was going to say (Lyman Briggs had the same way of speaking). Jim found her compelling. "She captivated you," he said, "with her eyes."[1]

Later in the courtship when Jim was invited to dinner, he met Chief for the first time. Still smarting over Ann's first marriage, Chief was not happy about her beginning a new relationship and was ill at ease with Jim. Fortunately, the conversation centered on a recent decision of the Supreme Court with which Jim, with some forethought, had familiarized himself. Afterward, Chief said to Ann, "Now *there* is a sound young man."[2] These salutary first encounters with both Isabel and Chief established the basis of what grew into happy relationships between Ann's parents and her husband.

The same was true with Lyman and Katharine, although Jim's involvements with Ann's grandmother were decidedly more guarded. After the engagement was announced, Katharine gave Jim a lecture on the logic of an employee owning stock in the company that he worked for and then proceeded to hand him a gift of shares in Rohm and Haas, manufacturer of industrial chemicals where he was employed, with the admonition that he should add to these at once.[3]

Jim and Ann were married in Swarthmore on January 17, 1953, and for seven months, lived in Philadelphia near Rohm and Haas. Ann taught and tutored in the German department at the University of Pennsylvania. In late summer, when a promotion took Jim to Houston, Texas, a stoic Isabel watched as Ann and Jim drove away from Dickinson Avenue. In his rearview mirror, Jim saw her weeping in Chief's arms.

———————————

*T*he four of them enjoyed a reunion in Europe the following summer, a trip Chief proposed when he learned that Jim had never been abroad. This time, when they toured the Continent in a rented car, Isabel introduced her plan for dividing driving responsibility. Rather than the expected apportionment of time for each person to be at the wheel, the plan assigned simultaneous road duties to all: One watched on the left, another on the right, another for approaching signs, and one drove. After a few hair-raising brushes with near accidents, Jim declined to participate.[4]

Isabel loved the quaintness of Europe and its depth of history. She preferred the countries, such as Switzerland and Germany, that were neat, clean, and well-organized; she disliked countries such as Italy and Ireland which she saw as less tidy and more "laid back." While touring, she took her photography seriously, framing and composing each shot with care, a procedure she obviously enjoyed. In recalling the trip, Jim Hughes observed that she never became so wrapped up in "the statistical details of the world that she lost track of things beautiful. She took time to 'smell the roses.'"[5]

Life was good in those years for the entire family. Isabel and Chief became grandparents, celebrating a coveted rite of passage, and Lyman and Katharine, now in their eighties, became great-grandparents. On May 26, 1955, Peter and Betty's son, Jonathan Briggs Myers, was born in Morristown, New Jersey, followed in December by Ann and Jim's daughter, Kathleen Ann Hughes. In her privileged role as maternal grandmother, Isabel went to Houston for two weeks to get acquainted with Kathleen and to help Ann. (Douglas James Hughes was born on April 18, 1958, and Jennifer Myers, adopted daughter of Peter and Betty, was born November 3, 1962.)

Almost as gratifying as the arrival of the grandchildren was the celebration of Lyman Briggs' eightieth birthday. His many recognitions now included honorary degrees from six universities, the Presidential Medal of Merit, the Gold Medal of the United States Department of Commerce, the National Geographic Society's Burr medal (three times), and election to the National Academy of Science and the American Philosophical Society.[6] Later, Michigan State University would cap this list by establishing in his honor an undergraduate facility, Lyman Briggs College, "created specifically for students interested in a broad liberal education in the biological and physical sciences and mathematics in the context of a small residential college."[7]

These symbols of respect and admiration from Briggs's colleagues were hardly more cherished than a private birthday message from his daughter. On May 6, 1954, Isabel wrote:

Dad Darling—

On this shining anniversary I want to thank you for the fifty-seven years of being my dad, and all the treasured things you have added to my life. All the questions you answered for me when I was little—and ever since—and the things we did together, the walks in the woods, the trips to camp, the paddling on the river, the baseball games you took me to, and always, all the way up to now, the being so *interested!*

And thank you, thank you, for not taking that job in California long ago. You told me it had been offered, and I wept a little, and you said tenderly, "Well, that settles it!" When I think what I would have missed, and Ann & Peter would have missed, if you and Mother had been so far away all these years—

And thank you for the background of science and research, the ingrained notion of fascination of finding out something that no one has known before—and what it takes in ingenuity and caution and patience.

And thank you for your faith and support in the type research which is clearly my destiny, being the application of the bent for research which I inherit from you to the field of research which Mother opened up by her creative insight into the type problem.

And thank you for finding Mother sixty-odd years ago and marrying her for our joint benefit. I am thankful to be the daughter of you two—

> With all my heart,
> Isabel[8]

In a separate letter, and in his inimitable way, Chief sent his appreciation "to a grand guy on his 80th birthday! One with thousands of friends, and, so far as I've heard, no enemies. One who has climbed all the way on his own two feet while pulling an increasingly greater load.... No airs, no pretense...and all the while an individual with radioactive mind of the non-toxic kind, never giving offense, always endearing...[and] I drink to your health. Lovingly, Chief."[9]

Chief's admiration of his father-in-law's mental agility at age eighty exacerbated his own resentment at being asked, on reaching age sixty-five, to retire from the law firm of Duane, Morris, and Heckscher, which he had served for thirty-seven years. Still solicitor for the Borough of Swarthmore, he enhanced his income for the next decade through private law practice that he maintained in the Dickinson Avenue house. Whenever Isabel needed help that was within his legal ability to provide, he responded generously. As the Indicator began to move into a professional world that required "counsel and contracts," he was at her side.

The first step that brought broader professional recognition for the *Myers-Briggs Type Indicator* was Isabel's pioneering work with medical colleges; the other involved Educational Testing Service.

After Lyman Briggs's first contact in 1947 with George Washington University Medical School and the testing that ensued, Dr. Leland Parr, a department head, advised Isabel to try to enlist more medical schools for a "large scale experiment."[10] After approaching five schools in the Philadelphia area and three in New York City, Isabel wrote Dr. Lawrence W. Hanlon at Cornell University Medical College that she now had "five big ones."[11]

With these conquests to strengthen her cause, she contacted John M. Stalnaker, Director of Studies for the Association of American Medical Colleges (AAMC), to seek his support.[12] Stalnaker was interested, but he realized that confirmation of her preliminary findings would need a much larger sample of medical students.[13] Not until the fall of 1951, at the time of the annual meeting of AAMC in French Lick, Indiana, was he able to discuss the matter with his Committee on Student Personnel Practices. Meanwhile, he wrote Isabel that "it would be unwise to approach many of the deans individually." (Evidently Stalnaker did not know that she had already approached fifteen schools!)[14] At his invitation, Isabel attended the AAMC meeting in late October.

On the way home from that meeting, she scribbled a triumphant note, in pencil, to Katharine Briggs: "We have met the Association, and they are ours." Hanlon had arranged for her to have lunch with Dr. Thomas Alexander Cumming Rennie, a psychiatrist on the medical faculty at Cornell. Before their discussion was over, Rennie had concluded, "If this device of yours is as good as it sounds, it is a very important device." When he asked her about her background and how she got into the work, she reluctantly told him, "It won' t qualify me." Rennie responded, "The hell with that."[15] It is no wonder that Isabel then wrote a friend, "Score another touchdown for Cornell."[16]

With the approval of a man of Rennie's stature, Stalnaker was ready to ask other medical schools whether they would like to participate in the research project. By the end of November, twenty-five had responded affirmatively.[17] Before the year was out, forty-five medical colleges had given the Indicator to a total of 3,605 students in the class of 1955.

Four years later, Isabel would follow up these students (others were added in the meantime) and compare their Medical College Admission Test scores, class standings, and grade point averages with Type profiles. She was less interested in validation as such than she was in helping to select the best students to survive the rigors of a medical education and become competent and respected practioners. She wanted a chance to tell "which students are likely to do the poorest work because of a deficit of perception, and which students are likely to have emotional difficulties because of a deficit of judgment,—and let the event verify the prediction."[18]

Working with the enormous body of data that the medical school study provided, Isabel was able to devise more sophisticated scoring methods that could provide three gradations of information useful in individualized, and even clinical, situations. For the most part, however, the most widely used application of the Indicator would be the first gradation, which provided a clear, standard description of each of the sixteen types that could readily be discussed with persons in a group.[19]

In taking on this enormous project, Isabel Myers had "a tiger by the tail." If she ever had moments of doubt or panic, there is no evidence of it in her correspondence. On the contrary, she countered resistance by requesting personal appointments so she could explain the Indicator and its theoretical underpinnings. (She had attended the AAMC conference at French Lick to be able to present personally her cause.) She regarded those who reacted negatively to her work as people who simply did not understand. In two instances, one with Jefferson Medical College, the other with Western Reserve School of Medicine, the Indicator was rejected by their respective psychological clinics and/or departments of psychiatry. Ironically, at both schools, the decisions were rendered by women.[20]

It is clear that Isabel felt a sense of betrayal from an angry letter she wrote—but apparently did not mail—to the dean at Jefferson: "I believe Dr. [Olive] Morgan feels, with considerable reason, that the entrance of another *woman* with another test would complicate a situation which is already difficult enough. May I suggest, that, if it does prove possible to find a period in which the Indicator could be given, I had better not put in an appearance. I could probably send a young man."[21] Eventually, Jefferson became part of the study but Western Reserve did not.

It is not surprising, however, that medical school deans, as well as persons in Stalnaker's office, not infrequently wrote to ask, after the Indicator was administered, when her reports to them would be forthcoming. In addition to scoring and tabulating the results, Isabel wrote hundreds of letters to medical personnel. Each school that agreed to participate would first let Stalnaker know, and Isabel would then follow up with a personal letter to each dean. When answer sheets poured in from the medical students, she had a cadre of Swarthmore neighbors trained to assist in the scoring, but the only full-time employee she ever had with the Indicator was Lisa McGaw, a young friend of Peter's.

A graduate of Holyoke College, with a Master's degree from Hartford Seminary in psychology and religious education, Lisa had had infantile paralysis, which left her physically disabled. When Peter was in the Navy, he met her at a Friends' Meeting in San Francisco and was indignant because of the blatant discrimination in the job market that a woman of her education and intelligence had suffered. Although largely because of her disability, the bias, in some instances, was merely because she was female.[22] The combination was insurmountable. Peter wrote to Isabel and Chief, both of whom immediately began to do something about the situation. Both wrote to possible employers on the west coast, and Isabel laid her case (unsuccessfully) before Donald MacKinnon at Berkeley.[23] "We are all shocked," Isabel wrote Lisa, "at the cumulative amount of discouragement that can be handed to one small and valiant girl."[24]

Lisa began scoring Indicators in early 1947 in San Francisco and, by September, Isabel was "delighted." In November, Chief drew up a contract of work with Lisa as a full-time employee of the Myerses at two hundred dollars per month.[25] Before making this commitment, Isabel talked the matter over with Katharine and Lyman Briggs. "They have therefore made a gift to the Type Indicator of several thousand dollars for working capital," Isabel wrote Lisa, "with instructions that it is to be *used*, not hoarded.... For the long pull, which we are now embarking on, it is infinitely more important for you to get back your health than to do any given amount of work. Remember that, will you my dear?... *Now* will you stop worrying about what I think of you? I think you are about the most valiant soul I ever ran into—and I think we are going to have a lot of fun from here on."[26]

The professional relationship between Isabel and Lisa continued, with Lisa in due course moving to the East Coast, first to Swarthmore and later to New York City. In the fall of 1960, Isabel wrote Lisa: "A very unexpected and distressing situation has arisen at Chief's law office. The firm has told him that since he has passed the age of 65 they will expect him to retire shortly. There is no provision for retirement pay or its equivalent. We have got to watch every penny from now on." This meant, of course, that Isabel could no longer afford to employ Lisa "beyond a very limited period."[27] Fortunately, Lisa had taken courses at Columbia University that enhanced her editorial skills. Having assisted Isabel during the medical school study, when Isabel had the greatest need for clerical help, Lisa was now able to move on to a position as a full-time freelance editor.[28]

---

*T*he part of the medical school study that began with George Washington University in 1947 and occupied Isabel for nearly ten years laid the ground work for the next leap in recognition for the Indicator. Dr. Harold C. Wiggers, dean of the Albany Medical College, knew that Henry Chauncey, president of Educational Testing Service, was interested in personality testing. In February 1956, at a meeting of educators at which both men were present, Wiggers mentioned that he had been favorably impressed with a new instrument called the *Briggs-Myers Type Indicator,* which provided a promising approach to the problem of student selection. Chauncey followed up immediately on Wiggers' suggestion.[29]

CHAPTER SEVENTEEN

First Publisher
for the Indicator

*I*n February 1956, when Henry Chauncey attended a meeting of the New York State Department of Education in Albany, he took with him David R. Saunders, a member of the ETS research staff whose field was personality measurement. Chauncey wanted Saunders to talk in more detail with Wiggers, also present at the meeting, about the Briggs-Myers instrument and, if indicated, to get in touch with the people who had developed the test. On March 23, Saunders wrote to "Mrs. Myers":

> In the course of a recent conference attended by both Dean Harold C. Wiggers of the Albany Medical College and myself I learned something of your work in testing medical students in cooperation with the American Association of Medical Colleges. Unfortunately, Dean Wiggers was able to tell me only very little concerning the details of your approach, but he did imply that he thought your approach was very promising.
>
> Since Swarthmore is not very far from here, I wonder if you would be willing to accept an invitation to visit us [ETS] in Princeton some afternoon in the near future for the purpose of exchanging our experiences in the testing of medical students. I expect that we could get together a group of a dozen or so to whom you might present your material in an informal discussion situation. We would, of course, be happy to reimburse you for your traveling expenses.[1]

Isabel was delighted at the prospect of making a presentation to ETS, the first time a professional organization of this stature had come to her.

On May 22, members of the research department at ETS gathered in a conference room in a rented building near 20 Nassau Street, in Princeton, to hear a guest speaker talk about a personality testing instrument. The audience was made up almost entirely of men with doctorates from universities such as Chicago, Illinois, and Princeton. Many of them were protegés of distinguished mentors in tests and measurements such as Raymond B. Cattell, J. Paul Guilford, Harold O. Gulliksen, and L. L. Thurstone. Also present were a group called Psychometric Fellows, who were selected and funded by ETS and studying for doctorates at Princeton University.

When Saunders walked in with Isabel Myers, heads flew up at the sight of an older woman with greying hair tucked in a bun at the back of her neck, a face free of make-up, and attire that could hardly be described as the latest in fashion. Only Chauncey and Saunders had ever heard of her. After her presentation, which received a polite if not enthusiastic reception from the research staff, Saunders lingered to look at some of her materials and to take the test. Immediately intrigued, he thought that the Indicator was "potentially the best personality instrument" he had ever seen. Henry Chauncey also believed that the Indicator was worth further study.[2]

By 1956, ETS was recognized as premier in the field of educational testing. It had begun operations in January 1948 when the testing activities of the American Council on Education, the College Entrance Examination Board, and the Carnegie Foundation for the Advancement of Teaching (through the Graduate Record Office) united to form a single organization. James B. Conant, president of Harvard University, was elected chairman of the new joint Board of Trustees, and Henry Chauncey, Director of the College Entrance Examination Board, was appointed president of ETS.

In Chauncey's first annual report to the Board of Trustees for 1949–50, this statement appeared under the heading of Personality Measurements: "The long-range goal of ETS in the personality area may be stated as the development of personality tests which ultimately can be administered to groups and scored objectively, and which yield reliable measures of aspects of personality that are useful in educational guidance and selection."[3] The 1956–57 annual report stated: "This year, we discovered one such test—the *Briggs-Myers Type Indicator*."[4]

From the examination of Henry Chauncey's diaries for the 1950s, it is clear that he was deeply interested in the study of personality traits and their bearing on education. In 1955, he noted, "Tests are neither good nor bad; it is the way they are used or the effects they have which may be good or bad. If one recognizes incorrect or exaggerated uses and if one is on the watch for bad influences, dangers may be avoided. Tests provide the 'paths through the woods.'"[5]

Chauncey's opinion that tests themselves were neither good nor bad, but it was how they were used that could have either a negative or positive effect, concurred with Isabel Myers' belief that the Indicator did not focus on whether people were good or bad, but rather focused on how people functioned. What she had not foreseen, however, were the rigid statistical criteria that ETS's quantitatively oriented research staff would apply in evaluating the Indicator.

In any event, in the spring of 1957, Isabel Myers reached a verbal agreement with Chauncey and Saunders that all parties would like ETS to publish the Indicator. For the next three months, Saunders, in the role of negotiator between ETS's attorney and Isabel Myers (carefully coached by Chief), prepared and revised numerous drafts of an agreement that was finally signed in July 1957.[6]

Both parties to the contract immediately faced two tasks: the collection of better standardization data to update Form C, and the preparation of a proper user's manual. It was agreed that ETS would (1) assist her by providing logistical and financial support and (2) "have sole responsibility for, and control over, all promotional activities, in accordance with accepted professional practice."[7] In addition, Isabel Myers and Henry Chauncey agreed that she would write an explanatory book about the Indicator.

She then devised Form D, which contained three hundred items to be pretested, and ETS produced a multilithed edition of this form that, in May 1957, was given to juniors and seniors in some thirty high schools selected by Isabel Myers in the Philadelphia area. A letter composed by Saunders on ETS letterhead was sent to each principal to enlist the school's participation. (The one hundred percent response from the principals suggested that ETS had impressive educational clout.)[8] Isabel prepared an answer sheet so that scoring could be done on ETS's special machine (the IBM 101) for test scoring—a huge step into the age of technology—and she was provided with computer support for the item analyses. In the spring of 1958, Form E, a shortened version for younger students, and Form F, "the complete MBTI to be used for further research," evolved. Form F would be the standard for another twenty years.[9]

In February 1959, Isabel Myers signed another agreement with ETS which identified Form F as "developed and ready for use."[10] Confident that the Indicator was effectively launched, Saunders returned to other research projects. At Isabel Myers's suggestion, Richard Cordray, her young tutor in statistics then teaching at Chico State College in California, was hired by ETS for the summer of 1959 as an interim project director. At the end of the summer, in a memo to Chauncey, Cordray wrote, "I have been trying for years to convince Mrs. Myers that she should do as little clerical work as possible, on the ground that her time was better spent elsewhere. Her reply has been that she has been disappointed with accuracy. I have now convinced her that the...accuracy of machine operations can be assured. She was impressed."[11] Cordray had also urged Isabel to publish her work in a refereed journal, but she steadfastly refused because she lacked a Ph.D.[12]

For the next year, John Ross, an Australian Psychometric Fellow, assumed responsibility for the Indicator.[13] Ross had hardly begun his work when rumblings of opposition were heard from sources other than the quantitively oriented research staff. The Cooperative Test Division (CTD), a part of ETS that was in the business of creating, acquiring, and marketing tests to be sold to qualified users, had appeared to be the logical home for the Indicator.[14] However, John Dobbin, head of CTD, and his staff strenuously objected to having the Indicator placed in their division but recommended, nevertheless, that ETS "give the instrument publication for a fairly long period (five years) as a research tool."[15] In June 1960, ETS then set up the Office of Special Tests to house activities related to the Indicator and various other research instruments.[16]

John Ross returned to Australia and left his recommendation that ETS publish the Indicator for one year, "perhaps two," as an experimental test, and that a manual be published. In an evaluation of the Indicator, Ross also stated, "A veil of suspicion hangs about it. It had an unorthodox origin, it is wedded to a somewhat unfashionable theory, and the enthusiasm it has aroused in some people has provoked sterner opposition in others. I am making an attempt to be...simply the dispassionate and impartial evaluator."[17]

Ross was then replaced by a new staff person in research, Lawrence Stricker, and, at about the same time, Henry Chauncey named Isabel Myers as a consultant to "spend at least one day a month [at ETS] on a regularly scheduled basis," with a fee of $250 per month, beginning in November 1960.[18] Stricker's first assignment was to work with Myers in writing a test manual, and by March 1961, he reported to Chauncey that a draft for most of the manual was "roughed out." He also outlined detailed plans for distribution of the Indicator.[19]

When Stricker, an articulate twenty-seven-year-old psychometrician trained at New York University, prepared a draft of the manual, he included in the text a stinging critique of the Indicator. A colleague who reviewed Stricker's draft commented, "This shouldn' t be called a manual, [but rather a] technical report on the test." The reviewer went on to say that Stricker's conclusions and recommendations were "too emotional" and should be revised.[20]

Stricker's criticisms were decidedly upsetting to Isabel Myers, who regarded this as an attack on both her and her work. In relaying her concerns to Chauncey, she stated that the critique contained "misinterpretations, distortions, and omissions."[21] She labeled her own file related to him as "Larry Stricker, Damn Him." In a lengthy letter to Stricker, she closed with a strong caveat: His position on the Indicator, she said, would be much more valuable and much more generally valued if it took "a tone of benevolent neutrality consistent with [the purposes of research]...than if it mars its usefulness by undertaking on its own initiative to cut off the dog's tail behind its ears. The dog just might turn out to be a champion."[22]

Later, Isabel Myers prepared a twenty-four-page rebuttal to Stricker for ETS Executive Vice President William Turnbull.[23] Thus began a scholarly feud that only intensified, despite Turnbull and Chauncey's attempts at mediation.[24] The imbroglio was finally resolved the following February when Stricker was replaced by Junius A. Davis (known as "Jay"), a clinical psychologist who had joined the ETS staff in September 1961 as assistant to the president.

Stricker's critique, prepared for publication, was held up until Myers's manual came out in September 1962, a delay that was decidedly displeasing to him.[25] Although Stricker declined to be interviewed, a colleague has described Stricker's assignment as untenable in that he was handed a research project to espouse and develop, about which positive conclusions had been drawn before he was given an opportunity to evaluate the material.[26]

On the other hand, Chauncey believed that Stricker was "unduly negative" and that "even if one does not want to dignify Mrs. M[yers]'s hypotheses by speaking of them as theory, one can consider them as ways of looking at human beings." In this respect, it seemed to Chauncey that the Indicator had much to commend it.[27]

The first task that faced Davis, to assist in completing the manual by the deadline of July 1962, entailed working many eighteen and some twenty-hour days. Even on this grueling schedule, Isabel Myers, who seldom went to the ETS cafeteria even for lunch, still worked with apparently limitless energy. The secret, she told an exhausted Davis, was Tiger's Milk, a mixture of brewer's yeast blended with milk and Hershey bars (kept in a large thermos) that made a "perfect high-energy diet."

Isabel Myers had enormous respect for Jay Davis, and as she wrote and rewrote the text of the manual to try to achieve her usual standards of perfection, she received his suggestions with minimal resistance. Davis was responsible for ensuring that the text "reflected well on ETS, the discipline, and on her, [without] getting into the insidious problems where her emotions were as high as Stricker's."[28]

Before the manual was finished, however, Saunders, who had left ETS in January 1961 to begin his own consulting business, was hired to assist with the final text. Isabel was happy to be working with him again. Saunders recalls that part of his role was to take what he knew she wanted to say and help her to say it in terms acceptable to ETS. He also performed some necessary computations for data that had to be included in the manual. Earlier, while working with Isabel on Form D, he had persuaded Isabel Myers to change the order of the names in the Indicator's title to "Myers-Briggs" instead of her earlier designation of "Briggs-Myers." Tests were usually known by their initials, he explained, and she was quick to see the implications of the acronym. Before giving her final consent, however, she determined from a survey of the scientific literature that it was conventional practice for more recent contributors of refinements to be named first in a series.[29] She also accepted Saunders's suggestion that the symbol for Intuition (I) be changed to "N" to eliminate confusion with the "I" that stood for Introversion.[30]

In September 1962, the manual was published, and Isabel Myers's jubilant colleagues at ETS feted her with a party. Later that same month, Isabel made her professional debut before the American Psychological Association in St. Louis. Sponsored by APA member David Saunders, she titled her paper "Inferences as to the Dichotomous Nature of Jung's Types, From the Shapes of Regressions of Dependent Variables Upon

Myers-Briggs Type Indicator Scores." The paper evoked virtually no response.

Then in December Davis sent a confidential memo to Chauncey and Turnbull, outlining some difficulties in relationships with Isabel Myers. His summary reads:

> Mrs. Myers has dedicated her life and that of her family to the concept of type; she believes it to be a profound and extremely important social discovery. She believes her Indicator provides the way to make this concept useful in educational and vocational guidance, marital and vocational adjustment, elaboration and diagnoses, and therapy of personality problems, etc. She is bright, energetic, compulsive, and very persistent. Anything that may further the development and promulgation of the Indicator and its acceptance by the professional public transcends any other code of behavior. The woman has worked day and night for…[many] years with this goal overriding all other personal goals; she is a kind of modern Joan of Arc, and her cause is as sacred; she simply doesn't anticipate being trapped and bound at the stake.

Davis specifically cited her talent for enlisting ETS personnel, some of whom allegedly asked for the day off or a place to hide when she came to Princeton. To circumvent bureaucratic procedures (to her, operational delays) she frequently worked at night, and according to Davis, at this time, she searched for data that she felt she needed in files inaccessible to her during regular working hours. Isabel's motivation, that of professional need, was, she thought, unquestionably legitimate, but many of the ETS staff viewed her after-hours searches as an intrusion. Davis recommended that the consultant relationship be terminated "at the end of the present contract period" and for the remainder of that time, Myers be given office space where "access to others is hampered."[31]

Although Turnbull requested soon thereafter that a staff member check to see "if by happy chance the problem has gone away," there is no record of a reaction from Chauncey other than his maintaining the consultant relationship with Isabel.[32]

Davis later informed Chauncey that, although ETS was "losing heavily on this operation," they had "gotten a good buy for the research dollar" because [Mrs. Myers] had "remained active in her own research…and her work has been timely, appropriate, sound, and responsible."[33]

A large part of Isabel Myers' active research focused on data from the medical schools. She had undertaken a longitudinal study of over four thousand medical students by following them up twelve years after she gathered the initial data in 1951. Using information from the AMA directory, she determined, among other things, that most of the students had selected careers and kinds of practice that was "attractive" to their Type.[34] With Jay Davis as coauthor, she reported on this study in September 1964 at the annual meeting of the American Psychological Association in Los Angeles. In an addendum to the paper, Davis wrote:

> Mrs. Myers has joined us in the best tradition of [Edward K.] Strong and [Lewis M.] Terman…. Her demonstrated concern for a carefully conceived program of research involving ultimate criteria sets a pace that one would hope more test authors may emulate…. Those of us [doing research in personality measurement] must take some envious note of the theoretical underpinnings…of the instrument. The relationships are logical and real.[35]

That fall, Isabel Myers began another enormous research project for which ETS provided materials at cost but made no funding available. The project, which would eventually become the Myers Longitudinal Nursing Study, involved testing over ten thousand nursing students. Despite Davis' praise of Isabel Myers' competence as a researcher, Chauncey was concerned about unfinished tasks that would be delayed even longer, such as a needed revision of the 1962 manual (this was never completed) and the book describing personality types that he continually and courteously inquired about during his regular consultations with her.

In retrospect, there is considerable irony in the fact that even Isabel Myers' advocates failed to take her caveat seriously about "strong intuitives," such as: "How easy it is for an intuitive in the grip of an inspiration to leap ahead to the possibilities without looking at the factors that count against."[36] Proceeding with the nursing study was far more important to her than routine projects such as revising and rewriting or setting down old ideas. Clearly, the ETS staff thought differently about her priorities.

The presentation of her paper at the meeting of the American Psychological Association, in collaboration with Jay Davis, marked the peak of Isabel Myers' association with ETS. Although her publishing contract would continue in force for another decade, Chauncey terminated the consulting arrangement at the end of 1965.

Clearly the initial plans for development and promotion of the Indicator first suggested by Stricker were not proceeding apace. After the manual was published, ETS had issued an 8 1/2-by-5 1/2, six-page typed brochure, with an order blank insert for potential users of the Indicator that Davis described as "dowdy."[37] He and others then at ETS have confirmed that the Indicator was never publicized or, in the administrative jargon, ever given "the Tiffany treatment."[38]

When Jay Davis and Henry Chauncey left the Princeton offices of ETS—Davis, in 1968, to head a satellite office in Durham, North Carolina, and Chauncey, in the spring of 1970, to retire—Isabel Myers lost her two strongest advocates. Although activity at ETS with regard to the Indicator virtually ceased, a small cadre of people outside of Princeton were doing important research.

One of these was Donald MacKinnon at IPAR in Berkeley. Another, Takeshi Ohsawa, was the first user to translate the MBTI into a foreign language. He had learned about the Indicator from a colleague, Sukeyori Shiba, professor of psychology at Tokyo University, who was sent to ETS in 1963 by the Ministry of Education of Japan to study aspects of test administration.[39] Ohsawa, an industrial psychologist, was immediately interested in the practical applications of the Indicator in management and in suiting the worker to the job. With his colleagues at the Nippon Recruit Center in Tokyo, he translated the MBTI to use experimentally, and in 1968, Ohsawa came to the United States to confer with Isabel Myers and to seek her approval to publish the MBTI in Japanese. She signed an agreement with Ohsawa on August 17, 1968, and the next year she received royalties on 40,000 copies. By the end of the decade, Ohsawa was using nearly 300,000 copies per year.[40]

In the early 1960s, Eleanor Barberousse, a doctoral candidate and student assistant in counseling at Auburn University in Alabama, was searching for a test to measure creativity, a topic she wanted to pursue for her dissertation. She found a study done by none other than IPAR and noted that the "MBTI results were significant in picking these [creative] people out." Hers became the first dissertation, completed in 1965, to use the MBTI.[41]

After ordering materials from ETS, Barberousse had presented the MBTI to the Auburn counseling staff, whose director was W. Harold Grant. Grant and his staff began to use the Indicator extensively, and they became interested in it as a research instrument. In the spring of 1966, in Washington, D.C., at a meeting of the American Personnel and Guidance Association, Auburn staff members presented a program on their MBTI research. At Grant's invitation, Isabel Myers traveled from Swarthmore for the APGA meeting and to have discussions with the Auburn group. Grant later recalled that she was delighted with their work (the first college to use the Indicator) and that they were "using it as she had intended." At the same time, she outlined "some corrections that she felt were appropriate."[42] She "peered intently at us through her glasses" as the presentations continued. Both as a faculty member at Michigan State University and later when he returned to Auburn, Grant directed a number of doctoral dissertations that used the MBTI.[43]

In the early 1970s, Cecil Williams, director of the counseling center at Michigan State University, became a frequent user of the Indicator and he, too, was responsible for its use in dissertations and other research.[44]

That some of these first dissertations came out of Michigan State University where her parents had been honor students in the 1890s was particularly gratifying to Isabel. With unflagging interest, she followed all of these increments of progress in the Indicator's use, progress that contributed to her dissatisfaction with the situation at ETS. However, abrupt changes and tragedies in her family during the next decade tended to divert her attention from the apparent bureaucratic stalemate.

Part Five

CHAPTER EIGHTEEN

Family Tragedies

On March 26, 1963, shortly before his eighty-ninth birthday, Lyman Briggs died at his home in Washington. His obituary, listing his numerous professional honors and achievements, was complemented by a succinct, poignant editorial in the Washington *Evening Star:*

> Dr. Briggs was indeed "a scientist's scientist," an intellectual explorer who set out in his early teen-age years to examine, to understand and eventually to find practical and valuable application of an almost limitless variety of little known scientific truths.
>
> Happily mixed with Dr. Briggs' great professional qualifications, however, was a personality that was a charm and delight to his friends. Only a few years ago, in 1959, Dr. Briggs was applying his scientific talents to one of his favorite pastimes, baseball. He wanted to know whether pitchers really can throw curves. He found that they can, and do. [Ideal curving speed: about 100 ft. per sec. Optimum amount of spin: so me 1800 revolutions per minute. See *Time,* April 4, 1959]. If this sort of preoccupation seems frivolous for a distinguished scientist in his middle 80s, his own…philosophy stands as a pretty good explanation for an always youthful interest in life. "Never look back; something may be creeping up on you…." Old age never really had a chance to creep up on Dr. Briggs.[1]

Lyman's ashes were placed in the Cedar Hill Mausoleum, in suburban Maryland, beside those of his small son, Albert Cook Briggs, and Isabel's two stillborn infants.[2]

Isabel accepted her father's death as a rite of passage for one so deeply loved and revered during his long life. She was immediately faced with the total responsibilty for the care of Katharine Briggs, whose faculties failed noticeably after Lyman's death. Isabel resolved the problem by buying a small house next door, at 317 Dickinson Avenue, in Swarthmore, where she and Chief could more easily monitor her mother's personal and legal needs. A relative remarked that "Katharine [once] did everything but breathe for Isabel."[3] Now the situation was reversed.

In the fall, Chief's sister, Parcie, then living in Florida, came up to be a companion to Katharine, an interlude from obligations that Chief seized to take Isabel on a much needed vacation. To have someone available immediately if any emergency developed with Katharine, Jim and Ann moved into 321 Dickinson Avenue while Chief and Isabel were away. In the spring of 1966, Chief and Isabel had a "rewarding seven weeks in seven [European] countries" with Peter, Betty, and Jonathan, then eleven, as their guests. (Jennifer, only four, stayed with friends in Swarthmore.) For a weary Isabel, the most immediate pleasure was the ocean crossing to England on the *Queen Mary,* with "calm seas, wonderful food, wonderful deck chairs to relax in, [and] wonderful nights for sleeping." However, she walked around the deck three times every day "to get in training for keeping up" with her "long legged family."[4]

The vacation served Isabel well because, in the next year, Katharine rapidly declined both mentally and physically. Isabel moved her mother to the Bishop Nursing Home in Media, Pennsylvania, where Katharine died on July 10, 1968, six months past her ninety-third birthday.[5] Her ashes were placed beside Lyman's in the Cedar Hill Mausoleum.

---

*P*aul Gemmill, now retired from the University of Pennsylvania, and Jane rented the house at 317 Dickinson Avenue. In 1969, the year after Katharine's death, they, with Isabel and Chief, had hosted the fiftieth reunion of the Awful Ate. All eight were present and, although none of them thought seriously that it would be their last get-together, it turned out to be so. Phyllis recalled that at their twenty-fifth reunion in 1944, Isabel had "analyzed" all of the Ate, and she was convinced that what Isabel told her had "worked out." Phyllis added, "We hear so much that is Freudian and have been steered into such an over-emphasis on sex, that it is refreshing to have another approach."[6]

Isabel's contacts with the Awful Ate decreased in proportion to the amount of time that went into the Indicator. The Indicator, along with her growing family, commanded most of her attention. In 1964, Peter and Betty had moved to southern California, where Peter would spend more than ten years with the Magnavox Research Laboratories, working on radio and satellite navigation. Isabel was able to visit the children when she was at the APA meeting in Los Angeles, and after Katharine's death, she, Chief, and Parcie took an extended train tour of Canada and Alaska that ended in southern California for a few days with the Peter Myers family.

In his role as grandfather, Chief was the faithful steward who remembered birthdays and Christmases with generous checks and who corresponded with the youngsters. As soon as they could manage a pencil and their alphabet, each grandchild wrote regularly to the grandparents, and often to the great-grandparents.

Peter's move to the West Coast was compensated by Jim and Ann's move in late 1956 back East. Jim had accepted a position with Atlas Powder Company in Wilmington, Delaware, where Douglas Hughes was born in April 1958. Isabel, in the midst of tasks at ETS, did not help Ann with this second baby, but she and Chief were within easy driving distance for quick visits to the Hugheses. After two years in Wilmington, Ann and Jim moved to Tamaqua, Pennsylvania, near Wilkes-Barre, the site of the Atlas main plant. Jim was made a manager with greatly expanded responsibilities. They lived in Tamaqua for almost six years.

During her children's preschool years, Ann, like Isabel before her, devoted full time to being a mother. She often wrote Isabel about clever things the grandchildren were doing, but she never reported to the extent that Isabel had to Katharine Briggs. Moreover, during those years, Isabel's mind was far more centered on the Indicator than on being a grandmother. Nor did Ann and Jim rely on the Indicator in rearing their children.

By the time Kathy and Doug started school, Ann and Jim had already taught them to read. Ann soon learned that the children in the

Tamaqua schools were generally poor readers and she set about to learn why. Thus Ann began what would be her life's work. Convinced that the reading methods in use were wrong, she talked with the superintendent. Instead of encouragement, she got a you-tend-to-your-business-and-we'll-tend-to-ours response. Undeterred, Ann thoroughly researched ways in which reading was taught, could be taught, and should be taught, a study that was expanded with a coauthor and published in an educational journal.[7] She then began to lecture and to make a name for herself. Present at one of her lectures in New York was M. Blouke Carus, president of Open Court Publishing Company, publisher of educational materials. Carus completely agreed with Ann's ideas. He then asked her to write a new program for language instruction, a work that was published by Open Court in 1966. Soon one of Open Court's main authors, Ann developed the *Foundation Program,* a highly effective reading program that by 1972 was being used by 400,000 first graders. She was the author of *Breaking the Code,* written for a remedial literacy program; she also wrote versions of the reading, writing, and mathematics portions of the Open Court kindergarten program. Ann believed that educating children from ages five through eight was "where the great breakthrough in education must come if we are ever to achieve our national resolve to educate every child up to his maximum potential."[8] Indeed, one educator said that Ann's work promised to be just as creative and could measure up to anything Isabel Myers ever did.[9]

Isabel was avidly interested in what Ann was doing, and she soon began to collaborate with her daughter in some of this work. Ann usually sent carbons of her professional correspondence to Isabel to keep her mother informed about each project. Ann would frequently drive down with the children from Tamaqua, and the two women would spend long hours discussing their work. Isabel wrote "how to" stories, devised games, composed poems (and added a few of her earlier ones) for Ann's curriculum projects.[10] If Ann could not commit herself to the Indicator, Isabel could join in her daughter's work. Their collaboration was made easier when Ann and the children moved to Swarthmore during Jim's yearlong assignment overseas for his company (Atlas Chemical Industries, Inc.).

With Kathy and Doug now in Swarthmore schools, Isabel and Chief were able to keep the grandchildren so that Ann could spend several weeks in Europe with Jim. The interlude with Ann in Swarthmore, supremely gratifying to Isabel, was disrupted when Jim, promoted to Marketing Specialist for Latin America in the summer of 1968, moved his family to Miami.

By now, Ann was "swept up and running and would never turn back."[11] Jim's work continued to call for more and more responsibility which, in turn, brought him more and more gratification. Both Jim and Ann were moving at high speed on diverging professional routes.

In the spring of 1969, at an Open Court board meeting in La Salle, Illinois, Ann met a young intellectual, Carl Bereiter, professor at the University of Toronto and professor of Applied Psychology and Curriculum at the Ontario Institute for Studies in Education. Ann attended the meeting in an advisory capacity; Carl, to give a paper. By that fall, Ann and Carl were collaborating on a kindergarten project for Open Court that required frequent discussion and interaction. The next spring, after trying to deny what was happening, Ann admitted to herself and later to Jim that she was in love with Carl and wanted to be free to marry him.

Ann then confided in Isabel and sought her counsel. Even though she was exceedingly upset, Isabel's chief concern was not to alienate her daughter. She, in effect, helped Ann in her plan to file for a divorce in Florida. Ann, Jim, and the children could remain in Miami under one roof until the decree would be final on August 6, 1970. These plans were kept from Chief, who first learned of Ann's intentions in a long letter that she wrote in the summer to both parents.[12] Isabel read the letter and sobbed that their world would never be the same again.

Unaware of Isabel's complicity, Chief, for whom frankness was standard procedure, wrote a blistering reply to Ann. "I love you, and I will always stand back of you, but I cannot forgive you for what you have done to Jim, Kathy, Doug, Jim and Emily [Jim's parents], Isabel and me." Chief considered himself to be an understanding person when marriages had gone sour, but he could not see that such applied to her. "Granted that you think...[Bereiter] is a soulmate...[but] since when does an honorable person decide to chuck overboard a wonderful marriage, distress everybody who loves her, and decide, at age 42, to pull up stakes; cut loose from most of her 'roots,' and take her children away to join his—hoping that the man's wife will eventually agree on a divorce? It sounds like one of those horrible movies! It is absolutely unbelievable." Still, Ann would always be "the little girl from whose fingers or knees I used to remove splinters."[13] At Isabel's urging, Chief softened his views somewhat. Sure of her feelings, Ann took the children and moved to Toronto to be near Bereiter.

Now in their mid-seventies, Chief and Isabel were trying to be stoic about the end of Ann's marriage and her relationship with Bereiter. They were unprepared for the next blow when, scarcely a year later, Peter told them that he and Betty were getting a divorce. The disappointment was intensified in each case because Chief and Isabel's own children had initiated the actions. Interestingly enough, Isabel's first move after hearing Peter's news was to call Ann to discuss it.[14]

Indeed, as the children's problems burgeoned, she turned more and more to her own work—work that would help her to survive the greatest tragedy to come in her lifetime.

Jim and Ann had made generous arrangements about joint custody of Kathy and Doug that enabled Jim to have them during school vacations and in the summer. In August 1972, the three of them were just back from a trip abroad when word came that Ann had died suddenly.

While Jim and the children were in Europe, Ann and Carl were living in a small apartment in Cambridge, where he was a lecturer at Harvard for the summer session. Ann had elected to make use of medical facilities in the Boston area to have remedial surgery to tighten her abdominal muscles.[15] She insisted that she could do without her mother's offer to come and help after she was released from the hospital. Uneasy about Ann, and despite her daughter's protestations, Isabel went anyway. Under circumstances that were anything but auspicious, she and Carl finally met. He bunked on the living room sofa to give Isabel a place to sleep. That first night, near dawn, when Ann had not come back to bed after going to the bathroom, Isabel went to check on her— and found Ann dead. She had been stricken with an embolism after surgery. Isabel soon called Chief with the tragic news. "I don't know how to tell you this—she's dead."[16] He flew up immediately. Completely rebuffed from any attempt to share the emotional stress, Bereiter left. They never saw him again.[17]

Isabel telephoned Kathy, and Jim, who was in Brazil, returned to Florida within hours so that he could tell Doug, still in Miami until school opened. Jim vowed to Douglas that he would never again leave him for any reason, and he kept his promise, obtaining a nontraveling position with his company at their headquarters in Wilmington, Delaware. He then moved back to Swarthmore, which he had long thought of as "no better place in the world for a kid to grow up" and that the children regarded as home. Until Jim could take care of obligations in Miami, Douglas lived for three months with his grandparents.[18]

---

*B*oth Isabel and Chief were devastated by Ann's death. Their grief was so profound that, at the time, both functioned as if under some kind of protective spell. Kathy, who met them in Toronto to help clear out the house, recalls that she had made a clay sculpture of her mother's head for an art class. When Chief found it, he and Isabel were so upset that they put in a bucket of water and melted it down.[19]

Back in Swarthmore, as one day moved into another, Isabel tended to Ann's personal matters, Chief to the legal. (The estate, not trivial because of the amount of her royalties, was complicated by Ann's residency in Canada.) Neighbors and friends—especially the Gemmills —wanted to offer comfort, but had difficulty penetrating Isabel's stoic facade. Jane later told Kathy Hughes that, at the time, Isabel had commented,"At least Kathy will never have to take care of Ann."[20] Isabel told one close friend the general details about Ann's death, then added, "Now we shall say no more about it."[21] She kept Ann's purse beside her large chair in the living room until her own last weeks. For fear that Ann's ashes would be discovered, she asked Jane Gemmill to keep them until later when the grandchildren were grown and away.[22]

Sometime after Jim was settled back in Swarthmore, he was out walking one night, saw the light on at 321 Dickinson Avenue, and stopped. Chief had gone to bed, and Isabel was in the living room, alone, playing solitaire. When he asked her why she was up so late, she said she couldn't sleep—and burst into uncontrolled weeping. Jim took her in his arms and held her. Finally, between sobs, she told him, "The light has gone out of my life."[23]

Katharine Briggs' words, written to Isabel seventy years earlier in "The Education of Suzanne," came back to haunt rather than comfort her: "If a great sorrow comes to you, my little girl, and I should not be there to help you bear it, remember this, the message from my grief to yours. Bereavement and sorrow are as much a part of life as birth and joy."

Later, Isabel wrote a coda to her mother's message that she called "A Credo for Living." It indicates that in her later years, she turned to a more orthodox religious belief. "In times of stress or hard decisions," she wrote, "most of us erring mortals need something to tie to, something greater than ourselves that will furnish more support and certainty than we can extract from our own everyday processes of conscious reasoning. Some of us find it, some of us don't." But, she added, "we must *seek* the help we need." She supported her thesis with scripture. She continued: "The old idea that God and the Devil are contending for our souls can be comforting in times of confusion because it gives us the chance to take sides in the fight even before we are out of the fog." Embodied in her next comment, taken from John Bunyan's *Pilgrim's Progress,* was the spirit of the Isabel of old: "Rejoice not against me, O mine Enemy! When I fall, I shall arise."[24]

Not long after Ann's death, Isabel confronted her own enemy and one that she would fight for the rest of her life: cancer. It had first struck sixteen years before and required removal of a malignant growth and lymph glands from her right arm. Surgery took place on May 12 and 18, 1956, after she had set the date with ETS to give her symposium on May 22. Much to the distress of her family, Isabel did not postpone the date with ETS, but appeared with her right arm in a sling.[25] Then, in 1970, the enemy recurred, when another "small lump" appeared on her upper right arm; in 1972, still another appeared above her right elbow. In a letter to Betty, Isabel asked her to "put up a little petition.... More things are wrought by prayer—which I do believe."[26]

*I*n the midst of these troubles and sadnesses, two people became an important and lasting part of Isabel's life: her beloved daughter-in-law, Betty Myers, and a young woman with a doctorate in clinical psychology (from Temple University), Mary McCaulley. Both women helped to fill the unfillable void left by Ann's death.

When Ann died, Betty wrote to Isabel and Chief that "I really can't imagine better parents than you —and I feel almost choked with grief and anger that this should have happened to you.... I keep wondering about you—worrying about you—wishing to be with you now. I love you both so much."[27]

While Peter and Betty's divorce action proceeded slowly, Chief and Isabel were concerned about Betty. Isabel was interested in helping her find her own niche in life, and Chief, in helping her find adequate security. Chief reviewed the divorce settlement and advised Betty like a father (both of her parents had died earlier); at the same time, he was careful to be unquestionably fair to Peter.[28] Isabel encouraged Betty to pursue her dream of studying law, a dream about which she said "if it be not practical, *make it so.*" When Betty acknowledged that Swarthmore felt more like home than anywhere else, Isabel lost no time in finding a small house near Dickinson Avenue for Betty and Jenny to rent. They came in June 1973. (That spring, shortly before his eighteenth birthday, Jonathan had entered the University of California at Santa Barbara). "You did say," Isabel wrote Betty, "that you would like to have been our daughter. *This we can have anyway*, whether you finally decide to be a lawyer or not."[29] Betty did both. Isabel helped her to complete a successful application for entry in the Villanova law school in Philadelphia. After getting a law degree, Betty added training in library science that led to her being a law librarian.[30] Continuing to live in Swarthmore, she became the daughter that Isabel and Chief needed in their old age.

During her public school years in Swarthmore, Jennifer Myers was often at 321 Dickinson Avenue. She was much closer to Chief, who shared activities with her; although she admired Isabel, it was "at a distance." Her grandmother was "almost totally engrossed in the Indicator." Later, Jennifer would find the Indicator enormously helpful in understanding herself, an extrovert and sensing type in the midst of "this family of intuitive introverts."[31]

———

*M*ary McCaulley, on the faculty at the University of Florida in the Department of Clinical Psychology, was involved in clinical and research supervision, assessment, and the psychology of women. One day, when she was looking through the *Mental Measurements Yearbook,* she stumbled on a test based on Jungian concepts called the *Myers-Briggs Type Indicator.* McCaulley ordered a copy from ETS "for research purposes," gave it to a few friends, and thought it made some sense. She then began to use it with clients, who reacted to their type descriptions in the manual with "it's O.K. to be my kind of person" and "that's just how I feel." McCaulley then decided the Indicator "really had something to it." She continued to use it for about a year. Then, when she searched in vain for a publication on type referred to in the ETS manual, McCaulley wrote Isabel Myers to ask about it. She also told her about using the Indicator with students at the university. Moved into action when more data were at stake, Isabel answered forthwith, wanting copies of McCaulley's data and confessing that the reference in question was "not printed."[32]

After this exchange of letters, the two women met in Philadelphia in October 1969 when the University of Florida sent McCaulley to a meeting at the Center for Studies of Sex Education in Medicine at the University of Pennsylvania. Thus, a conversation began that, effectively, lasted for ten years. Both women, Phi Beta Kappas, were INFPs, a pattern that Isabel said was characteristic of "everyone who has fallen in love with the Indicator without anyone else telling them about it."[33]

Just after Isabel had had one of the malignant nodules removed from her arm, she received a letter from Mary McCaulley suggesting that the two of them work together on MBTI research. Finding a compatible investigator who had proper academic credentials and who was unquestionably hooked on the Indicator now gave added impetus to Isabel's will to live. In 1972, when she again had surgery on her right arm, she and Mary McCaulley were close to realizing their dream of establishing a center for research on the MBTI. She later told McCaulley that every major step forward with the Indicator had come at a time when there was a recurrence of cancer.[34]

Coincidental or not, these breakthroughs in Isabel's professional life helped her to face the fact of her incurable disease. In the time that was left to her, she was determined to refine the Indicator as much as possible and to complete the book that Henry Chauncey had wanted fifteen years earlier. She would finally have to rely on outside help in both instances.

CHAPTER NINETEEN

A New
Alliance

By the time Mary McCaulley and Isabel Myers began their professional association, Isabel had become increasingly dissatisfied with the situation at Educational Testing Service. McCaulley's professional enthusiasm about the Indicator reinforced Isabel's own convictions that it was proving to be more and more valid, valuable, and applicable as the results came in from her continuing studies.

Although by 1971 Isabel felt that the contract with ETS should be terminated, she reasoned that at least ETS was making the MBTI available to interested persons and that she, in turn, was relieved of the burden of having to package and mail materials. She confided to Mary McCaulley that ETS hardly knew they had the Indicator, a situation that was a grave concern to both women.[1]

Both Isabel and McCaulley had conferences with ETS management with no positive results.[2] Indeed, a newly named vice president for testing programs, Winton Manning, probably expressed the consensus of the organization when he stated that, in the 1970s, compared to other large and complex activities under his review, the MBTI was "a very small fly on the wall."[3] Even so, Manning offered help from ETS in future research on the MBTI in the form of "critiques, advice, and counsel on the study designs and analyses, and critiques of the reports on finished work."[4]

To Isabel, this was not a satisfactory resolution, nor was the subsequent transfer of the Office of Special Tests (under which the MBTI was housed) to the Atlanta office of ETS, where even less support from Princeton was forthcoming. Agreement to terminate the contract with ETS was finally signed in April 1975, to be effective in December, despite efforts of some of the staff in Atlanta to "save" the Indicator.[5]

When ETS had approached Isabel in 1956 about the possibility of publishing the MBTI, she was indeed enthusiastic. When Chauncey had arranged the consultant relationship, she was appreciative because this legitimized her efforts as professional. Peter Myers remembers that she regarded the unfavorable response of some of the research staff as a serious problem, but she was convinced that these young men were attacking her, and not the Indicator, even though she was puzzled as to why they were doing this. Just as she had regarded the objections of some of the medical school personnel to be based on fallacies or misunderstandings of what the Indicator was all about, she was sure this, too, explained most of the objections at ETS. She was sure of her position, of the rightness of her cause, and that God was on her side because she was right![6]

Thirty years after the fact, Henry Chauncey, although not au courant as to the status of the MBTI, still believed that his first hunch about it was sound. He was fully aware that a compromise was unlikely between the pro-MBTI people and the research staff; he also felt that ETS had given Myers significant support, but "her continuing desire for even more assistance became intolerable."[7]

When David Saunders had left ETS in January 1961, he was not unaware of the storm of controversy that was beginning to develop. He recalled that Myers' presentation to the research group in the spring of 1956 was iconoclastic. Although in developing the Indicator, she did, some things that would shock a conventional statistician, she had good reasons for what she did, "things that the conventional statisticians had never thought of."[8] According to Saunders, Isabel Myers "broke the rules," and the presumption followed among the research staff that this was done out of ignorance because she lacked recognized professional credentials. In his opinion, her lack of credentials merely deprived her of suitable language to describe what she had done. Her own language and terminology were clear to her, but often meant something else to people with whom she needed to communicate. Years later, after doing some statistical research on the Indicator (and developing Form J), Saunders observed to colleagues that Isabel Myers had "an intuitive grasp of statistics that psychology hasn't caught up with yet."[9]

John Ross, currently at the University of Western Australia and whose association with the MBTI ended when he left ETS in 1961, stated recently that before he met Isabel Myers, he thought it "distinctly unlikely that an amateur, even one with so distinguished a father...could have developed an instrument of any value.... The woman I met was middle-aged, plain and plainly dressed, obviously intelligent, and sane (I had expected she might be otherwise). She was confident of her work and quite prepared to have it examined critically and skeptically. I remember that she was stubborn."[10]

Other than Chauncey, Saunders, Ross, and Stricker, the psychologist who worked longest and most closely with Isabel Myers during the ETS period was Junius A. Davis. When interviewed in 1987, he obviously still felt the intensity of her devotion to her cause, recalling that she had such utter faith in it and was so profoundly convinced of its integrity that to her it was "almost god-like in its power."[11]

Apparently unaware of any of Davis' critical reaction to her efforts to get information and to move things along, she was always positive in her attitude toward him. She damned the ETS system of management with faint praise for its failure to push the Indicator, but she commended various individuals in the system. The association with ETS had allowed her to gather data and apply sophisticated procedures to the analyses and to complete and see a manual published. Furthermore, under its auspices, the first bibliography of MBTI research was compiled, and Form F, which would be the standard for approximately two decades, was developed.[12] A person of less brilliance, self-assurance, and commitment than Isabel Myers might have been defeated by the opposition and waning support from a prestigious organization like ETS.

If it ever occurred to her that antifeminism could possibly have complicated the situation at ETS, as it had done in the beginning of the medical school research, she did not leave evidence of this awareness Although antifeminism generally pervaded the workplace in the years when the MBTI was developed and launched, ETS had actually been a leader in hiring women with doctorates, though largely in administrative positions.[13] Even so, all of the professional women on the ETS staff concurrent with Isabel Myers and J. Davis later readily acknowledged the presence of sexism in the 1960s; Davis recalled that some of the men on the staff referred to Isabel Myers as "that horrible woman,"while others called her "the little old lady in tennis shoes."[14]

Yet she was not to be discouraged nor deterred. Fortunately, as the years with ETS moved to a close, other contacts became highly significant in the life of the Indicator. One of these was Mary McCaulley; the other, to begin in the fall of 1975, was Consulting Psychologists Press in Palo Alto, California.

*W*hen Isabel and McCaulley agreed to work together on the Indicator, one of the first things that McCaulley accomplished was to put all of Isabel's hand-worked data on the computer. This provided a readily accessible data base for research and a convenient method of storing and organizing new data that became available. In due course, McCaulley would provide a program to score the Indicator on the computer. One enormous project that she and Isabel completed was a clear, concise monograph, *The Myers Longitudinal Medical Study,* in publishable form.[15]

In a letter to McCaulley, Isabel said she wanted to supply all the help she could if the clinic at the University of Florida would agree to a consultant arrangement whereby she could "shepherd the...interpretation of the Indicator.... One basic aim, as I see it, is to make the concept of type contribute to mental health by cure or prevention or both."[16]

They discussed the need for funds, both for research and to pay for Isabel's services, and this meant that McCaulley would have to apply for grants. Isabel decided that this was a waste of valuable time. "Forget about my consulting fee," she wrote McCaulley, "and I don't like the idea of a consulting fee anyway. I'd rather work on my own, creating materials that people anywhere can buy and use if and as they want to. If the materials are good, they will reach many more people than I would ever reach by 'consulting,' with the added advantage that they can go on operating without me, in both space and time."[17] Indeed, Isabel and McCaulley had unsuccessfully approached ETS as a possible source of funds for research on the Indicator. In typically succinct fashion, Chief summarized the outcome: "ETS is unenthused. Stuffy bastards!"[18]

Isabel approved of McCaulley's idea to give the MBTI to several hundred freshman (class of 1974) at the University of Florida, which would provide data, she said, from which she could establish needed norms for the "present generation" and add significantly to the data bank.[19]

Since these activities took place before the ETS contract ended, McCaulley was concerned lest a computer scoring service conflict with ETS interests. Surely with tongue-in-cheek, Isabel doubted that "ETS would mind." (In the contract she had retained author's rights to reproduce and use materials on all levels.) Although she told McCaulley at this time (January 1971) that she had decided to terminate the contract in another eighteen months, it was ETS, not Isabel, who had made the first move.

By 1974, interest at the University of Florida had grown until over 150 faculty members and graduate students were engaged in research and action projects that related type differences to "teaching, career choice and satisfaction, marital adjustment, and counseling."[20] In the five years following McCaulley's introduction of the Indicator, twenty-four related doctoral dissertations and eleven Master's theses came out of the university. McCaulley was indefatigable in seeking funds for further research as well as in planning and leading workshops and symposia to promote the Indicator.

This center of activity encouraged Isabel and McCaulley to decide to establish a nonprofit corporation in Gainesville for the study of psychological type, an idea that became a reality in 1974.[21] The goals for the "Typology Laboratory," agreed upon by McCaulley and Isabel, were to "provide...guidance in the application of current knowledge of Jungian types to practical problems, particularly education and manpower, and to conduct...research to improve the usefulness of the Type Indicator for work with individuals."[22] At first associated with the University of Florida, the Laboratory, with the aid of outside research grants (chiefly from the American Medical Students Association), became an independent entity in 1975.[23] Known as the Center for the Applications of Psychological Type (CAPT), its name was chosen by Isabel, who also designed the logo.

Beginning in 1970, Isabel visited Gainesville several times each year for periods of two to three weeks. She participated in training users of the MBTI and in supervising work designed to individualize the Indicator reports. She was a highly effective drawing card as the keynote speaker in 1975 at the first national MBTI conference organized by McCaulley in Gainesville. Her topic: "Making the Most of Individual Gifts."[24] From the time of CAPT's inception until her health prohibited, Isabel was deeply involved in its work and goals. At times when the financial situation was fragile, she provided funding. She gave CAPT the rights to publish and promote *Introduction to Type,* which, with Ann's help, she had completed in 1970. In addition to providing royalties to Isabel, this widely used pamphlet was instrumental in helping to maintain CAPT's solvency until the organization became self-sustaining in 1979.[25]

The idea to establish the Typology Laboratory was sound, but the struggle to make it work took its toll on both McCaulley and Isabel Myers. With similar personalities that were more oriented toward research than toward the extraverted task of raising money, both women exploited valuable time and energy that might have been more happily spent on the Indicator.[26] Isabel still answered inquiries about the MBTI that ETS forwarded to her (except for requests for material), and this amounted to a staggering amount of correspondence from all over the United States.[27] Much of the time, McCaulley served in the multiple roles of teacher, lecturer, fund raiser, manager, and researcher. Isabel noted that McCaulley is "not an administrator…[and] does not even want to be. She wants to do research and writing [and] she is worn out by the load she has been carrying." Understandably concerned about McCaulley, Isabel wanted her to "get some rest each day."[28]

Mary McCaulley came into Isabel's professional life at a crucial time, but the importance of her personal support and care for Isabel during the bleak years after Ann's death cannot be overestimated. Chief thought highly of Mary McCaulley as well. He told Isabel: "I like her. She's direct and open. She laughs easily. She makes me think of Ann."[29] McCaulley also provided a kind of nurturing that was apparently difficult, if not impossible, for Chief to give. "As for me," he wrote to a cousin of Isabel's, "I've had enough to do trying to be a lawyer to really get interested in type." His part, he said, was "driving her anywhere she wanted to go." However, he recognized how important the Indicator was to Isabel, and whatever mattered to her, mattered to him. He was ready to provide any legal advice that Isabel needed, but he did not have the kind of resources to solve problems such as how to continue the life of the Indicator after the contract with ETS terminated. (His thought, that the University of Florida "take over" the MBTI, was not feasible for any of the parties concerned.[30]) Chief knew that in helping Isabel to find a suitable home for the Indicator, McCaulley could be more effective. As a thinking type, he approached problems with unfailing logic, and when those means were exhausted, he saw little purpose in continuing the fight on hunches.

When faced with the task of finding a suitable home for the Indicator, both McCaulley and Isabel believed in one of Isabel's favorite quotes from Samuel Johnson: "Nothing will ever be attempted if all possible objections must first be overcome."[31] When McCaulley looked at the growth in use of the Indicator since its introduction in Florida, she wrote Miriam Bryan, head of the Office of Special Tests in Atlanta, that she was "almost afraid to think what would happen if ETS promoted the Indicator 'through normal professional channels' as they promised in Isabel's contract."[32]

With the help of John Dobbin, who had retired from ETS, and Miriam Bryan, who wanted to postpone her retirement until the MBTI was in "friendly hands," McCaulley approached the Psychological Corporation in New York City, a large and well-known publisher of psychological tests. She sent materials about the MBTI to its president, Roger T. Lennon, with whom she and Miriam Bryan were finally able to meet when they were in New York in late October 1974 for an ETS Invitational Conference. Following McCaulley's chat with Lennon, Isabel herself talked with him and was promised a decision in due course.[33] By the time eight months had passed with no response from Lennon, McCaulley had found another publisher, Consulting Psychologists Press, in Palo Alto, California.[34]

CHAPTER TWENTY

A New
Publisher

On July 10, 1975, Mary McCaulley telephoned Consulting Psychologists Press (CPP) in Palo Alto, California. She did not know any of the staff at CPP, but she was aware that the company was a small and highly reputable publisher of psychological tests. In her search for a home for the *Myers-Briggs Type Indicator,* McCaulley's contacts with two larger and more prestigious organizations, ETS and Psych Corp, had been disappointing.

On the day the call was made to CPP, Isabel Myers was in Florida with McCaulley discussing the future of CAPT. Inevitably, the subject came up of the MBTI's future. The deadline approached for the ETS contract to end, and there had been no response from Psych Corp. It suddenly occurred to McCaulley that one option would be to approach "this small company" in California. She left the meeting, went to a public telephone booth, and placed the call.

McCaulley first spoke with Janice Strom, administrative assistant to Dr. John (Jack) D. Black, president of CPP. Strom listened to what McCaulley had to say, then promised to get back to her after talking with Black. Feeling that Strom was pleasantly neutral, McCaulley was surprised when, on the same day, Jack Black himself called back, with obvious enthusiasm about the Indicator, and asked that materials be sent for him to examine. McCaulley and Myers reacted with mutual elation and relief at what seemed to them a "virtual yes."[1]

On July 25, Black wrote to "Dr." Isabel Briggs Myers:

The materials sent me by Dr. McCaulley finally reached me and I want to study them in more detail than I have been able to do so far, but in any event, I want to assure you that we would be honored to add the *Myers-Briggs* to our repertory of assessment devices. We like to think that we have the most distinguished list of personality tests of any publisher and we try to confine new publications to those which will enhance our offerings. I certainly feel that this is true of the Type Indicator.

I will be sending you for your perusal our standard contract and I hope it will meet with your approval. Although our standard royalty is ten per cent, I would like to increase this to twelve per cent in recognition of the fact that yours is not a brand new venture but a test which already has a considerable following.... I am assuming that you would agree that a revision of the content of the manual is called for and that you would be willing to prepare or collaborate on a revision.[2]

When she returned home from Florida on July 28, Isabel found Black's letter waiting. She answered immediately: "I am gratified by the promptness of your decision to adopt the Type Indicator, and touched (being a feeling type) by the appreciation implicit in your generosity as to the royalty. Whatever I can do to help with the transition, I shall be blithe to do so.... As to revision of the Manual, obviously something new is now called for, and I would far rather do it myself than leave it to anyone else." She suggested that he solicit ideas about the content for the new manual from McCaulley.[3]

Isabel was concerned about the misuse of test results and informed Black that she did not want the Indicator exported beyond the Iron Curtain for fear that it might be used to "finger dissenters," who were "almost certain to be intuitives." An unfortunate experience was still fresh in her mind when a bank, after giving the MBTI to its employees, fired all of the intutitives "because they were trouble makers."[4]

After incorporating several provisions from the ETS contract that she valued, Isabel Briggs Myers, on September 5, 1975, signed an agreement with John D. Black for CPP. It was a landmark decision for both parties.[5]

As early as the late 1940s, Jack Black had heard favorably about the MBTI when he was a graduate student at the University of Minnesota.

After completing his doctorate, he went to Stanford as director of Counseling and Testing Services. A colleague of Black's, Harrison Gough, also a graduate student at Minnesota, had developed the *California Psychological Inventory* (CPI) and was a research psychologist on the IPAR staff at the University of California at Berkeley.[6] Meanwhile, in addition to his academic duties, Black had set up a center in Palo Alto for private clinical practice called Consulting Psychologists Associated.

In the summer of 1955, after talking informally with Gough about the need for a publisher for the CPI, Black decided the time had come to expand the operations of Consulting Psychologists Associated to include the publication of psychological tests. The *California Psychological Inventory* would be their first publishing venture, and Consulting Psychologists Press would be the name of their new operation.[7]

Incorporated in 1956, CPP was initially financed, according to Black, by friends, relatives, and personal funds. Black and Gough designed the test booklet, answer sheets, and scoring stencils for the CPI, while graphic artists and marketing personnel were hired as independent contractors.[8]

Just as the *Myers-Briggs Type Indicator* began as a family affair, so did CPP. Black's father, Alexander G. Black, a retired metallurgist, became CPP's Jack-of-all-trades. The warehouse was located in a room in back of his house in Palo Alto.[9]

By mid–1956, CPP opened its first office in Palo Alto at 270 Town and Country Village. At the end of 1956, the balance sheet showed fifteen hundred dollars in the red—the only year that CPP would ever show a loss.

At that time, Stanford University Press published a half-dozen or so psychological tests, including the widely used *Strong Vocational Interest Blank,* but Stanford did not have a staff with expertise in psychological testing. Black persuaded them that it would be mutually advantageous for CPP to market their tests; by mid–1957, a contract was signed that gave CPP editorial control of their tests and distribution rights.[10]

The following year, CPP issued its first catalog for "Psychological Tests and Services," an understated, twenty-one-page 8 1/2-by-5 1/2 inch pamphlet with a qualifications form to be filled out by users and a purchase order blank inserted inside the back cover. The number of tests offered had grown to eighteen. In an introduction to individual descriptions of the tests, CPP stated the following:

Consulting Psychologists Press is now one of the four largest
exclusive publishers of tests in the United States.... It is the
policy of Consulting Psychologists Press to devote its full
resources to the publication of worthwhile testing devices.
Because tests require specialized skills and techniques not only
in their development but in their production, handling, and
distribution, the best interests of all concerned are served by a
publisher concentrating exclusively on them. The professional
staff of Consulting Psychologists Press is employed to assist
members of the profession at large in bringing their tests to
fruition.[11]

In 1962, CPP opened new offices at 577 College Avenue and
added, among other tests, the *Frostig Developmental Test of Visual Perception,* to assess the perceptual skills of young children. This became a
leading seller.

Issued approximately every two years, the catalogs showed a
steady expansion of materials available, until, in the tenth anniversary
year, CPP offered thirty-four "measures, inventories, rating devices,
and tests," and Science and Behavior Books, as well as the *Mental
Measurements Yearbooks.* The introduction to the 1965–66 catalog stated
the following:

Sales this year will approach a quarter of a million dollars and
this catalog records the volume of items now published.

Mere quantity has never been a primary goal of the Company,
however, for it has concentrated on publication of specialized
testing instruments for use by psychologists concerned with the
assessment and prediction on many facets of human behavior.
While some of the tests listed in this catalog are widely used by
schools and colleges, business and industry, or clinics and
hospitals, many of the devices are designed for the unique
problems of behavorial scientists working in laboratories and
assessment centers.

Progress in the field of psychology—both theoretical and
applied—depends heavily upon the development of new and
improved techniques for measuring human characteristics, for
understanding and predicting behavior. The tests described in
this catalog and others to be published soon offer the profession promising methods for attacking many of the unsolved
problems of human behavior.

The twentieth anniversary catalog in 1976 listed for the first time the *Myers-Briggs Type Indicator,* and with this addition, catalogs began to be issued annually. The Indicator would gradually become a leading seller. The increased volume of business required many more full-time people on the staff.[12] The physical plant was gradually expanded at 577 College Avenue, and the warehousing, which had long outgrown one room, moved several times to more spacious quarters. The same year that CPP signed the contract with Isabel Myers, they purchased a large warehouse in Redwood City.[13]

Jack Black now had had twenty years of experience in publishing tests, and he confidently set about to redesign answer sheets and test booklets for the MBTI. His aim was to make them "more attractive and easier to read" for those both administering and taking the Indicator.[14] He was not a little startled on learning that every minute detail about typeface, indentations, spacing, and so forth, was a grave concern of Isabel Myers. In fact, settling these matters promised to take more of Black's time and tact than negotiating the contract.

Exasperated but undaunted, Black finally wrote Isabel:

> I would like to suggest that in an enterprise of this kind, it seems to me that the parties involved have to respect one another's competencies. Your unique and irreplaceable contribution lies in your intutitive ability to devise items with high potential for defining types, in your persuavive skills in obtaining normative and validational samples, and in your managing the data and writing the manual, etc.... Conversely, I think we [at CPP] know more about design, format, type selection, layout, paper and ink selection than you do.... Furthermore, you have to remind yourself that I have as much interest as you in broadening the market for the MBTI and I do not intend to produce materials that jeopardize that goal.

Black softened his caveats in a closing paragraph: "Finally, Isabel, please do not upset yourself or waste too much of your valuable time and energy on minute production matters." He added that if she objected strongly to something, CPP would try to accommodate her wishes or to explain why they could not.[15]

At first he was concerned about Isabel's apparent "fragility," but he found out soon enough that she was "anything but fragile." Although he was often frustrated by her persistence and pervasiveness, her "staggering" accomplishments enabled him to keep a sense of perspective.[16] After he met Peter Myers and her at the MBTI conference in Gainesville, he spoke of her "charming and remarkable family" and said how delighted he was that "our publishing the Type Indicator is turning out to be so much more than just a business matter."[17]

Isabel acquiesced to many of Black's suggestions and he later complimented her on her ability to accept suggestions from a "Johnny-come-lately," inasmuch as she had spent a lifetime bringing the Indicator to its "present level of effectiveness," and he knew that it must be "very hard to tolerate the meddling of an 'outsider.'"[18] Sales figures began to show tangible proof that CPP's decision to publish the MBTI was sound. In 1976, sales figures averaged about $3000 per month. In the next year, they increased by $4500, establishing a sales curve that continued steadily upward.[19]

The collegiality established early in the working relationship of Jack Black and Isabel Myers was highly important. Where ETS had not prevailed with either Isabel Myers or the Indicator, Jack Black had succeeded. Black's task of marketing the MBTI was made easier because of the already widespread knowledge and use of the instrument. Black's decision whether to publish the MBTI, unlike Henry Chauncey's, was not influenced by the opinions of a group of psychometricians with impeccable credentials who objected to the unorthodox statistical logic behind the structure of the MBTI. Black was free to follow his own hunches and to rely on his own judgment, which eventually paid off handsomely.[20]

Black's hunches also paid off for Isabel. She lived to see the Indicator, her life's work, at last in the hands of a publisher who valued its potential almost as much as she thought it deserved.

CHAPTER TWENTY-ONE

Last Years
With Chief

*I*n addition to having found a good home for the Indicator, Isabel was heartened by Peter's remarriage to a woman who had grown up in Swarthmore. "The big news is that Peter is about to marry again, and to a wonderful former sweetheart he has always loved," Chief wrote to English friends, Agatha and Maurice Pocock. "A classmate at Swarthmore High School...she is Katharine Downing Heisler, ex-wife of Charles Heisler...of Mobile, Alabama...[and mother of four children]. We, of course, have known Kathy for years, and she claims to have always loved Pete's family."[1]

This was the Kathy Downing who had grown up in Swarthmore and had graduated from high school in the same class with Peter and Ann. Kathy had continued her education as a scholarship student at Vassar, at that time strictly a woman's college. She and her classmates were nevertheless swept up in the uncertainties of World War II. Majoring in economics, she finished in three years, an option offered by the college so that students could help in the war effort. Kathy then applied for admission to the Wharton School for graduate work, but was told by the dean, "We don't admit women. All they do is get married." She then enrolled in the graduate school of arts and sciences at the University of Pennsylvania where she took most of the courses she could have had at Wharton.[2] Instead of writing her Master's thesis, Kathy opted to go to work immediately at Edward N. Hay Associates in Philadelphia. In due course, she met and married Charles Heisler. They settled in Pennsylvania and for twelve years lived in Swarthmore.[3]

When Kathy, only child of Katharine (Mrs. Hugh) Jaeger Downing, lost her mother in 1958, Isabel went to her and said, "No matter how old you are, you still need a mother, and I'll always be available."[4]

With Kathy now an official member of the family, Isabel wrote her: "Welcome home and bless you for making Peter happy. Ever since Peter told me of his hopes, I have been putting it in my prayers that things should come out in the best of all possible ways for the two of you."[5] Kathy responded: "In my heart you have always been my family and I do indeed feel that I am at last coming home. And, that you should both be able to overcome your uncomfortable feelings about divorce to welcome me with love and acceptance makes it even more important." She was touched by their "generous wedding gift to us and of your thoughtfulness in sending half directly to me—it gives me a most welcome safety margin for this interim period."[6]

A year after Peter and Kathy's marriage, they, along with Kathy's youngest daughter, Michele, then thirteen, returned to the Washington area, where Peter had been reassigned by Magnavox. This made Isabel and Chief very happy. Settling in suburban Maryland, Peter and Kathy were closely associated with his parents during their last years.

Tutored by Isabel, Kathy became involved in Isabel's main focus in life—the Indicator. Now working in public school education, Kathy found that the MBTI could have some interesting applications. She later commented that when Isabel conversed, the only subject was the Indicator. If you talked with her, you talked Indicator.[7]

Chief continued to take care of family correspondence and family matters, remembering the grandchildren at special times. He and Isabel widened their hearts and added the four Heisler children to the list of young people, all of whom received identical, generous checks at Christmas. However, their first grandchild, Peter's son, Jonathan, now in a rebellious mood, was a cause of concern. Always motivated to work hard and to achieve success and financial security, Chief could not understand Jon's dropping out of college in favor of a self-sufficient lifestyle.

Using his usual well-reasoned approach, Chief wrote to Jon:

> Your letter about becoming a carpenter led Isabel to recall
> the adage about "three generations from shirt sleeves to shirt
> sleeves." Before Granddad Briggs, his family was shirtsleeves
> (mostly farmers). Then came Granddad, Isabel, Peter, who
> primarily work with their heads rather than their hands;
> come you, and back to shirtsleeves (T-shirts) as a seriously
> considered mode of living, with minimum use of the head.

I'm not derogating skill with the hands, keen sight, steady nerves and good coordination, but why not both head and hands?... Perhaps you *should,* for the coming academic year, continue to plop around in bare feet and T-shirts until you get the claustrophobia out of your system, but it would be tragic, indeed, if you deliberately downgrade that fine mind you have...[and] acquire an understanding of the universe via television and the daily and Sunday papers.[8]

Although Jon respected and loved both Lyman Briggs and Chief, he was unmoved by Chief's arguments. Chief continued to write affectionate but firm letters to his grandson (and Isabel always sent her love). Jon finally spelled out *his* views in a letter written on his grandfather's eightieth birthday, in which he explained that money in itself had little value to him, and he did not want to be a part of the nine-to-five tread mill that trapped most people striving for economic gain. He preferred simple living over conspicuous consumption and waste. With rare insight for a teenager, Jon told Chief that he might share Jon's views had he been born in 1955, and had Jon been born before 1900, he might be more positive about education and a professional career.[9]

The dialectic continued until Chief apparently gave up. Neither changed his point of view.[10] What Isabel may have thought is not recorded, but if Jon's lifestyle disturbed her, she could ignore it by immersion in the Indicator.

Yet Isabel's almost total immersion was, at times, hard for Chief to tolerate. In his letters to family and friends during the 1970s, when Isabel was spending large blocks of time in Florida or at conferences and meetings with McCaulley, Chief regularly commented that she was "off MBTIing." He was coping with almost constant pain caused by osteoarthritis and trying to effect his own therapy. "Isabel is so wrapped up in her Type Indicator work that I don't think she would feel any pain if it were present," he wrote to the Pococks; "some of her Jungian disciples down in Gainesville, Florida, have set up a Typology Lab, employing computers, and just at present it's hard even to get her out to a movie."[11]

While Isabel spent most of her time on the Indicator and with professional colleagues, Chief held a small, private law practice and his job as solicitor for the Swarthmore Borough Council. (He retired as solicitor in January 1978, before his eighty-fourth birthday in May, after fifty-three years of service.)[12] As Chief's hearing became more and more impaired, Isabel read to him at night; hers was the one voice that was still easily audible. He coveted more of her company, but from her point of view, while she worked, "just knowing he is there" was enough.[13] As age began to take its toll on them, they felt fortunate to be together. They had watched the slow deterioration of Paul Gemmill, first in the house at 317 Dickinson and, then, until his death in 1974, in a local nursing home.[14]

There is no doubt that watching Paul's decline motivated Chief to coax Isabel to leave her work for trips abroad while they were still mobile. He disregarded his own pain, even when the osteoarthritis "complained of too much driving," and he coped by walking "bent over at right angles, with frequent stops." His tendency to watch out for Isabel was justified when, in 1971, outside of Paris, she left her handbag, containing money, papers, and passport in a taxi; this caused several hasty trips to the American embassy for an emergency passport. The bag, which was turned in to the embassy by an "honest taxi driver," arrived in Swarthmore several months later.[15]

In the spring of 1975, Chief thought it was time for another get-away abroad—to France, the Netherlands, and England. He told Isabel that he was going to Europe one more time and asked if she were coming. She went.[16] Gone for six weeks, they crossed on the "Queen II" in deference to Isabel's refusal to fly. (She always went by train when she traveled in the States.) Chief arranged for Britrail passes for their travel on land. He was eighty-one, Isabel, nearly seventy-eight.[17]

---

*W*hen Jim Hughes and his children moved to Swarthmore in the fall of 1972, Douglas, then fourteen, lived with his grandparents for the first three months so that he could start to school on time. After he and his father (Kathy was at the University of Wisconsin) were in their own home, Doug saw Chief and Isabel frequently. This association came at a time in Doug's life when the impressions were well-etched in his memory.

His first memory of Isabel was seeing her bent over papers and data and, later, either working on the Indicator or playing cards. She rarely watched television and seemed to have very little "kitchen instinct." Although Isabel tended to be more talkative than Chief, there was rarely banter or joking. Doug also recalled that during those years in Swarthmore after Ann's death, Isabel and Chief rarely mentioned her name.

As a somewhat romantic teenager, Doug could not understand the obviously mutual appreciation that Chief and Isabel had for each other. Often the two would eat a "silent" breakfast because "nothing new had happened since each had gone to bed." They had separate bedrooms that enabled each to respect the other's rather different working and sleeping habits, an arrangement that young Douglas found even harder to understand. Once, during a meal, he listened to a rare discussion of politics about George McGovern and Richard Nixon, who were running for president of the United States. Isabel said some uncomplimentary things about McGovern, to which Chief listened silently, then announced, "Well I'm going to cancel your vote tomorrow!" The impact on Isabel was very obvious indeed. Chief was unmoved.

Chief related to the grandchildren much better than Isabel, and he liked to instigate fun. Douglas described his grandfather as one who was tireless about entertaining children. Chief built "creative toys" that became more and more complex as the grandchildren got older. Douglas remembers an excavated space under the house at Dickinson Avenue known as the bomb shelter, which was supplied with enough food and water to last for two months. Built by Chief in the late fifties, it was to provide fireproof storage for Isabel's papers, but his pragamatic bent led him to prepare the space to use "just in case."[18]

Although Kathy Hughes was away at college when her father moved back to Swarthmore, she was often at home for vacations and academic recesses. During one of these times, she was working in the basement at 321 on a term paper that called for explanations of "three different theories for the existence of God." Isabel came downstairs at one point to see how it was going, and not surprisingly, began to discuss with Kathy the theory that "there must be a God because the environment is so perfectly suited for man." When Isabel said she was certain there must be a God, Kathy asked what made her so sure. After a thoughtful silence Isabel replied, "The humor in a rabbit."[19]

"She was not a traditional grandmother," Kathy recalls. "She alternated between sternness and levity. She once said her nickname had been 'Joy' when she was young and she laughed a lot. But she could also be very stern. She seemed to be in her chair working every morning by eight at the latest and she was frequently there when we went to sleep at night. I mostly remember her in that chair." Kathy, like Doug, recalls that cooking was not one of their grandmother's notable talents. Isabel often served frozen dinners, but she did make "excellent scrambled eggs!"[20]

If Chief were lonely in his last years, he rarely revealed his feelings to anyone. At one point, Peter found an opportunity to praise his father when Chief had given young Katie Heisler a car that he and Isabel were not using. Peter wrote:

> Thank you, Dad, so very much for making Katie so happy.... It is so typical of you to see a need and just quietly provide it. And you have provided so much for me and my family(s) over the years.... You have always been quietly there, backing my aspirations and endeavors...[and] I appreciate more than I will ever be able to tell you —though I have tried on occasion. As long as I can remember I have always appreciated you, as well as loved you and respected you.[21]

Chief had been prescient about their having "one more time" in Europe. In July 1977, for the fourth time, Isabel had a recurrence of cancer. Her trusted surgeon, Dr. Jonathan Rhoads, suspected that she might have an abdominal aneurysm and proceeded to operate. What he found instead was cancer of the liver. After consultations, the decision was made not to use radiotherapy or chemotherapy.[22]

Her family and friends rallied around, all equally distressed. One colleague wrote her that he had "just assumed" her "indestructibility."[23] Jack Black, at Consulting Psychologists Press, and Hellen Guttenger, a friend at the University of Florida, both sent her an article by Norman Cousins from the May 28 *Saturday Review* on coping with illness. She tried very hard to apply the Cousins precepts.[24] She was enormously pleased when a young colleague and user of the MBTI, Tom Carskaden, on the faculty at Mississippi State University, sent her, by special delivery, the first copy of a journal to be devoted to research on psychological type.[25]

Mary McCaulley, in the Washington area for an MBTI workshop in which Isabel had been scheduled to participate, visited her in the hospital. McCaulley found her in a tangle of tubes, with an open brief case by her bed, working diligently. She had requested no flowers — they would obviously clutter the limited space needed for more important things. The nurses and doctors were appalled.[26]

A deadline of August 1 hung over Isabel to finish the supplementary manual for the new Form G of the MBTI, which she had prepared to replace the old Form F, developed at ETS in 1958. With Peter's help while she was in the hospital and during her first weekend at home, she met the deadline. Peter took the materials to the airport to expedite their arrival in California.[27]

Before McCaulley returned to Florida, she went to Swarthmore to see Isabel, now at home. McCaulley found her "pale and fragile" but with a "quick step." She told McCaulley that everyone had a "sword of Damocles" hanging over them —they were just not so aware of it. She and Chief had agreed that there was no point in "being miserable over things you can't help." There would now be no more travel, because it "takes away from work…[and] from Chief for no good purpose." That evening, Chief, who had met McCaulley at the Swarthmore train station, took her out to dinner. Isabel was too frail to join them. In the conversation over dinner, the only time that McCaulley had ever had alone with Chief, he talked about the past. It was as if he needed to review his life with Isabel, which he sensed was almost over. In an open and loving way, he told McCaulley about Isabel's miscarriages many years ago and her bravery in facing those disappointments.[28] It seemed that Chief wanted to reassure himself that Isabel could be just as brave in facing the uncertainty that lay ahead. McCaulley hoped that it would be so.

Back in Gainesville, in a personal letter, McCaulley said to Isabel that she wanted to put in writing "some things very near my heart which I have never said to you, though I am sure you know them without my words."

> I believe firmly that it is absolutely essential for our country that people value differences, easy as this is in the abstract and difficult as it is in particular…. When I discovered your work…it seemed as if I had found something I was looking for all my life—something truly worthwhile for human life and understanding, and something so complex it would never become boring. It was as if I had come home, and I knew that somehow, this was the task for the rest of my life.

> I truly believe that what you have done will be seen in another decade as a major event in moving people toward deeper understanding and compassion. I know that there will be all levels of use of the MBTI, and some of those won't please either of us: But you have set a foundation that will keep bringing people back to an essential respect for differences, and what you have written will inspire young people long after both of us are gone.

> Working with you is a challenge and a constant inspiration. You know I admire you, but even more, I love you very

deeply, and cherish each moment we have together, and each contact, however banal and brief.[29]

Jane Gemmill, Isabel's devoted friend of more than sixty years, began an intensive campaign to persuade Swarthmore College to give Isabel an honorary degree at the June 1979 commencement. Jane wrote letters to Isabel's colleagues, classmates, and friends, to her surgeon, Jonathan Rhoads, and to nationwide members of the League of Women Voters. In September 1978, Jane took a folder full of recommendations to Swarthmore alumnus Kendall Landis, then vice president of Swarthmore College and secretary of the joint faculty/board nominating committee for honorary degrees. In February, Landis wrote Jane that although the committee "did not find its way to nominating Isabel Myers...it is regrettable that a Swarthmorean who has devoted herself so long and successfully to an aspect of psychological testing was not so honored. I can only say that deliberations were most difficult and that many, many other worthy candidates were considered too." Jane was bitterly disappointed.[30]

Isabel's health took another grave turn in June 1978. She was admitted to the University of Pennsylvania hospital for removal of a malignant mass at the back of her left knee. Again, the decision was made not to use radiation or chemotherapy.[31]

Isabel now recognized that in the face of an uncertain future, the problem of priorities had become acute. When she discussed this with Peter, he "put up an overwelming argument in favor of 'the book.'" This was a manuscript that had "lain neglected for years with a big gap in it where the chapters on the practical applications of type belonged." (It was the same book that Henry Chauncey had waited and hoped for twenty years earlier.) Isabel finally agreed with Peter, but with misgivings. Knowing that his mother did not have the luxury of continued procrastination, Peter also realized that he would have to help. He and Kathy spent every weekend for the next two months working with Isabel. He went through all of the old chapters, and Isabel found that he was an "expert both at working out the general structure and at pointing up the details with exactly the right words." The whole book was, Isabel said, "better than I could have made it alone." Somewhat to her dismay, Peter told Jack Black about the book, and Black offered a contract "before the manuscript had been submitted." The book, to be called "Gifts Differing," owed its "resurrection and much of its quality to Peter," Isabel said. For his contributions, she requested that he be made a junior author.[32]

While his mother needed inordinate amounts of time, Peter faced a crisis in his career. Magnavox, the company he had been with for over twelve years, wanted to reassign him to the West Coast, but he preferred to stay in the East for family reasons. In January 1979, Peter accepted a position with the National Academy of Sciences as staff director for the board on radioactive waste management.

Meanwhile, as work continued on *Gifts Differing,* Peter was happy to see that his mother "looked better, ate better, and [her] writing was less jerky & everything seemed to be going well."[33] When the text of *Gifts Differing* was finally finished, Isabel wrote a friend that it was her "pride and joy," although "something less than half the length of the two mystery novels" she had written long ago. *Gifts* was the hardest work she had ever done in her life, and it was her "contribution to the future." There was a great deal more to be done, she said, but "at least this blueprints all the groundwork. There are lots of people in the world who [can] take it from here."[34]

She had been unable to attend the second international conference on type held at Michigan State University. This disappointment receded in the joy of "MBTI Conference III," held in Philadelphia in October 1979, which both she and Chief attended. The celebration, in honor of Isabel's eighty-second birthday, was a bittersweet farewell.

CHAPTER TWENTY-TWO

"What Is
To Be Desired?"

In 1971, Edward S. Golden founded Organizational Renewal Associates (ORA), a management consulting company in Moorestown, New Jersey. A clinical psychologist and an ordained Presbyterian minister, Golden had become an enthusiastic user of the MBTI. In the spring of 1979, at a conference in Gainesville, he, Mary McCaulley, Peter and Kathy Myers, and others, arrived at the idea that the next national meeting of Indicator users should be held in honor of Isabel Myers on her eighty-second birthday. Although the meeting would follow the usual format with presentation of papers and a keynote speaker, the thrust of the conference—to fete her—was to be a secret. Ed Golden consented to be the conference chairman, and his wife, Sally, also on the ORA staff, was the organizer. As a committee began to make plans, another idea evolved: to form an organization of those who used the MBTI and who did research in the field of psychological type. Attached to the registration form for the October meeting in Philadelphia was an option to pay a fee and become a charter member of a professional organization, separate from CAPT, to meet biennially and to be known as the "Association for Psychological Type," or simply, APT. About 150 persons responded favorably, a working treasury resulted, and APT was effectively launched. Kathy Myers was the first president.[1]

By the time of the national meeting in October 1979 at the Philadelphia Stadium Hilton hotel, Isabel Myers was very frail indeed. Dr. Harold Wilkinson, her Swarthmore physician, told Peter that the cancer was on the move and that the time left would depend on "when it hits a vital organ."² When she herself asked Dr. Wilkinson how long he thought she had, he told her he didn't know, and he was glad he didn't. She soon discovered lumps on the right side of her abdomen, began to run a fever, and developed anemia, which required periodic transfusions.³

Isabel had hoped *Gifts Differing* would be ready in time for the meeting so she could inscribe copies, but on learning that it would not be, she designed a self-adhering bookplate that she could sign for prepublication purchasers, who could then attach it to their copy when the book came off the press. She had the plate imprinted: "May you enjoy the full use of all your gifts."

Her own frailty notwithstanding, she participated in the Careers Workshop at the Philadelphia conference—and paid her registration fee as any other attendee. (Sally Golden, the new treasurer of APT, returned it.)⁴ Preconference workshops were held on Wednesday, the 17th, and late that afternoon, a block of time was set aside for videotaped interviews with Isabel. She also spent considerable time signing bookplates for purchasers of prepublication copies of *Gifts Differing*. A room was provided at the Hilton for her to have a place to rest during the day and to eliminate the tiring drive back to Swarthmore at night.

The conference began with registration on Thursday morning, October 18, Isabel's birthday. That evening, the conference banquet took place with Edward Golden as master of ceremonies. If Isabel was suspicious when, at a nearby table, she saw Jane Gemmill, Chief, Kathy Hughes, and, of course, Peter and Kathy Myers, she kept her counsel. Jane Gemmill and Kathy Hughes had never attended MBTI conferences, and this was the first, last, and only time that Chief was present at one. Isabel was seated with Ed Golden and the keynote speaker, David Keirsey. Chairman of the department of Counseling/School Psychology, California State University, Fullerton, Keirsey had recently published a book, *Please Understand Me,* about character and temperament types.

After Keirsey's talk, Ed Golden introduced Jack Black, who, as it were, let the cat out of the bag. His remarks, a mixture of humor and sobriety, surprised Isabel and touched her deeply. Black commented that Isabel did not look her age but "I think the reason we are here is that Isabel doesn't *act* her age. No eighty-year-old is supposed to engage in an active research program, devising a new form of a test, writing a major book, revising a test manual." Black then gave a brief history of "a select list of giants in the field of psychological measurement" and ended this list with the name of Isabel Myers, "a diminutive giant, perhaps, but a giant nonetheless." Black described some characteristics that these "giants" had in common:

> An obvious one is intellectual power—a creative form of intelligence, probably limited to the upper one-half of one per cent of the population. Another attribute I have noticed is what I call a "puzzle-solving mentality." If you say to one of these people, "it won't work or it can't be done," you have waved a red flag.... In the development of these pioneering instruments, these people have solved problems that most psychologists said were insoluble.
>
> Even more important, perhaps, is that all these people have shown a single-mindedness that is extremely rare. They become convinced that they are "on to something" and that that something is extremely important and must take precedence in their lives. Furthermore they are able to maintain that conviction with very little encouragement or external reinforcement. They all went through long periods without much support from colleagues. I might say that such single-mindedness can make a person a little difficult to live with, and perhaps Mr. Myers could comment on that.[5]

Much to everyone's astonishment—particularly Isabel's—when Ed Golden asked if anyone else had anything to say, Chief announced, "I do." The champion orator of sixty-some years ago at Swarthmore College, with permission to speak readily granted from the master of ceremonies, rose from his chair and went to the rostrum. "I am the husband of Isabel Myers," he said, "and they tell me [looking at his name tag] I am an ISTJ." For several minutes, he spoke spontaneously about Isabel and their years at Swarthmore College, and he shared some memories from their early life together. He concluded by saying she had lost none of her charm and youthful enthusiasm, and he still marveled at why she would have married "someone like me." Although they were of totally different types, he said, they fell in love. "Need I tell you," he concluded, "that I am still in love with her?"[6]

Sally Golden ended the program by presenting Isabel with the letters "INFP" handcrafted in gold and suspended on a gold chain.[7] When Ed Golden had asked Isabel about her dream for the future, she said: "I dream that long after I am gone, my work will go on helping people." The Philadelphia conference encouraged her to believe that the dream would not die.[8] Later, at home, "as she settled comfortably into bed," her last words to Chief were, "I really should have burst the bubble by telling people that I have been extremely fortunate in being able to do just exactly what I wanted to all my life—doing what I did was my idea of fun."[9]

Isabel told a friend that while she planned to "live long and prosper" (in the words of the Rip Van Winkle toast) she knew that her life expectancy would depend somewhat on her "powers of natural resistance, which my surgeon considers to be unusually good."[10] It became more and more clear, however, that her strength was ebbing.

Isabel wrote McCaulley that she was "getting along fine," but "things can happen suddenly. At present... my frame of mind resembles Kipling's old Roman general who consulted his sword every morning and said 'This day too is granted Rutilanus to live.'"[11]

Her positive frame of mind was heightened by the activities of her grandchildren. Kathy Hughes, after graduating from the University of Wisconsin with a major in history, studied for a year at the Sorbonne. Now living in New York, she was on her way to being a staff writer with the *Wall Street Journal*. Douglas Hughes, a senior at Cornell University and a prelaw major, would follow Chief in choice of a career and graduate *cum laude* from Georgetown Law School. Jonathan, in Hawaii, was living what he believed; if Isabel questioned his lifestyle, she could not quarrel with his philosophy. Jennifer, the youngest of the four, was a junior at Swarthmore High School.

Isabel did not have Ann, but she had Betty and Kathy, both loving and attentive. And she and Chief had, in addition to Peter's unfailing help and caring, Jim Hughes. After Chief and Isabel's sixtieth wedding anniversary, Jim wrote an intimate, touching letter saying how much they had meant to him both before and after Ann's death. "You both have been towering and enormously positive influences in my life and...I love you very much."[12] In one of the final letters Mary McCaulley wrote Isabel, she said, "You have...given me through your support of my work more than I could repay in a hundred years.... What I have done in the past earlier stage was done of my own free will, and I have been repaid a hundredfold by the privilege of working with you."[13]

By late January, it was getting harder for Isabel to concentrate, but she still faced the task of proofreading the text of *Gifts Differing* that CPP promised to send her sometime in February. She asked Kathy Hughes to prepare an index for the book (that was never used). When Kathy arrived from New York to help out, she could see how tired her grandmother was and knew that Isabel often prayed, "Lord, make me whole," sometimes when she was lying down to rest on the oriental rug in front of the sofa.[14]

On a wintry Sunday afternoon, as she lay on the couch in her living room, Isabel spent several hours talking with David Saunders, her first supporter at ETS, about the possibilities of needed research on the Indicator. Obviously in some physical pain, she was impressively astute mentally.[15]

Chief was clear mentally, but he, too, was getting more frail. He did not want to accept what lay ahead for Isabel, and he was trying to convince himself that if he could get through "this hard time, all will be O.K." Then he realized it would not be all right, because "she will be gone."[16]

As winter gave way to spring, Isabel, with Peter and Kathy's help, finished proofing *Gifts Differing*. However, she was not to hold a published copy in her hands. She was now able to sit up for a part of the day, usually wrapped in a soft tiger blanket that Jack Black and staff at CPP had sent her. On an April afternoon, she welcomed two visitors from CPP: Lorin Letendre, who had joined the staff in February as a senior vice president and Janice Strom, who had first received the telephone call about the Indicator from Mary McCaulley. For almost five years, Strom had talked regularly with Isabel on matters pertaining to the Indicator, and she was excited about finally getting to meet "Mrs. Myers." Isabel, too, was pleased to be able to "put a face to a voice." Strom recalls that, although Isabel was "very frail," her health in no way diminished her interest in even the smallest detail about the Indicator, its users, and about CPP.[17]

For Letendre, the half hour he spent alone with Isabel was a treasured memory. As they discussed the future of the MBTI and his goals for CPP, he felt a "comfortable synchronicity." Letendre was deeply moved by this woman, who, almost at the point of death, projected an aura of "other-worldliness." He felt as if he were in the presence of someone greater than a mere human being. The meeting had such an impact on him that it helped to influence his decision to stay at CPP when other tempting opportunities arose.[18]

Isabel no longer had the strength to write letters, so she asked Kathy to let Jack Black know that her talk with Letendre had increased her "security about the future and direction of the MBTI."[19] Kathy also wrote to Letendre: "Part of dying is a gradual detachment—a cutting loose of this world—and you came [to Isabel] at a point when there seemed little that...[was] important enough to bring up from her dwindling reservoir the strength to focus. But you and Jan did, and it was a beautiful gift to her."[20]

During the last weeks, Peter ordered a hospital bed that was set up in the living room for his mother. Isabel did not want to go to a hospital, and she and Chief had long agreed that there would be no chemotherapy or radiation treatments. Dr. Wilkinson had prescribed medication for pain and, as needed, for restlessness. Chief began to isolate himself more and more, apparently unable to bear the sight of Isabel's relentless deterioration.

In April, Kathy Myers began to stay at 321 Dickinson instead of coming up every weekend with Peter. By then, despite her being barely able to move, a wraithlike Isabel insisted that Kathy take her to the bank to be sure some checks were properly deposited. The teller, in an aside to Kathy, wondered how Isabel could be out of bed and *walking*. This was her last venture out of the house. Near the end of April, practical nurses were hired around the clock.

On Friday evening, May 2, Peter drove up after work to find his mother not "consistently with us." She would recall things about her childhood and sometimes talked in a "little girl voice." On Monday morning, May 5, before Peter returned to Washington, Isabel looked at him and asked, "Peter, what is your understanding of the word 'lethargy'?" He told her he thought it was "a warm glow that comes when out of all the things you could possibly be doing none seems interesting or important enough to make the effort to do it.... You can relax and think comfortably about what has been—and not worry any more." Smiling at him, she said, "How nice. That is just how I feel." She reached out to Peter and then settled back, apparently asleep. Peter left to return to Washington.[21]

In late morning, Jane Gemmill came in, stroked Isabel, and talked gently to her. Jane went home, and as the afternoon wore on, Kathy sat beside Isabel's bed, writing notes. It was still light outside when Kathy looked up and realized that Isabel was no longer breathing. She gently told Chief, who then came in, and for a few silent minutes, stared at Isabel. "It's going to take a long time to get used to her not being here," he said. Jane Gemmill, Kathy, and Chief were standing together, mute, when a strange and sudden gust of wind blew through the house, moving doors and curtains. Very late that evening, when Peter arrived back at Dickinson Avenue, he found Isabel lying peacefully under her tiger blanket.

On Wednesday, the seventh, a brief memorial service was held in the living room of Isabel's home, now cleared of its sick-room furnishings. The Reverend Warren C. Skipp, rector of Trinity Episcopal Church in Swarthmore (Kathy Myer's girlhood church) read from I Corinthians 12:4, a passage that began: "Now there are varieties of gifts, but the same spirit," and briefly from the church liturgy for the dead.[22] Chief sat quietly among his family—Peter, Kathy, Betty; Jim, Kathy, and Douglas Hughes; and neighbors and friends, Jane Gemmill, Jim and Edna Hornaday, and Nancy and Merle Zimmer. After the service was over, Chief took everyone to lunch at his and Isabel's favorite restaurant, the Ingleneuk. Almost totally detached during Isabel's last days, Chief had relegated the final arrangements to Kathy and Peter because (he told Peter) that he was not good at "these feeling things."

The next morning before dawn, while Chief was still sleeping, Peter, Kathy, Betty, and Jim took the ashes of Isabel and Ann and scattered them in a beautiful spot in the woods that had been a favorite place of Isabel and Chief. Separated for eight years, daughter and mother were once again united. [23]

Found in a stack of Isabel's papers was a single page, in Isabel's handwriting, of a credo of her philosophy. Titled "What Is To Be Desired?" it shows how Isabel finally tried to guide her life:

What Is To Be Desired?

Self-respect—to be part of the solution, not part of the problem

Love—to love the human beings that mean the most to me [be a help and comfort to them when and if they need it] & contribute to their lives if I can

Peace of Mind—to avoid mistakes that make me regret the past or fear the future

Involvement—always to be tremendously interested

Understanding—to be able to incorporate the things [&] people & ideas that happen to me in a coherent concept of the world

Freedom —to work at what interests me most

Abbreviations
in the Notes

AMH	Ann Myers Hughes
APT	Association for Psychological Type
CAPT	Center for Applications of Psychological Type
CGM	Clarence Gates Myers
CPP	Consulting Psychologists Press
DRS	David R. Saunders
DWM	Donald W. MacKinnon
EMD	Elizabeth Monk Devlin
ENH	Edward N. Hay
ETS	Educational Testing Service
GH	*Good Housekeeping*
GWSM	George Washington School of Medicine
HC	Henry Chauncey
IAM	Isabel Ann Myers
IBM	Isabel Briggs Myers
IMB	Isabel McKelvey Briggs
IPAR	Institute for Personality Assessment Research
JAD	Junius A. Davis
JAH	James A. Hughes, Jr.
JBM	Jonathan Briggs Myers
JDB	John D. Black
JMS	John M. Stalnaker
KCB	Katharine Cook Briggs
KDM	Katharine Downing Myers
LJB	Lyman James Briggs
MBC	Mary Baldwin Cook
MHM	Mary H. McCaulley
MSC	Michigan State College
MSU	Michigan State University
NYU	New York University

PBM	Peter Briggs Myers
RSB	Ray Stannard Baker
SEP	*Saturday Evening Post*
SS	*Scattered Seeds*
TOST	The Office of Special Tests
WHC	*Woman's Home Companion*
WM	*Writer's Monthly*
WWT	William Watson Turnbull
Youth	*Youth's Companion*

Notes

Chapter 1

1. IBM to KCB, Jan. 8, 1942, IBM Papers.
2. *Reader's Digest*, Jan. 1942, p. 12.
3. IBM to KCB, Jan. 8, 1942, IBM Papers.
4. IBM to ENH [Jan. 8, 1942], IBM Papers.
5. IBM to KCB, Jan. 8, 1942, IBM Papers.
6. *Ibid.*
7. MHM to author, notes on conversations with IBM, 1971, MHM Papers.
8. *Ibid.*
9. Interview with PBM, Oct. 1988.
10. They were her maternal uncle, Cyrus G. Baldwin, president of Pomona College, and her maternal great-uncles James H. Fairchild, president of Oberlin College, Edward Henry Fairchild, president of Berea College, and George Thompson Fairchild, president of Kansas State Agricultural College (now Kansas State University).
11. Harvard University and Harvard Medical School archives.
12. KCB, "At Present," manuscript fragment, typed, IBM Papers.
13. *Catalog of the Officers and Students of the State Agricultural College of Michigan,* 1890–91; John Sanford, University Archivist to author, July 31, 1987.
14. Office of the Registrar to author, Feb. 1, 1989; transcripts of KEC and LJB; MSU Archives.
15. MBC to KCB, July 23, 1895, IBM Papers.
16. *Ibid.,* Aug. 13, 1895.
17. Interview with PBM, Jan. 13, 1989; KCB referred to her visual incapacitation as "injured eyesight." See KCB, "The Education of Suzanne," typed ms. IBM Papers. Hereinafter, KCB, "Suzanne."

18. MCB to KCB, Sept. 10, 1895. The Baldwins in Ohio were apparently collateral relatives of Mary Julia Baldwin after whom Mary Baldwin College, Staunton, VA, was named.

19. MBC to KCB, Aug. 13, 1895; KCB, "Suzanne."

20. Marriage license of KCB and LJB, IBM Papers.

21. John Hopkins Alumni Records; Tony Lush, *Lyman Briggs: A Biography,* Michigan State University, 1969, p. 10. Hereinafter, Lush.

22. KCB, "Suzanne."

23. KCB, Record book, 1897–1910, IBM Papers.

24. KCB, "Suzanne."

Chapter 2

1. KCB, "Suzanne."

2. *Ibid.*

3. *Ibid.*

4. *Ibid.* Spencer, who also showed contempt for the humanities and advocated science as the principal instrument of education, was criticized by a contemporary as "the most immeasurable ass in Christiandom." See Sir Paul Harvey, *The Oxford Companion to English Literature,* 4th ed. rev., Oxford University Press, 1969.

5. KCB, "Suzanne."

6. *Ibid.*

7. *Ibid.*

8. *Ibid.*

9. IBM on tape, June 17, 1979, IBM Papers.

10. IMB to LJB, Aug. 26, 1901, IBM Papers.

11. *Ibid.,* May 13, 1902, IBM Papers.

12. IMB, three untitled stories, 1902, IBM Papers.

13. KCB to Edwin G. Rich, March 1, 1929, IBM Papers.

14. IBM on tape, June 17, 1979, IBM Papers.

15. KCB, "Suzanne."

16. *Ibid.*

17. IBM on tape, June 17, 1979, IBM Papers.

18. KCB, Record book, p. 23, IBM Papers. On a separate piece of paper, undated, inserted between blank leaves of the Record, is a list of IMB's reading: Henry Cabot Lodge's *History of the Colonies* and *Life of George Washington;* in the American Statesmen series, biographies of Alexander Hamilton, Daniel Webster, Henry Clay, Abraham Lincoln, and John Calhoun; Ulysses S. Grant's memoirs (2 vols.); James Schouler's *History of the United States Under the Constitution* (4 of 7 vols.); Henry Wadsworth Longfellow's *Evangeline* and *Miles Standish;* poetry of James Russell Lowell and John Greenleaf Whittier; Lord James Bryce's *American Commonwealth;* John Adams' *Right of Petition;* Albion W. Tourgee's *A Fool's Errand;* and Harriet Beecher Stowe's *Uncle Tom's Cabin.*

19. KCB, "Suzanne."
20. IMB, "The Diary of a Girl Going Traveling, 1904," IBM Papers.
21. KCB, "Suzanne"; IBM on tape, June 17, 1979, IBM Papers.
22. IMB, "Her Book," Diary, June 8, 1906 through Feb. 12, 1912, IBM Papers.
23. KCB to E. G. Rich, March 1, 1929, IBM Papers. Asaph Hall (1829–1907) was a distinguished American astronomer who taught at the U.S. Naval Observatory and at Harvard University.
24. IBM on tape, June 17, 1979; Diary, 1906–1912; KCB, "Suzanne"; report card of IMB, 1911–1912, Western High School, District of Columbia, IBM Papers.
25. Diary, 1912–1915, entries in 1913.
26. Emerson W. Matthews to KCB, May 6, 1913, IBM Papers.
27. IBM on tape, June 17, 1979, IBM Papers.
28. *Ibid.*
29. Interview with PBM, Jan. 22, 1989.
30. KCB to Edwin G. Rich, March 1, 1929, IBM Papers.
31. Diary, April 16, 1911.
32. *Ibid.*
33. KCB, Manuscript fragment, "At Present," IMB Papers.
34. *Ibid.*
35. *Ibid.;* KCB, "Suzanne."

Chapter 3
1. Grace Dunlop Peter and Joyce D. Southwick, *Cleveland Park, An Early Residential Neighborhood of the Nation's Capital,* 1958.
2. *Ibid.,* interview with Mrs. Philip Sidney Smith.
3. Quoted in Constance McLaughlin Green's *Washington, A History of the Capital, 1800–1950,* 1962, pp. 195–196.
4. RSB to KCB, Nov. 29, 1910, IBM Papers. Baker later was director of the press bureau for the American Commission to Negotiate Peace, Paris 1919, and authorized biographer of Woodrow Wilson.
5. RSB to KCB, Dec. 12, 1910 and Jan. 12, 1911, IBM Papers.
6. RSB to KCB, July 28 and Oct. 5, 1911 and Dec. 22, 1912, IBM Papers.
7. Edward W. Bok to KCB, April 17, 1911, IBM Papers.
8. *Ladies Home Journal,* October 1912, pp. 41, 42.
9. *Outlook* to KCB, Dec. 19, 1912, IBM Papers. On the back of this letter KCB noted in pencil her earnings for the year.
10. *Outlook,* Jan. and March, 1915.
11. IMB, Diary, 1906–1912; *Ladies Home Journal* to KCB, Jan. 16, 1912, IBM Papers.
12. *Woman's Home Companion* to IMB, Oct. 14, 1914, IBM Papers.
13. Diary, 1912–1915.
14. *The Washington Times,* Sept. 24, 1912; Diary, 1912–1915.

Chapter 4

1. Diary, Jan. 15, 1915, IBM Papers.
2. *Ibid.,* Feb. 24, 1915.
3. *Ibid.,* Feb 18, 1915.
4. *Ibid.,* Jan. 10 and 15, 1915.
5. *Ibid.,* summer of 1915.
6. Quoted in Richard J. Walton, *Swarthmore College, An Informal History,* p. 4.
7. *Ibid.,* p. 25.
8. "The Book of Me, September 1910," fragments, IBM Papers.
9. Interview with Jane Brown Gemmill, May 10, 1987.
10. IMB to KCB, Sept. 21, 1915, IBM Papers.
11. IMB, transcript from Swarthmore College; IMB to KCB, Sept. 11, 1915, IMB Papers.
12. Diary, 1915–1916.
13. Handwritten "chronology" of CGM's early life, July 1980, PBM Personal Papers.
14. CGM, General Memo Book, 1980, p. 122, PBM Personal Papers.
15. Myers Family Records, IBM Papers; interview with PBM, Feb. 1, 1989.
16. Telephone conversation with PBM, June 29, 1987.
17. CGM to JBM, Nov. 14, 1976.
18. CGM, General Memo Book, 1980, p. 122, PBM Personal Papers.
19. Interview with Eleanor Atkinson Smith, June 14, 1988.
20. Interview with Jane Brown Gemmill, May 10, 1988; transcripts of CGM and IMB, Swarthmore College archives.
21. IMB to KCB, Oct. 12 and 13, 1915.
22. IMB to KCB, Dec. 16, 1915.
23. Diary, 1915–1916; IMB to KCB, Dec. 11, 1915, IBM Papers.
24. IMB, Diary, 1915–1916; IBM on tape, June 17, 1919, IBM Papers.
25. Diary, 1915–1916.
26. *Ibid.*
27. *Ibid.*
28. CGM to KCB, May 18, 1916, IBM Papers.
29. Wilson Myers, a clarinetist, had taught his three children to play instruments; Parcie played the piano and harp, CGM the bass fiddle, Milton the trumpet, and Ella Myers the violin (CGM, General Memo Book, p. 122).
30. According to Peter Myers, Chief destroyed Isabel's letters to him after her death.
31. CGM to KCB, Oct. 27, 1916.

Chapter 5

1. CGM and Paul F. Gemmill to IMB, Oct. 2, 1916, IBM Papers.
2. Transcripts of CGM and IBM, Swarthmore College archives.

3. CGM to KCB, Jan. 25, 1917, IBM Papers.

4. Preserved in IBM's private papers, the letter apparently escaped Chief's eye because it was addressed to Katharine.

5. CGM to KCB, April 29, 1917, IBM Papers.

6. IMB to Lyman Briggs, April 29, 1917, IBM Papers.

7. IMB to KCB, April 12, 1917, IBM Papers; Walton, pp. 25–26.

8. CGM to IMB, Aug. 30, 1917, IBM Papers.

9. IMB to KCB and LJB, May 7, 1917, IBM Papers.

10. KCB to IMB, May 19, 1917; IMB to KCB, May 19, 1917; CGM to KCB, May 22, 1917, IBM Papers.

11. KCB to IMB, May 19, 1917, IBM Papers.

12. IMB to KCB, May 10 and 17, 1917, IBM Papers.

13. CGM to IMB, April 2 and 26, 1917, IBM Papers.

14. CGM to KCB, April 29, 1917, IBM Papers.

15. Walton, p. 25; CGM to LJB, May 24, 1917, IBM Papers. Chautauqua was originally established in 1874 in Chautauqua County, New York, as a Sunday school assembly. Later, it became a summer center that offered concerts, lectures, classes, and recreational programs. Based on the New York plan, the Swarthmore Chautauqua traveled to small towns to provide cultural enrichment. The Chautauqua was expected to operate at a profit.

16. *The Phoenix,* March 20, 1917, p. 3.

17. Ella G. and Parcie Myers to CGM, c. May 1917, IBM Papers.

18. Parcie Myers to IMB, July 9, 1917, IBM Papers.

19. IMB to KCB, May 29, 1917, IBM Papers.

20. Transcript, IMB, 1915–1919, Swarthmore College Archives.

21. Link and Link, *The Twentieth Century: An American History,* p. 86.

22. Frances Williams Browin, "How We Won the War," p. 46, in *Swarthmore Remembered.*

23. IMB to KCB, April 5, 1917, IBM Papers.

24. CGM to IMB, Aug. 9, 1917, and CGM to KCB, Aug. 6, 1917, IBM Papers.

25. CGM to IMB, July 28, 1917, IBM Papers.

Chapter 6

1. IMB to KCB, Sept. 22, 1917, IBM Papers.

2. *Ibid.,* Sept. 24 and 25, and Oct. 1, 2, 4, and 20, 1917.

3. IMB to KCB, Oct. 1, 1917, IBM Papers.

4. Chief's three specifics were the Bolshevik take-over of the Russian government in late 1917, after which they sued for peace, thus releasing forty German divisions to be thrown against the Allies on the western front; the opposition of Wisconsin's Senator Robert M. LaFollette to America's entry into the war and his criticism of President Wilson's policies during the war; and the crushing defeat of the Italians in October 1917 at the hands of a combined German-Austrian army. See Link and Link, *The*

Twentieth Century, CGM, p. 86.

5. CGM to IMB, Nov. 8, 1917; IBM to KCB, Nov. 5, 1917, IBM Papers.

6. IMB to KCB, Dec. 6, 11, 17, and 19, 1917, IBM Papers.

7. *Ibid.,* Jan. 10 and 28, 1918.

8. *Ibid.,* Jan. 12 and 14, 1918. Later in her life when IBM reminisced with KDM about her college years, she said that in her freshman year, she changed her major from science to English as a subject that would be more useful as a mother (IBM on tape, June 17, 1979). That same year, she told Gordon Lawrence that she started out as a physics major (Gordon Lawrence to author, Jan. 26, 1989). However, her transcripts, diaries, and detailed letters written during her college years to Katherine Briggs contradict these memories.

9. IMB and CGM to KCB, Jan. 29, 1918, IBM Papers.

10. Alexander Leitch, *A Princeton Companion,* Princeton University Press, 1978, p. 252.

11. Link and Link, *Twentieth Century,* pp. 87–88.

12. IMB to KCB, March 4, 1918, IBM Papers.

13. CMG to IMB, April 28, 1918, IBM Papers.

14. IMB to KCB, May 3, 1918, IBM Papers.

15. *Ibid.,* May 6, 1918.

16. CGM to IMB, June 1, 1918, IBM Papers.

17. *Ibid.,* May 17, 1918.

18. Quoted in CGM to IMB, June 6, 1918, IBM Papers.

19. Paul Gemmill to IMB, June 13, 1918, IBM Papers.

20. Telegram, CGM to IMB, June 14, 1918, IBM Papers.

21. CGM to IMB, June 6 and 10, 1918, IBM Papers.

22. Parcie and Ella Gates Myers to CGM, June 11 and 15, 1918, IBM Papers.

23. CGM to IMB, May 28, 1918, IBM Papers.

24. Marriage certificate of CGM and IMB, June 17, 1918; handwritten news release, IBM Papers.

Chapter 7

1. IBM to KCB, June 19, 20, 21, and 22, 1918, IBM Papers.

2. *Ibid.,* June 25 and 27, 1918.

3. *Ibid.,* June 21 and 22, and July 15, 1918.

4. *Ibid.,* July 9, 1918.

5. *Ibid.,* June 29, 1918.

6. *Ibid.,* July 19, 1918.

7. *Ibid.,* July 14, 1918.

8. *Ibid.,* July 17, 1918.

9. *Ibid.,* July 19, 1918.

10. *Ibid.,* July 26, 1918.

11. Ten loose-leaf pages, four in KCB's handwriting, six in IBM's, c. 1918, IBM Papers.

12. IBM to KCB, Aug. 1 and 2, 1918, IBM Papers.
13. *Ibid.*, Aug 16 and 21, 1918.
14. *Ibid.*, Aug. 22, 1918.
15. CGM to KCB, Sept. 14, 1918, IBM Papers.
16. CGM to IBM, Nov. 9, 1918, IBM Papers.
17. *Ibid.*, Nov. 21, 1918; CGM to the Adjutant General, Dec. 1, 1918, IBM Papers.
18. CGM to IBM, Dec. 17 and 19, 1918, IBM Papers.
19. CGM to IBM, Dec 29, 1918, and Jan. 13, 1919, IBM Papers.
20. Notes "From the Desk of Jane Gemmill," July 23, 1986; CGM to KCB, Jan. 27, 1919, IBM Papers; *The Swarthmorean,* May 16, 1980, p. 4.
21. "Somerville" was begun in 1871 as a literary society in honor of a Quaker intellectual, Kate Fairfax Somerville (1788–1872), after whom the first woman's college at Oxford University was named.
22. CGM to KCB, April 12, 1919, IBM Papers. Reichard received a doctorate in anthropology from Columbia University and was later professor and executive officer in the department of anthropology, Barnard College.
23. IBM to KCB, April 4, 1919, IBM Papers.
24. CGM to KCB, April 12, 1919, IBM Papers.
25. CGM, General Memo Book, 1981, pp. 123–124, IBM Papers. In his memoirs, Chief wrote that he thought the "Awful Ate" took themselves too seriously and that the conventional students mostly regarded the eight as "anarchists."
26. IBM to KCB, April 25, 1919; and KCB to IBM, May 5, 7, and 16, 1919, IBM Papers.
27. In 1988, the four surviving members of the "Awful Ate" were Eleanor, Jane, Phyllis, and Katherine.
28. IBM, transcript, Swarthmore College, 1915–1919.
29. *Halcyon,* 1920, p. 66.
30. Interview with Eleanor Atkinson Smith, Feb. 17, 1989.

Chapter 8
1. Lush, 1969.
2. LJB to IMB, July 4, 1914, IBM Papers.
3. LJB to KCB, July 16 and Aug. 3, 1914, IBM Papers.
4. *Ibid.*, Oct. 6, 1914.
5. *Ibid.*, Oct. 7, 1914.
6. Lush, pp. 9, 12, and 13.
7. Lush, p. 5.
8. IMB to KCB, June 2, 1917, IBM Papers; interview with PBM, March 27, 1989.
9. WHC, Oct. 1912. Woolf's essay lay dormant until "rediscovered" by the feminist movement of the 1960s.
10. KCB, "Suzanne"; Julia Clark Hallam, "The Price of a Home," and

reply by Elizabeth Childe, *New Republic,* Oct. 20 and Nov. 17, 1917.

11. According to PBM, KCB's poor eyesight and extreme introverted personality contributed to her isolation. Interview with PBM, Feb. 12, 1989.

12. Dewey's *The Child and the Curriculum* was published in 1906, and *The School and the Child* in 1907.

13. Manuscript, 2pp typed, c. 1918, IBM Papers.

14. Quoted in manuscript by Elizabeth Childe, 4 pp. typed, c. 1918, IBM Papers. The magazine was not identified.

15. U.S. Patent Office to KCB, Jan. 23, 1918 and March 15, 1919, and Eugene Brown to KCB, March 17, 1919; undated, typed list of luggage manufacturers, IBM Papers.

16. Interview with PBM, Feb. 12, 1989.

17. *Ibid.;* IBM on history of the MBTI, tape, APT conference, Oct. 6, 1974; IBM on tape, June 17, 1979, IBM Papers.

18. IBM on tape, June 17, 1979, IBM Papers. KCB spent five years writing, revising, and trying to publish her novel, "The Guesser," in which she interwove her theory of type with the narrative. The result was cumbersome. See correspondence about "The Guesser" between KCB and publishers, 1924–1928, IBM Papers.

19. IBM could not recall what biographies KCB read; IBM on tape, June 17, 1979, IBM Papers.

20. KCB to IBM, Oct. 10, 1928, IBM Papers.

21. Polti's work was translated from the French by Lucile Ray and was likely the edition that KCB read. External evidence places her undated manuscript in 1923 before she had read Jung.

22. IBM to Carl Jung, June 8, 1950, Jung Archives, ETH-Bibliothek, Zurich; IBM on tape, Oct. 6, 1974, IBM Papers. Jung's book was critically reviewed by J. B. Watson in *New Republic,* Nov. 7, 1923 and a rebuttal by James Oppenheim appeared on Nov. 14, 1923.

23. KCB to Carl Jung, Aug. 23, 1927, IBM Papers. The copy in KCB's papers is a draft with emendations. The original has not been found in the Jung Archives, but Jung had no "reliable office before 1930" (Dr. Peter Jung to author, Dec. 10, 1990).

24. Because of the restrictions imposed by client confidentiality, the content of these letters is inaccessible (author to Beat Glaus, Peter Jung, Yvonne Voegeli, and Sibylle Franks, June 21, Aug. 6, and Sept. 26, 1990; Voegeli, Franks, and P. Jung to author, June 28, July 30, Sept. 21, Oct. 3, and Oct. 24, 1990; PBM to P. Jung, Oct. 29, and P. Jung to PBM, Nov. [12], 1990).

25. IBM to Carl Jung, June 8, 1950, ETH-Bibliothek, Zurich. In this letter, IBM recapitulated the visit in 1937 in New York between Jung and KCB. After their meeting in New York, the correspondence between KCB and Jung appears to have ceased. If further exchange occurred, the

letters are missing from both KCB's papers and the Jung Archives. In *C. G. Jung, Letters*, Gerhard Adler, ed., Princeton University Press, 1973, there is one letter to KCB (July 4, 1930). There is no mention of KCB or IBM in Gerhard Wehr's *Jung: A Biography*, translated by David M. Weeks, 1988.
26. Interview with PBM, Feb. 12, 1989.
27. Certificate of Flight to "Mrs. L. J. Briggs," Nov. 4, 1919; IBM to KCB, Nov. 7, 1919, IBM Papers.
28. Interview with PBM, Feb. 12, 1989.
29. For a discussion of women and higher education, see Carol Smith-Rosenberg, *Disorderly Conduct*, Knopf, New York, 1985, pp. 245–296.

Chapter 9
1. IBM to KCB, June 15 and 18, 1919; IBM on tape, June 17, 1979, IBM Papers.
2. IBM to KCB, June 4, 1919, IBM Papers.
3. *Ibid.*, July 8, 1919.
4. *Ibid.*, July 11, 1919.
5. *Ibid.*, July 25, 1989.
6. IBM and CGM to KCB, Oct. 7, 1919, IBM Papers.
7. Joseph Swain to IBM, and IBM to KCB, Oct. 13, 1919, IBM Papers.
8. IBM to KCB, Oct. 7 and 27, 1919, and Jan. 19, 1920, and CGM to KCB, Oct. 7, 1919, IBM Papers.
9. IBM to KCB, Oct. 4, 13, 16, 26, and 27, and Nov. 2, 12, and 21, 1919; IBM to the "Ate," Jan. 27, 1920; IBM on tape, June 17, 1979, IBM Papers.
10. IBM to KCB, March 4, 1920, IBM Papers.
11. CGM to KCB, Feb. 24, 1920, IBM Papers.
12. "Mrs. John Doe," typed ms., 22 pp., 1920; IBM to KCB, Feb. 24, March 4, and June 15, 1919, IBM Papers. Chief was undoubtedly still smarting over his father's treatment of his mother.
13. IBM to KCB, March 4, April 21, 30, and May 14, 1920, IBM Papers.
14. Jane Brown to IBM, March 25, 1920, IBM Papers.
15. IBM to KCB, Jan. 19, 20, and 23, 1920, IBM Papers.
16. CGM to Joseph Willets, July 2, 1920, IBM Papers.
17. IBM to KCB, June 8, 1920; CGM to Joseph Willets, July 2, 1920, IBM Papers.
18. IBM to KCB, June 8, and KCB to IBM, June 9, 1920, IBM Papers.
19. KCB to IBM, June 9, 1920, IBM Papers.
20. CGM to IBM, Aug. 2, 1919, IBM Papers.
21. CGM to Joseph Willets, Aug. 8, 1919, IBM Papers.
22. CGM to IBM, July 22 and 27, 1919, IBM Papers.
23. *Ibid.*, Aug. 4, 1920.
24. *Ibid.*, Aug 24, 1920.
25. IBM on tape, June 17, 1979, IBM Papers.

26. Miscellany of lists, c. 1921–1922, IBM Papers.

27. IBM to KCB, April 5, 1921; IBM to the "Ate," June 4, 1921, IBM Papers.

28. IBM to the "Ate," June 4, 1921, IBM Papers.

29. IBM to KCB, April 13 and 30, 1921, IBM Papers.

30. *Ibid.*, May 5, 1921; Ella G. Myers to KCB, May 10, 1921, IBM Papers.

31. CGM to KCB, June 9, 1921; IBM to the "Ate," June 4, 1921, IBM Papers.

Chapter 10

1. Ella G. Myers to IBM, April 2, 1923, IBM Papers.

2. KCB to IBM, May 10, 1923, IBM Papers.

3. *Ibid.*

4. KCB to IBM, July 8, 1923; IBM on tape, June 17, 1979, IBM Papers.

5. IBM to KCB, Feb. 2 and March 1, 1921; GH, Jan. 13, *Youth,* Jan. 17, SEP, Jan. 19, and WM, Jan. 16, 1923 to IBM, IBM Papers.

6. Palmer Photoplay Corp. to "Katherine McKelvey," July 6 and 30 and Oct. 6, 1920; Feb. 1, March 17, April 4, July 18 and 28, Oct. 13, and Dec. 12, 1921, IBM Papers.

7. Contract between KCB and Emile Offman, Jan. 18, 1923, IBM Papers.

8. KCB to IBM, July 8, 1923, IBM Papers.

9. *Washington Post,* March 25, 1923.

10. KCB to IBM, July 29, 1923, IBM Papers.

11. *Ibid.*, July 29, 1923.

12. Phyllis Komori to IBM, March 12, 1923, IBM Papers.

13. Fragment, IBM to Vera [Denworth], c. Nov. 1923, IBM Papers.

14. Jane Gemmill to IBM, Oct. 13, 1924, IBM Papers.

15. "A Line A Day Diary," Jan. 1, 1924, IBM Papers.

16. *Ibid.*

17. *Ibid.,* June 15, 18, 25, 26, 27, 28, and 30, 1924.

18. *Ibid.,* June 28, 1924.

19. *Ibid.*, Feb. 14–July 7, 1924.

20. CGM to IBM, telegram, July 8, 1924.

21. *Ibid.*, July 8, 1924.

22. Diary, May 20 and July 17, 1924.

23. *Ibid.,* Aug. 25, 1924.

24. *Ibid.,* Aug 31, 1924.

25. *Ibid.*

26. *Ibid.*

27. *Scattered Seeds,* Seventh Month, 1923, p. 107. From 1923–1925, IBM sold eleven poems and seven stories to SS.

28. KCB to CGM, March 26, 1925; LJB to IBM, April 8, 1925, IBM Papers. Dr. Baldwin found that KCB had 39 gall stones, which he removed in a second operation after the tumor.

29. J. F. Baldwin to KCB, March 21, 1925, IBM Papers.

30. Diary, April 24, 1926, IBM Papers.

31. Jane Gemmill to IBM, April 25, 1926, IBM Papers.

32. CGM to KCB, and CGM to IBM, April 29, 1926, IBM Papers.

33. CGM to PBM, Dec. 1, 1927, IBM Papers.

34. Edna and James Hornaday on tape, Jan. 7, 1983.

35. Diary, 1924–1927, IBM Papers.

36. Copy of birth certificate of IAM, IBM Papers.

Chapter 11

1. IBM to KCB, Oct. 5, 1928, IBM Papers.

2. *Ibid.*, Dec. 12, 1928.

3. *Ibid.*, fragment, c. 1928.

4. IBM to KCB, Oct. 5, [1928,] IBM Papers.

5. KCB to IBM, Oct. 10, 1928, IBM Papers.

6. Thomas Y. Crowell Co. to KCB, Nov. 26, 1926, IBM Papers.

7. D. Appleton & Co. to KCB, Aug. 13, 1928, IBM Papers.

8. J. Walter McSpadden to KCB, Nov. 9, 1928, IBM Papers.

9. *Ibid.*, Nov. 21, 1928.

10. *New Republic*, Dec. 22, 1926, p. 124.

11. *New York Times,* Dec. 18, 1926, p. 16.

12. *New Republic,* Dec. 5, 1928, pp. 61–63.

13. *Ibid.*

14. Rexmond C. Cochrane, *Measures of Progress: A History of the Bureau of Standards,* U.S. Dept. of Commerce, 1966, p. 314; KCB to IBM, May 8, 1927, IBM Papers.

15. IBM to Curtis Brown, Ltd., Dec. 20, 1928, IBM Papers.

16. IBM to KCB, Jan. 6, 1929, IBM Papers.

17. *Ibid.*

18. *Ibid.*

19. Telegram, Edwin G. Rich to IBM, Feb. 26, 1929, IBM Papers. Ironically, the telegram was opened first by the Gemmills because the Myers family was in Washington when it came. Paul telephoned the news.

20. Edwin G. Rich to IBM, Feb. 27, 1929, IBM Papers.

21. KCB to Edwin G. Rich, March 1, 1929, IBM Papers.

22. *Smart Set,* Aug. 1929, p. 4.

23. IBM to KCB, May 4, 1929, IBM Papers.

24. CGM to IBM, Feb. 26 and March 1, 1929, IBM Papers.

25. Pricilla Griffin to IBM, March 5, 1929, IBM Papers.

26. Katherine Miller, Phyllis Sellers, Dorothy Lucas, and Viola Martin to IBM, March 6, 16, 17, and 19, 1929, IBM Papers. Letters from Esther O'Neil and Eleanor Atkinson are missing.

27. IBM to KCB, LJB to IBM, IBM to Edwin G. Rich, May 4, 8, and 21, and IBM to CGM, Aug. 10, 1929, IBM Papers; interview with PBM,

March 27, 1989.

28. F. A. Stokes, Co., to IBM, Nov. 22, 1929, IBM Papers.

29. IBM to KCB, Oct. 12, 1929, IBM Papers.

Chapter 12

1. *Saturday Review,* Feb. 8, 1930.

2. *MSC Record,* Feb. 1930.

3. *Philadelphia Inquirer,* Jan. 13, 1930; IBM to "E.C.M.," typed ms., c. Jan. 13, 1930, IBM Papers.

4. *Daily News,* Jan. 1, 1930.

5. *Manchester Evening News,* Jan. 25; *Birmingham Post,* Feb. 4; *Irish Statesman* Feb. 8; and *Country Life,* Feb. 15, 1930.

6. *Detroit News,* "Manhattan Days and Nights" by Herbert Corcy, Feb. 14, 1930.

7. *Waterloo Daily Courier,* Jan. 8, 1930.

8. F. Carstarphen to IBM, Dec. 11; IBM to Edwin Rich, Dec. 13; Edwin Rich to IBM, Dec. 14; and IBM to F. Carstarphen, Dec. 16, 1929, IBM Papers.

9. IBM to Edwin G. Rich, and IBM to F. Stokes, Feb. 10 and Sept. 6, 1930, IBM Papers.

10. IBM to F. Stokes, Dec. 3, 1930, IBM Papers.

11. IBM to Edwin G. Rich, Aug. 9, 1930; Edwin Rich to IBM, Feb. 1, 1930; Curtis Brown to IBM, Sept. 28, 1934, IBM Papers.

12. IBM, typed fragment, background material for "Miss Kern," c. 1930, IBM Papers.

13. IBM to KCB, to F. Stokes, and to Edwin Rich, Dec. 14, 1929, Feb. 6 and 10, 1930, IBM Papers.

14. IBM to KCB, July 15, 1932, IBM Papers.

15. IBM to Barbara Pearson, May 30, 1931, IBM Papers.

16. IBM to KCB, March 21, 1931, IBM Papers; *Philadelphia Public Ledger* [May 16, 1931]; playbill of the Players Club of Swarthmore, May 4–8, 1931.

17. IBM to Barbara Pearson, May 23, 1931, IBM Papers.

18. *Philadelphia Public Ledger,* May 18, 1931, "Stage Sidelights"; agreement between IBM and Lawrence Shubert Lawrence, May 15, 1931, IBM Papers.

19. Playbill, Buck Hill Falls Auditorium, June 20, 1931; *The Morning Sun,* East Stroudsburg, PA., June 22, 1931; Barbara Pearson to IBM, May 24, 1931, IBM Papers.

20. IBM to KCB, Jan. 6, and KCB to LJB, Oct. 29, 1929, IBM Papers.

21. KCB to IBM, May 12, 1931, IBM Papers.

22. *Ibid.,* Feb. 5, 1933.

23. F. Stokes to IBM, Oct. 9, 1931, IBM Papers.

24. IBM to F. Stokes, Oct. 15, 1931, IBM Papers.

25. F. Stokes to IBM, Oct. 19, 1931, IBM Papers.
26. Program, "Theatre, Arts, and Letters," April 11, 1930; Matinee Musical Club of Philadelphia, invitation, Nov. 17, 1931; Philadelphia Club of Advertising Women to IBM, Oct. 23, 1931; Board of Public Education, Philadelphia, to IBM [Nov. 7, 1931], Narbeth Junior Club to IBM, Jan. 21, 1933; Business and Professional Women's Club to IBM, mid-Feb. 1933, IBM Papers; *Philadelphia Public Ledger,* Oct. 18, 1931.
27. *Ledger,* Oct. 18, 1931.
28. Taped interview with Edna and James Hornaday, Jan. 7, 1983; interview with PBM, Oct. 3, 1987; interview with Jane Gemmill, May 10, 1988; interview with Douglas Hughes, July 27, 1987.
29. F. Stokes to IBM, March 4, 1932, and IBM to F. Stokes, March 26, 1931, IBM Papers.
30. Jerry Stagg, *The Brothers Shubert,* pp. 286, 304.
31. IBM to KCB, March 28 and July 15; F. Stokes to IBM, March 4, 29, and July 15; Curtis Brown to IBM, March 29 and Aug. 2; IBM to F. Stokes, July 12, 1931, IBM Papers.
32. F. Stokes to IBM, July 15, 1931, IBM Papers.
33. Quoted in IBM to KCB, July 15, 1931, IBM Papers. KCB's original letter to IBM is missing.
34. IBM to KCB, July 15 and Oct. 30, 1932, IBM Papers.
35. PBM to KCB, June 25, 1934, Jan. 12, and March 11, 1935, IBM Papers; *New York Times,* Oct. 21, 1934. IBM noted on a small scrap of paper her total earnings from the two books as $11,000.
36. IBM to KCB, Jan 13, March 11, and April 5, 1935, IBM Papers.
37. *Ibid.,* May 8 and 14, 1933. Beckhard's successful plays were *Another Language* and *The Comic Artist.*
38. *Keene Evening Sentinel,* Aug. 9, 1934; playbill, Peterboro Drama Festival, Aug. 8, 9, 10, and 11, 1934; PBM to KCB, June 25, and IBM to KCB, Oct. 11, 1934, IBM Papers.
39. IBM to Nora [Waln], fragment, July 18, 1934, IBM Papers.

Chapter 13
1. Link and Link, p. 139.
2. Cochrane, p. 309.
3. *Ibid.,* p. 313.
4. *Washington Star,* Feb. 21, 1937.
5. Lush, p. 14.
6. *Ibid.,* p. 15.
7. Cochrane, p. 316.
8. Paul Gemmill to IBM, Aug. 22, 23, 24, and 30, and IBM to Jane and Paul Gemmill, Aug. 29, 1929, IBM Papers.
9. IBM to Jane and Paul Gemmill, Aug. 29, 1929.
10. IBM to KCB, Oct. 12, 1929.

11. IBM to KCB and LJB, Oct. 29, 1929, IBM Papers.

12. *Ibid.*, Oct. 27, 1929.

13. IBM to KCB, March 28, 1932, IBM Papers.

14. Interview with June Ullman Thomas, May 23, 1990.

15. Marguerite Pohek to Theresa Young, Nov. 17, 1931, IBM Papers.

16. Frank Morey to IBM, Nov. 29, 1932, IBM Papers.

17. IBM to KCB, March [1933], IBM Papers.

18. KCB to IBM, Nov. 20, 1932, IBM Papers.

19. IBM to KCB, Nov. 25, 1932, fragment, IBM Papers.

20. *Ibid.*, Dec 12, 1932.

21. Interview with PBM, Oct. 3, 1987; interview with KDM, April 9, 1989.

22. KCB to IBM, April 9, 1933, IBM Papers.

23. Walton, p. 37; *Phoenix,* March 21, Nov. 14, 17, 21, and 28, and Dec 5, 1933.

24. Interview with Jane Gemmill, May 10, 1988.

25. Interview with KDM, July 7, 1987; IBM to Carl Jung, June 8, 1950, Jung Archives, ETH-Bibliothek, Zurich.

26. CGM to KCB, Jan. 23, 1934, IBM Papers; *The Swarthmorian*, Jan. 8, 1976.

27. Interview with June Allman Thomas, May 23, 1990; interview with Lisa McGaw, Nov. 27, 1988.

28. Interview with Douglas Hughes, July 27, 1987.

29. CGM to Editor, *The Swarthmorean,* May 26, 1941, IBM Papers.

30. Curtis Brown to IBM, Oct. 21, 1941, IBM Papers.

31. KCB to IBM, April 9, 1933, IBM Papers.

32. IBM to KCB, July 22, 1937, IBM Papers.

33. *Ibid.*, Aug. 11, 1932.

34. PBM, diary of a trip, May 21–24, 1938; IBM, diary of a western trip, May 21–31, 1938; IBM to KCB, June 12, 1938, IBM Papers.

35. Interview with Richard Cordray, Oct. 19, 1988; IBM to HC, April 20, 1959, Folder 641, Frame 01846, Henry Chauncey Papers, ETS Archives. Hereinafter, HC Papers.

36. Interview with PBM, March 27, 1989.

37. IBM to KCB, Sept. 11, 1942, IBM Papers.

38. Cochrane, pp. 360–362. The other two physicists were Eugene P. Wigner, Princeton University, a Nobel Prize winner in 1963, and Leo Szilard, Columbia University.

39. Cochrane, p. 363.

40. KCB to IBM, Mar. 18, 1943; class schedule, PBM [March 1943], IBM Papers.

41. Ann Myers to KCB, June 17, 1943, and PBM to CGM, c. March 1943, IBM Papers; commencement program, Swarthmore High School, June 3, 1943.

42. CGM to [Swarthmore] School District, Jan. 11, 1943, IBM Papers; interview with Richard Cordray, April 20, 1989.
43. CGM to Register of Copyrights, May 5, 1943, IBM Papers.
44. IBM to KCB, Dec. 15, 1943, IBM Papers.

Chapter 14
1. For a more thorough discussion, see Myers, *Gifts Differing,* CPP (10th Anniversary Edition), 1990.
2. *Manual,* 1962.
3. For this dialogue, with names deleted, the author is grateful to Elaine Waples, a staff member at CAPT.
4. "Conversations with Isabel," June 1, 1977, CAPT publication.
5. IBM, *Introduction to Type,* 1970, p. 11.
6. *Ibid.,* p. 9.
7. Pricilla Griffin to IBM, March 5, 1929; Phyllis Sellers to IBM [June 1944], IBM Papers.
8. Interview with EMD, July 16, 1988.
9. IBM on tape, June 17, 1979, IBM Papers.
10. Interview with Jane Gemmill, May 10, 1988.
11. IBM to KCB, July 22, 1937, IBM Papers.
12. IBM to John A. Clark, Esq., Jan 31, 1978, IBM Papers.
13. Interview with Richard Cordray, Oct. 19, 1988.
14. IAM to IBM, Feb. 23, 26, and 28, 1948; PBM to IBM and CGM, Feb. 18, 1948; Richard Cordray to IBM, Dec. 26, 1943, March 13 and May 30, 1944; PBM diary, April 7, 1944; IBM to Richard Cordray, March 9, 1944, and IBM to John A. Clark, Esq., Jan. 31, 1978, IBM Papers.
15. "Duncan" and Timothy Hobson to IBM, June 26 and July 5, 1944, IBM Papers.
16. Interview with Richard Cordray, Oct. 22, 1988; IBM on tape, June 17, 1979, IBM Papers.
17. *Introduction to Type,* p. 12.
18. Notes on IBM visit, March 1971, MHM Personal Papers.
19. ENH to Vance Jewson, Sept. 24, 1945, Edward N. Hay Papers, Labor Management Documentation Center, M. P. Catherwood Library, Cornell University. Hereinafter, ENH Papers. Hay was a pioneer in personnel management through career development, job evaluation, executive career development, executive salary structure analysis, basic salary policies, and psychological evaluations. He was also publisher and editor of the *Personnel Journal.*
20. Copy of contract between IBM and Edward N. Hay, June 13, 1945; Hay was also coauthor of *Manual of Job Evaluation* and *Values of Psychology in Industrial Management,* booklets used in industrial consulting by Hay and Tomlinson, 220 S. 16th St., Philadelphia (newsletter fragment, Spring 1943), IBM Papers; interview with John Harker, April 7, 1989.

21. ENH to Vance Johnson, Sept. 24, 1945, ENH Papers.

22. DWM to IBM, Dec. 5, 1947, IBM Papers.

23. Harrison Gough and Wallace B. Hall to author, Feb. 16 and 20, 1990; Thorne and Gough, *Portraits of Type: An MBTI Research Compendium,* 1991, CPP.

24. "Conversations with Isabel," CAPT transcription, June 1, 1977. It is not clear with whom LJB first discussed the Indicator, Parr or Parks. IBM's initial correspondence with GWSM, following a telephone call, was to Katherine Brown, assistant to Dean John Parks (IBM to KB, June 24 and July 21, 1949); however, her subsequent correspondence was with Parr (Leland Parr to IBM, June 19 and Oct. 4, 1951, and March 25, 1954; IBM to L. Parr [Sept. 1951], IBM Papers).

25. The three instruments were the *Allport-Vernon Study of Values* (1931), The *Bernreuter Personality Inventory* (1933), and the *Minnesota Multiphasic Personality Inventory* (1942). For a discussion of these, see Cronbach, *Essentials of Psychological Testing,* Second Edition, Harper and Row, 1960, and Anastasi, *Psychological Testing,* Third Edition, Macmillan, 1968.

26. Interview with Richard Cordray, Oct. 22, 1988; IBM to HC, April 20, 1959, Folder 641, Frame 01846, ETS Archives; IBM to PBM, Feb. 28, 1944, IBM Papers.

27. IBM to PBM, Feb. 28, 1944, IBM Papers.

28. IBM to LJB, Oct. 18, 1949; KCB to IBM, Oct. 15, 1954, IBM Papers.

29. KCB to IBM, Oct. 14, 1959, IBM Papers.

30. IBM to KCB, Dec. 15, 1943, IBM Papers.

31. Certificate of Briggs-Myers Type Research, Nov. 13, 1947, IBM Papers.

32. Interviews with PBM, Oct. 3, 1987 and March 27, 1989.

33. Interview with Richard Cordray, Oct. 22, 1988; KCB to IBM, March 8, 1944, IBM Papers.

34. IBM on tape, June 17, 1979; KCB to IBM, July 29, 1923; KCB to Harriet Roman, Dec. 23, 1932, Jan. 11 and March 1, 1933; H. Roman to KCB, Jan 5, 1932 and Jan. 24, 1933; Tina Skeer to KCB, June 5, 1935–Jan. 18, 1943, passim; IBM's diary, "A Line A Day," Jan. 1, 1924–July 7, 1927, passim, IBM Papers.

35. IBM on tape, "Reflections on the History of the Type Indicator," n.d., transcription, CAPT library.

36. IBM to [Richard Cordray], c. April 1945, IBM Papers.

Chapter 15

1. IBM to KCB, Dec. 15, 1943, IBM Papers.

2. *Ibid.*

3. IBM diary fragment, March 12, 1946, IBM Papers.

4. IBM to KCB, Feb 29, 1944, IBM Papers.

5. *Ibid.*, March 3, 1944.

6. IBM to PBM, March 23, 1944, IBM Papers.

7. PBM diary, April 9, 1944, IBM Papers.

8. *Ibid.*, April 3, 1944.

9. KCB to IBM, Dec. 5 and 9, 1943; Tina Skeer to KCB, Nov. 19, 1942 and Jan. 18, 1943, IBM Papers; Book Notes, *Herald Tribune*, Jan. [18], 1943.

10. PBM diary, March 11, 18, and 19, 1944, IBM Papers.

11. Research Paper, PBM, Nov. 11, 1945; IBM to KCB and LJB, Dec. 1 [1945], IBM Papers.

12. IBM to KCB and LJB, Dec. 1, 1945, IBM Papers.

13. PBM to IBM, and PBM to KCB, Oct. 27 and Nov. 25, 1945; and IBM to KCB, Dec. 1, 1945; PBM to LJB, May 29, 1946, IBM Papers; interview with PBM, March 27, 1989.

14. Interview with EMD, July 16, 1988; CGM to John Nason, Dec 23, 1946, IBM Papers.

15. IAM to IBM, March 30 and April 3, 1944, Jan. and April 25, [1945,] IBM Papers; interview with Richard Cordray, April 19, 1989.

16. Howard Pennell to CGM and IBM, July 22, 1945, IBM Papers; interview with Alice Pennell Allen, April 26, 1989.

17. Résumé, John W. Secord, IBM Papers.

18. IBM to John Secord, April 18, [1948,] IBM Papers.

19. Interview with Jane Gemmill, May 10, 1988.

20. IAM to IBM, Sept. 22, 1948, IBM Papers.

21. IBM to PBM, Oct. 22, 1949, IBM Papers.

22. Divorce decree, IAM from JWS, Nov. 15, 1949, Clark County, Nevada.

23. Interview with PBM, May 21, 1989; interview with Carl Bereiter, May 4, 1989.

24. Thirtieth Reunion booklet of the class of 1919, Swarthmore College, June 4, 1949, p. 4.

25. *Ibid.*

26. CGM to John W. Bodine, Sept. 12, 1950, IBM Papers.

27. IBM to Carl Jung, June 8, 1950, ETH-Bibliothek, Zurich.

28. "Secretary" to IBM, June 15, 1950, ETH-Bibliothek, Zurich.

29. C. G. Jung to IBM, July 1, 1950, IBM Papers.

30. IAM, Diary, June 9–Oct. 8, 1950, IBM Papers.

31. Interview with JAH, June 1988.

Chapter 16

1. Interview with JAH, June 14, 1988.

2. *Ibid.*

3. *Ibid.*

4. *Ibid.*

5. *Ibid.*

6. The six universities were Michigan State, University of Michigan, South Dakota School of Mines, George Washington, Georgetown, and Columbia.

7. "Lyman Briggs College," a brochure, Michigan State University, 1968–1969. IBM and Chief visited the college shortly after its creation in 1967 after LJB's death but while KCB was still living (CGM to Julia Young Murray, IBM Papers).

8. IBM to LJB, May 6, 1954, IBM Papers.

9. CGM to LJB, May 6, 1954, IBM Papers.

10. An early finding showed that among medical doctors, introverted intuitives (INs) occurred six times more frequently than in the general population, and extroverted, sensing, feeling types (ESFs) were much less frequent among physicians than in the general population (4.4% to 39%), IBM to GWSM dean's office, June 24, 1949; IBM to Leland Parr, c. Sept. 3, 1950, IBM Papers.

11. The five were University of Pennsylvania, Women's Medical, Jefferson, New York University, and New York Medical College, IBM to L. Hanlon, Sept. 14, 1950, IBM Papers.

12. IBM to JMS, Sept. 4 (fragment), and JMS to IBM, Sept. 5, 1950, IBM Papers.

13. IBM to Dr. [Henry Walter] Brosin, Aug. 29, 1951, IBM Papers.

14. JMS to IBM, Sept. 12, 1951, IBM Papers. The schools were Buffalo, Cincinnati, Cornell, George Washington, University of Pennsylvania, Jefferson, Women's Medical, New York Medical, New York University, Ohio State, Pittsburgh, Rochester, Temple, Western Reserve, and Yale.

15. IBM to KCB [Nov. 6, 1951]; IBM to Lisa McGaw, Nov. 6, 1951, IBM Papers.

16. IBM to Lisa McGaw, Nov. 6, 1951, IBM Papers.

17. JMS to IBM, Nov. 12, 21, and 26, 1951, IBM Papers.

18. IBM to Baldwin L. Keyes, c. Sept. 26, 1950, IBM Papers.

19. IBM denoted these gradations as Levels I, II, III, and IV. Level II extended the interpretation of the four letters of type to be more intensely focused on the respondent in his or her own real-life situation and called for highly individualized feedback. Level III interpretations required a kind of scoring in which responses to items were rearranged to show "clusters" that could then receive a more detailed interpretation. These clusters identified three personality characteristics that IBM referred to as sufficiency indices (later termed *comfort scales*): stamina, conscious strain, and unconscious strain, all recognizable factors in the success or failure in a profession such as medicine. Level IV uses the Indicator as a predictor.

20. The women were Olive J. Morgan, Ph. D., Director of the Psychological Clinic, Jefferson Medical College, and Jane Kessler, instructor in psychiatry, Western Reserve School of Medicine. Olive Morgan to IBM, Sept. 25, 1950; Normand L. Hoerr to IBM, Oct. 12, 1951, IBM Papers.

21. IBM to Baldwin L. Keyes [after Sept. 25, 1950]; Olive J. Morgan to IBM, Sept. 25, 1950, IBM Papers.

22. Lisa McGaw to IBM, Sept. 9, 10, and 29, and IBM to Lisa McGaw [mid-Sept.], fragments, 1946, IBM Papers.

23. IBM to Lisa McGaw, Sept. 1, 1947; undated draft of letter, IBM to DWM, attached to above, IBM Papers.

24. IBM to Lisa McGaw, typed fragment [Sept. 1946]; Lisa McGaw to PBM, Sept. 3, 1946, IBM Papers.

25. Draft of typed letter, IBM to Lisa McGaw, with emendations in pencil by CGM, Nov. [10], 1947.

26. IBM to Lisa McGaw, Oct. 25, 1947, IBM Papers.

27. *Ibid.*, Sept. 27, 1960.

28. *Ibid.* McGaw kept thinking that the research possibilities IBM had originally proposed would develop, but "they never did." With McGaw in NYC, IBM would "call at any odd hour to ask for something almost immediately." Even though IBM was always courteous, McGaw began to feel "like a scoring machine." The relationship that had lasted well over a decade did not end on an entirely sanguine note (interview with Lisa McGaw, Nov. 27, 1988).

29. Trip Report, visit of HC and DRS to New York State Department of Education, Feb. 2, 1956, Folder 697, Frame 00299, HC Papers; DRS to IBM, March 23, 1956, IBM Papers; interview with DRS, Aug. 28, 1987.

Chapter 17

1. DRS to IBM, March 23, 1956, IBM Papers; Trip Report, Feb. 3, 1956, Folder 697, Frame 00299, HC Papers.

2. Interview with DRS, Aug. 28 and 29, 1987.

3. *Annual Report,* 1949–1950, p. 23, ETS Archives.

4. *Ibid.,* 1956–1957, p. 18.

5. HC Diary, Nov. 7, 1955, Folder 1073, Frame 00671, HC Papers.

6. Draft agreements, April 4, June 13, 20, and 25, and July 11, 1957, WWT Papers, ETS Archives, and DRS Personal Papers.

7. Draft agreement between ETS and IBM, July 11, 1957, WWT Papers.

8. Interview with DRS, Aug. 25 and 26, 1987; IBM to Evelyn Brehm, May 13, 1958, IBM Papers, University of Florida Archives.

9. Interview with DRS, Aug. 28 and 29, 1987.

10. Agreement between ETS and IBM and KCB, Feb. 3, 1959, IBM Papers.

11. Richard Cordray to HC, Aug. 5, 1959, Folder 642, Frame 02040, HC Papers.

12. Interview with Richard Cordray, Oct. 18, 1988.

13. IBM to HC, April 20, 1959, Folder 641, Frame 01846; HC to Richard Cordray, and HC to John Dobbin, May 1, 1959, Folder 642, Frame 020-23, HC Papers.

14. Interview with DRS, Aug. 25, 1987.

15. John Dobbin to HC, May 19, 1959, Folder 642, Frames 02029–02032, HC Papers.

16. As early as 1954, the Research Policy Committee had concluded that ETS should be willing to "consider preparing, distributing, and publicizing experimental tests submitted by others," but action was not taken until the Indicator needed a home (history of TOST, TOST Records, ETS Archives).

17. RM–60–02; John Ross to HC, July 7, 1960, Folder 643, Frame 00128, HC Papers.

18. HC to WWT, Oct. 18, 1960, Folder 641, Frame 01858, HC Papers.

19. (1) mention in *ETS Developments* (a quarterly publication that was distributed to the public); (2) comprehensive display of materials at the ETS main campus in Princeton; (3) entry in the Cooperative Test Division catalog; (4) copies to reviewers *(Mental Measurements Year Book, Annual Review of Psychiatry and Neurology,* etc.); (5) complimentary specimen sets to past users; and (6) letter and description to members of appropriate APA divisions (about 8,000 psychologists), LJS to HC, March 8, 1961, Folder 642, Frames 02139–02142, HC Papers.

20. Scarvia Anderson notes on LJS and John Ross's Draft Research Bulletin on the MBTI, 1962, WWT Papers.

21. HC memo, June 26, 1961, Folder 641, Frame 01906, HC Papers.

22. IBM to LJS, May 4, 1061, Folder 641, Frames 01900–01901, HC Papers; carbon, fragment, c. 1961, IBM Papers.

23. IBM to WWT, Jan. 6, 1962, WWT Papers.

24. HC memo, June 1, 1961, Folder 641, Frame 01902, HC Papers.

25. ETS RB–62–06; interview with Fred Kling, Oct. 7, and with JAD, Oct. 29, 1987. Two articles on the MBTI by Stricker and Ross (1964) were "Some Correlates of a Jungian Personality Inventory," *Psychological Reports, 14,* 623–643 and "An Assessment of Some Properties of the Jungian Personality Typology," *Journal of Abnormal and Social Psychology, 68,* No. 1, 62–71.

26. Interview with Fred Kling, Oct. 7, 1987.

27. HC Memo, May 3, 1961, Folder 641, Frame 01897, HC Papers.

28. Interview with JAD, Oct. 29, 1987.

29. Interview with DRS, Aug. 28, 1987.

30. *Ibid.,* Oct. 7, 1987.

31. JAD to John K. Hemphill, Dec. 17, 1962, WWT Papers.

32. John K. Hemphill to WWT, Dec. 17, 1962, and WWT notes thereon, WWT Papers.

33. JAD to HC, May 22, 1964, Folder 641, Frame 01986, HC Papers.

34. Monograph II, Aug. 1977, CAPT Library.

35. RM–64–15, ETS Archives.

36. IBM on tape, Feb. 18, 1979, IBM Papers.

37. MBTI order form, ETS Archives.

38. Telephone interview with JAD, March 17, 1988. Anna Dragositz, Director Evaluation and Advisory Service during the early years of the contract with IBM, has confirmed that "practically nothing was done to effect the distribution of the Indicator" (telephone interview with Anna Dragositz, Nov. 18, 1987). From 1962 through 1970, the MBTI did appear in the ETS *Publications List* under the heading of "Special Research Instruments" (microfiche records 447& 447.1, ETS Archives). The records of TOST note for fiscal year 1962–63, "a great burst of activity [with regard to the MBTI]; large mailing to APA list." A year later, TOST records show "considerable demand for the MBTI" (history of TOST, ETS Archives).

39. Gary Saretzky to author, May 29, 1990; Takeshi Ohsawa to author, May 17, 1990.

40. Ohsawa to IBM, Aug. 6, 1968, Sept. 5, 1969, and Dec. 13, 1977; IBM to Ohsawa, Feb. 5, 1969, and Agreement with Nippon Recruitment Center, Aug. 17, 1968, IBM Papers; Takeshi Ohsawa to author, Dec. 14, 1989. Ohsawa is currently president of the Human Resource Research Institute, Inc., Tokyo.

41. Eleanor Barberousse to author, June 23, 1989.

42. Barberousse and Harold Grant to author, June 23, 1989 and Jan. 16, 1990.

43. In 1969, Grant returned to Auburn, and in 1982, he became director of the Missionary Cenacle Volunteers at the Blessed Trinity Shrine Retreat, Holy Trinity, AL. For the past fifteen years, in additional to teaching courses on typology and spirituality, he has focused on what can be gained "from both theology and psychology." He coauthored a related book, *From Image to Likeness,* published in 1983 by Paulist Press, Ramsey, NJ (H. Grant to author, Jan. 16, 1990).

44. Interview with Cecil Williams, May 26, 1990.

Chapter 18

1. *Washington Evening Star,* March 27, 1963.

2. LJB's ashes were placed in niche 35, west wall, in the Cedar Hill Mausoleum, Prince George Co., Md., on April 6, 1963.

3. CGM to John and Betty Cook, Oct. 21, 1966, IBM Papers.

4. *Ibid.;* EMD to author, May 20, 1990; IBM to KCB, May 20, 1966, IBM Papers.

5. Interview with PBM, Oct. 4, 1987. Parcie Myers died in 1969 at age 83.

6. Eleanor Atkinson Smith, "A Memoir"; Phyllis Komori Sellers to IBM, May 14, 1974, IBM Papers.

7. Gurren, Louise, and Ann Hughes, *The Journal of Educational Research,* Vol. 58, No. 8, April, 1965.

8. Blouke Carus, "A Short History of the Development of the Open Court Reading & Language Arts Pedagogy," Oct. 1981; editorial, *Open Court Newsletter*, Oct. 1972.

9. Interview with Carl Bereiter, May 4, 1989.

10. Open Court Materials, Drafts and Notes, and IBM and AMH, Open Court Materials and Correspondence, 1969; Sherwood Sugden to IBM, Sept. 3, 1969, IBM Papers; Kathy Hughes to author, [July 27] 1990; Blouke Carus to author, Sept. 7, 1988.

11. Interview with JAH, June 14, 1988.

12. *Ibid.*, July 22, 1990.

13. CGM to AMH, April 24, 1970, IBM Papers.

14. CGM, typed memo, "Re Peter and Betty," Nov. 18, 1971, IBM Papers; interview with Douglas Hughes, July 27, 1988.

15. CGM, Diary, 1973, PBM Personal Papers; CGM to Ruth Lindsay, Sept. 14, 1972; Peter Hilton to IBM, Sept. 6, 1972, IBM Papers.

16. CGM to Ruth Lindsay, Sept. 14, 1972, IBM Papers; diary of CGM, 1973, PBM Personal Papers.

17. Interview with Carl Bereiter, May 4, 1989.

18. JAH to author, Aug. 3, 1990.

19. Kathy Hughes to author, [July 27,] 1990.

20. *Ibid.*

21. Interviews with Jane Gemmill, May 10, 1987, and Mary McCaulley, April 26, 1988.

22. Interviews with Jane Gemmill and Douglas Hughes, May 10 and July 27, 1988.

23. Interview with JAH, June 14, 1988.

24. IBM, "Ask and It Shall Be Given You. A Credo for Living," 3 typed pp, c. 1959, IBM Papers.

25. MHM notes on a visit to IBM in Swarthmore, July 20 and 21, 1977, MHM Papers; AMH to IBM, May 16 and 20, 1956; Parcie Myers to IBM, May 22, 1956, IBM Papers. David Saunders recalls seeing IBM with her arm in a sling, although he cannot associate this with her first visit to ETS. He does recall that she down-played the bandages, saying, "it was only a biopsy." Chief probably drove her to Princeton. Interview with DRS, Aug. 25 and 26, 1987.

26. Harold A. Wilkinson, M.D., to author, May 29, 1990; IBM to EMD, Nov. 13, 1972, IBM Papers.

27. EMD to IBM and CGM, Sept. 13, 1972, IBM Papers.

28. CGM to EMD, Feb. 23 and June 22, 1972; CGM to PBM, Nov. 5 and 18, 1972; PBM to CGM, Oct. 9, 1972, IBM Papers.

29. IBM to EMD, Oct. 22, 1972; CGM to Ruth Lindsay, July 1, 1973, IBM Papers.

30. IBM to EMD, Oct. 22, 1972; CGM to Agatha and Maurice Pocock, Feb. 2, 1973; IBM to Admissions Office, University of Pennsylvania Law

School, Feb. 19, 1973; CGM to Alastair and Adrienne Geddes, May 18, 1973, IBM Papers. Married in 1981 to an old friend, John Devlin, Betty is a law librarian at Villanova and continues to live in Swarthmore.

31. Interview with Jennifer Myers, July 16, 1988.

32. Interview with MHM, April 26, 1988. The unfinished manuscript was published by Consulting Psychologists Press in 1980 as *Gifts Differing*.

33. Interview with MHM, April 26, 1988.

34. CGM to AMH, Feb. 7, 1970, IBM Papers; MHM notes on visit to IBM in Swarthmore, July 20 and 21, 1977, MHM Papers; taped interview with MHM, April 26, 1988.

Chapter 19

1. IBM to MHM, Jan. 31, 1971, MHM Papers; interview with PBM, Oct. 4, 1987.

2. IBM to MHM, April 18, 1971 and April 23, 1972; MHM to Winton Manning, May 9 and Winton Manning to MHM, Sept. 27, 1972, MHM Papers; IBM to Winton Manning, Feb. 2, 1972, IBM Papers.

3. Interview with Winton Maning, May 19, 1988.

4. Winton Manning to MHM, Sept. 27, 1972, CAPT Archives.

5. The two were Miriam Bryan, head of TOST in the Atlanta office, and John Dobbin, acting head of the Atlanta office from March to September, 1973, who, under MHM's influence, had become an advocate of the MBTI. See F. Saunders, "Isabel Myers and Educational Testing Service: The Lost Frontier?" unpublished manuscript, ETS Archives. The decision to terminate TOST was made by consensus among pertinent ETS staff, with executive vice-president Robert Solomon issuing the actual order (Robert Solomon to author, April 1, 1989).

6. Interview with PBM, Oct. 4, 1987.

7. Interview with HC, Sept. 20, 1987, and telephone interview, May 18, 1988.

8. Interview with DRS, Aug. 25 and 26, 1987.

9. Telephone conversation with MHM, Jan. 14, 1988.

10. John Ross to author, Oct. 13, 1987.

11. Interview with JAD, Oct. 29, 1987.

12. Interview with DRS, Aug. 25 and 26 and Oct. 8, 1987; interview with PBM, Oct. 4, 1987; IBM to MHM, April 18, 1971, MHM Papers.

13. Interview with HC, Sept. 20, 1987.

14. Interviews with Lois Crooks, JAD, Anna Dragositz, and Rae Carlson, Oct. 23 and 29, and Nov. 18, 1987 and May 31, 1988; Scarvia Anderson to author, June 10, 1988.

15. Reprinted in 1983, the monograph is available at CAPT.

16. IBM to MHM, Jan. 30 and July 4, 1970, MHM Papers.

17. *Ibid.*, July 4, 1970.

18. CGM to EMD, Feb. 23, 1972, IBM Papers.

19. IBM to MHM, July 25, 1970, MHM Papers.

20. Brochure, "Information About the University of Florida Typology Laboratory," typed manuscript, c. 1974, CAPT Archives.

21. IBM to MHM, Jan 3, May 19, 1971, and Jan. 11, 1974; MHM to IBM, Feb. 14, May 17, and Nov. 27, 1971, and Feb. 8, 1974, MHM Papers.

22. Brochure, "Information About the University of Florida Typology Laboratory" [1974], CAPT Archives.

23. The first significant grant came from the Department of Health, Education, and Welfare through an application made by the American Medical Students Association (AMSA). In the early years CAPT was established as a field office of the nonprofit AMSA Foundation. This grant enabled IBM and MHM to prepare the monograph on the medical study (interview with MHM, May 3, 1990).

24. The first MBTI conference was held at Gainesville, the second at Michigan State University (1977), the third in Philadelphia (1979).

25. Janie Sweet to IBM, Jan. 10, 1978, IBM Papers. Telephone interview with MHM, May 3, 1990; telephone interview with KDM, May 26, 1990.

26. Telephone interview with MHM, May 7, 1990; MHM to IBM, Aug. 10, 23, Sept. 3, and Nov. 2, 1975; Jan. 13, and MHM, telephone notes, Oct. 2, 1977; June 15, Nov. 14, and Dec. 23, and MHM memo, July 27, 1978; Feb. 6, 1979 and Jan. 2, 1980; MHM to KDM and PBM, July 27, 1978, MHM Papers.

27. For a comprehensive study of the quantity of IBM's correspondence, see IBM Papers, University of Florida Archives.

28. MHM telephone notes on call from IBM, Feb. 6, 1979, MHM Papers. IBM had thoughts about supporting CAPT, but "the family" was "neither willing nor able to support it (IBM notes on "CAPT" [Oct. 1971], IBM Papers).

29. IBM to MHM, March 22, 1972, MHM Papers.

30. CGM to Albert and Margaret Cook, Aug. 28, 1980, IBM Papers; IBM to MHM, MHM Papers.

31 Quote typed in red on fragment, n.d., IBM Papers.

32. MHM to Miriam Bryan, April 21, 1974, MHM Papers.

33. MHM notes on a telephone conversation with IBM, April 21, 1975; MHM to IBM, April 21 and May 22, 1974; MHM to Roger T. Lennon, June 10, 1974 and March 25, 1975; MHM to John Dobbin, Oct. 16 and Nov. 19, 1974, MHM Papers.

34. McCaulley sent off an indignant letter to Lennon that said, in part: "While I continue to have sincere personal regard for you...I must admit this experience has caused me to lose a great deal of confidence I formerly had for Psychological Corporation. Whether you were unwilling to take steps needed to acquire information for your decision, or were unwilling to make the decision, or were unwilling to communicate a decision—any or all of these strike me as very poor business. Leaving professional colleagues

without vitally needed answers, even after deadlines were promised, seems to me to be unprofessional. MHM to Roger T. Lennon, Nov. 10, 1975, MHM Papers.

The Psychological Corporation has been unable to find any "relevant material" in their records with regard to IBM and the MBTI (John Dilworth to author, March 7, 1990).

Chapter 20
1. Telephone interview with MHM, May 11, 1990.
2. JDB to IBM, July 25, 1975, CPP Archives.
3. IBM to JDB, July 29, 1975, CPP Archives.
4. Telephone interview with Richard Cordray, Oct. 22, 1988.
5. IBM to JDB, Aug. 12, 1975; copy of *Agreement,* Sept. 5, 1975, IBM Papers.
6. Later Gough became chairman of the Department of Psychology at Berkeley and, in 1973, became IPAR's director.
7. Interview with JDB, Dec. 9, 1987; Harrison Gough to author, Feb. 16, 1990; Wallace Hall to author, Feb. 20, 1990. The CPI, in use as a research instrument at IPAR, had been rejected for publication by both ETS and Psych Corp.
8. Interview with JDB, March 8, 1989. In addition to Black and Gough, on the first board of directors were Louis Levine, San Francisco State College; Robert Jensen, attorney, Douglas Aircraft Co.; Arnold Horowitz, Hearst Enterprises; and DWM, who served as chairman of the Board of Editors.
9. *Ibid.* Alexander Black served in this capacity until his mid-nineties.
10. *Ibid.*
11. CPP catalog, 1958–1959, p. 2.
12. Interview with JDB, March 8, 1989. One of JDB's neighbors, Annette ("Bunny") Brown, became general office manager and retired in 1983.
13. Interview with JDB, March 8, 1989. In July 1990, CPP moved to its present location at 3803 East Bayshore Rd., Palo Alto.
14. JDB to IBM, July 25, 1975, CPP Archives.
15. *Ibid.*, Jan. 14, 1976.
16. Interview with JDB, Dec. 9, 1987.
17. JDB to IBM, Dec. 1, 1975, CPP Archives.
18. *Ibid.*, Oct. 21, 1977.
19. *Ibid.*, Feb. 16, 1977 and Feb. 8, 1978.
20. Interview with JDB, Dec. 9, 1987. IBM knew that MBTI sales had tripled from 1976 to 1979.

Chapter 21
1. CGM to Pococks, Feb. 2, 1973, IBM Papers. The Heisler children were Roland, 22, Hugh, 20, Katie, 18, and Mary Ellen, 12.
2. Telephone interview with KDM, April 9, 1989.

3. Much of the time, the Heislers lived in or near Swarthmore, and, as long as Peter and Betty were in the East, the two couples were friends. Later, the Heisler children visited Peter and Betty in California (interview with EMD, July 16, 1988; telephone interview with KDM, April 9, 1989; CGM to Pococks, Feb. 2, 1973, IBM Papers).

4. Telephone interview with KDM, April 18, 1989.

5. IBM to KDM, Jan. 29, 1973, KDM Personal Papers.

6. KDM to IBM and CGM, Feb. 9, 1973. PBM and KDM were married on Feb. 9, 1973, in California.

7. Telephone interview with KDM, April 18, 1989.

8. CGM to JBM, July 23, 1973, IBM Papers.

9. JBM to CGM, May 25, 1974, IBM Papers.

10. CGM to JBM, June 2, 1974; CGM to PBM, Dec. 3, 1975, IBM Papers.

11. CGM to JAH, Nov. 12, 1970, to Pococks, July 12, 1972, to J. E. Anderson, May 29, 1973, to KDM, Nov. 14, and Mildred Johnson, Dec. 15, 1974, IBM Papers.

12. After fifty years of service, CGM was honored by the Swarthmore Borough Council with an official resolution and an evening of speeches (*The Swarthmorean,* June 20, 1975). This was followed by his flying to Pittsburgh to be honored at the annual meeting of the Pennsylvania Association of Boroughs for "more than forty years of service" (CGM to JBM, Nov. 26, 1975, IBM Papers). When he retired in 1978, the Borough Council honored him with a dinner and citations (*The Swarthmorean,* Jan. 6, 1978).

13. JAH on tape, June 14, 1988.

14. Telephone interview with Jane Gemmill, May 24, 1988.

15. Itinerary, 1971 European trip, May 10, 1971; CGM to Jim and Emily Hughes, May 10, 1971, and to Pococks, Feb. 2, 1973, IBM Papers.

16. Itinerary, IBM and CGM, May 1, 1975, IBM Papers; conversation with KDM, July 7, 1987.

17. Itinerary, IBM and CGM, May 1–June 12, 1975, IBM Papers.

18. Interview with Douglas Hughes, July 27, 1988; interview with PBM, June 4, 1990.

19. Kathy Hughes to author, [July 27,] 1990.

20. *Ibid.*

21. PBM to CGM, Nov. 18, 1977, IBM Papers.

22. Harold A. Wilkinson, M.D., to author, May 29, 1990.

23. Gordon Lawrence to IBM, July 15, 1977, IBM Papers.

24. IBM to Hellen Guttenger, Aug. 3, 1977, IBM Papers. The article, "An Anatomy of an Illness," was reprinted in the June *Reader's Digest* and later appeared in book form under the same title.

25. Carskaden had the idea for such a publication in 1975 after attending the first MBTI conference in Gainesville, FL. He and Marcie Carlyn, of

Michigan State University, compiled and edited the first issue, which appeared in the summer of 1977. In 1984, it became a refereed publication, *The Journal of Psychological Type.*

26. Interview with MHM, April 26, 1988.

27. IBM to John A. Clark, Esq., Jan. 31, 1978, IBM Papers.

28. MHM notes on trip to Swarthmore, July 20 and 21, 1977, MHM Papers; interview with MHM, May 21, 1990.

29. MHM to IBM, Sept. 3, 1977, IBM Papers.

30. MHM, Rae Carlson, Jane Gemmill, and Harold Grant to K. Landis, Aug. 24 and 28, Sept. 5 and 12; Jane Gemmill to Jonathan Rhoads, Eleanor Stabler Clarke, and Boyd T. Bernard, Sept. 5 and 6, 1978; to PBM and KDM, Feb. 13, 1979; K. Landis to Jane Gemmill Sept. 6, 1978 and Jan. 30, 1979, IBM Papers. The four alumni who did receive honorary degrees in June 1979 were Sadie Tanner Mosell Alexander, Stephen Cary, Norman Bruce Hannay, and William Hardy McNeill.

31. Harold A. Wilkinson, M.D., to author, May 29, 1990.

32. IBM to John A. Clark, Esq., Jan. 31, 1978, IBM Papers. Mary McCaulley also helped with suggestions (PBM to MHM, Sept. 1; MHM to IBM, Sept. 8; notes on MHM visit to Swarthmore, July 20 and 21, 1977; MHM notes on a telephone call, Oct. 2, 1977, MHM Papers). KDM and Kathy Hughes also helped to finish *Gifts Differing* (interview with KDM, April 18, 1989).

33. PBM to MHM, Sept. 1, 1977, MHM Papers.

34. IBM to John A. Clarke, Esq., Jan. 31, 1978, IBM Papers.

Chapter 22

1. APT now has over 3,300 members located in all fifty states and seventeen foreign countries.

2. MHM notes on a telephone call to IBM and from PBM, Sept. 28, 1979, MHM Papers.

3. IBM to MHM, Nov. 25, 1979, MHM Papers; Harold Wilkinson, M.D., to author, May 29, 1990.

4. Sally Golden to IBM, Dec. 14, 1979, IBM Papers. The workshop on careers was a postconference event on Sat., Oct. 20 (brochure, "The Third National CAPT-MBTI Conference on the Use of the *Myers-Briggs Type Indicator,* " Oct. 17–20, 1979).

5. Remarks by John D. Black, *MBTI News,* 2:4, July 1980, p. 5.

6. CGM to CAPT, Nov. 13, 1979, IBM Papers. CGM's remarks also appeared in *MBTI News,* 2:4, July 1980; interview with PBM, June 4, 1990.

7. Interview with Sally Golden, May 23, 1990.

8. Quoted in *MBTI News,* 2:4, July 1980, p. 1. Events prior to and during the conference were reconstructed from interviews with Sally and Ed Golden, PBM, KDM, and others, and from the *MBTI News.*

9. CGM to CAPT, Nov. 13, 1979, IBM Papers. Chief, who had not understood that PBM was to drive to Swarthmore on Thursday afternoon and pick up Jane Gemmill and himself for the evening banquet, had to do some rapid, last-minute getting ready.

10. IBM to "anonymous" [fall of 1977], IBM Papers.

11. IBM to MHM, [early 1980], hand printed, 2 pp., MHM Papers.

12. JAH to CGM, July 7, 1978, IBM Papers.

13. MHM to IBM, Nov. 29, 1979, MHM Papers.

14. Kathy Hughes to author, [July 27,] 1990.

15. Interview with DRS, Aug. 26, 1987.

16. MHM notes on a telephone call from PBM, Jan. 31, 1980, MHM Papers.

17. Interview with Janice Strom, Aug. 6, 1990.

18. Interview with Lorin Letendre, July 6, 1990.

19. KDM to JDM, April 26, 1980, CPP files.

20. KDM to Lorin Letendre, May 1, 1980, CPP files.

21. *Ibid.*; interview with PBM, May 21, 1989.

22. IBM chose the title for *Gifts Differing* from Romans 12:6 ("Having gifts that differ according to the grace given to us, let us use them"), the scripture that the family intended to be read. However, the minister mistakenly read the passage from I Corinthians.

23. The last days of IBM were reconstructed from interviews with PBM (May 21, 1989), KDM (April 18, 1989 and May 26, 1990), and Jim Hughes (May 23, 1990). Chief continued to live alone until the summer of 1983 when he was no longer able to cope. PBM then brought him to the Althea Woodland Home, in Silver Springs, MD., where he died on Aug. 11, 1984. Both houses on Dickinson Avenue were subsequently sold.

Chronology

May 7, 1874	Birth of Lyman James Briggs near Battle Creek, Michigan
Jan. 3, 1875	Birth of Katharine Elizabeth Cook in East Lansing, Michigan
March 1888	Katharine Elizabeth Cook enters Michigan Agricultural College
Sept. 1889	Lyman James Briggs enters Michigan Agricultural College
May 1893	Katherine Elizabeth Cook and Lyman James Briggs graduate from Michigan Agricultural College
May 25, 1894	Birth of Clarence Gates Myers in Waterloo, Iowa
Dec. 23, 1896	Lyman James Briggs and Katharine Elizabeth Cook marry in Claremont, California; move to Washington, DC, where he is employed at Department of Agriculture
Oct. 18, 1897	Birth of Isabel McKelvey Briggs
Sept. 23, 1899	Birth of Albert Cook Briggs
July 2, 1901	Death of Albert Cook Briggs
June 11, 1901	Lyman James Briggs receives Ph.D. from Johns Hopkins University
1903	Briggses move to Mt. Pleasant area
April 1909	Briggses move to 3208 Newark Street (Cleveland Park)
Sept. 1913	Clarence Gates Myers enters Swarthmore College on the Swarthmore Western Scholarship
Sept. 1915	Isabel Briggs Myers enters Swarthmore College
Spring 1917	Isabel Briggs Myers and Clarence Gates Myers become engaged
June 1917	Clarence Gates Myers graduates from Swarthmore College, Phi Beta Kappa, then enters University of Pennsylvania Law School

Dec. 7, 1917	Clarence Gates Myers enlists in Army Air Division
June 17, 1918	Clarence Gates Myers and Isabel Briggs marry at her home in Washington, DC
Nov. 11, 1918	Armistice signed; Clarence Gates Myers joins Isabel Briggs Myers in Swarthmore; he reenters law school at University of Pennsylvania
June 1919	Isabel Briggs Myers graduates from Swarthmore College, Phi Beta Kappa, major in political science
Summer 1919	Clarence Gates Myers and Isabel Briggs Myers both on Chautauqua circuit
1919–1920	Clarence Gates Myers and Isabel Briggs Myers in Swarthmore, she, assistant in economics at college; he, teaching assistant at University of Pennyslvania while in 2nd year of law school
Sept. 1920	Clarence Gates Myers and Isabel Briggs Myers move to "little house" on Myrtle Avenue, Morton
June 1921	Clarence Gates Myers finishes law school
Sept. 1921	Clarence Gates Myers obtains first job with Biddle, Paul & Jayne
Spring 1923	Clarence Gates Myers joins law firm of Duane, Morris, and Heckscher in Philadelphia
1923 and 1924	Isabel Briggs Myers loses a boy and a girl infant
August 1924	Clarence Gate Myers and Isabel Briggs Myers purchase house at 321 Dickson Avenue in Swarthmore, Pennsylvania
April 24, 1926	Birth of Peter Briggs Myers
Dec. 29, 1927	Birth of Ann Isabel Myers
Feb. 6, 1929	Isabel Briggs Myers writes a mystery novel, *Murder Yet to Come,* and wins $7500 prize
1931	Isabel writes a play, *Death Calls for Margin*
Dec. 1932	Roosevelt appoints Lyman James Briggs Director of National Bureau of Standards
Spring 1934	Isabel Briggs Myers's second novel, *Give Me Death,* is published
August 1934	Isabel Briggs Myers's second play, *Hostage to Fortune,* produced at Peterborough, New Hampshire, Dramatic Festival
Jan. 1942	Isabel Briggs Myers reads about *Humm-Wadsworth* in Readers' Digest; with advice from Katharine Cook Briggs, begins to develop her own instrument on "type"
1943	Forms A and B of MBTI developed
June 1943	Peter and Ann graduate in same class from Swarthmore High School
1944	Form C of MBTI developed

1943–47	Peter at Worcester Technology in Navy; Ann at Middlebury College
Sept. 1947	Peter enters Oxford as Rhodes scholar
June 1948	Ann graduates from Middlebury, Phi Beta Kappa
June 26, 1948	Ann marries John Secord
July 28, 1948	Peter marries Elizabeth (Betty) Monk
Oct. 1949	Ann divorces Secord in Las Vegas
June 1950	Peter recieves Ph.D. in physics from Oxford
Jan. 17, 1953	Ann and James A. Hughes, Jr., marry in Swarthmore
Summer 1954	Clarence Gates Myers, Isabel Briggs Myers, Ann and Jim in Europe
May 26, 1955	Birth of Jonathan Briggs Myers (Morristown, New Jersey)
Dec. 31, 1955	Birth of Kathleen Ann Hughes (Houston, Texas)
May 1956	Isabel Briggs Myers has malignant growths removed from right arm
April 16, 1958	Birth of Douglas James Hughes (Wilmington, Delaware)
1958	Form F of MBTI developed under auspices of Educational Testing Service (ETS)
July 1959	Isabel Briggs Myers signs contract with ETS to publish MBTI
Nov. 3, 1962	Birth of Jennifer Myers; adoped by Peter and Betty
March 26, 1963	Death of Lyman James Briggs
Summer 1963	Isabel Briggs Myers moves Katharine Cook Briggs next door a 317 Dickinson Avenue, Swarthmore
July 10, 1968	Death of Katharine Cook Briggs
Late 1969	Isabel Briggs Myers meets Mary McCaulley in Philadelphia
April 22, 1970	Jim and Ann announce break-up of their marriage; Ann gets Florida divorce, August 6, 1970
1970	Recurrence of cancer on Isabel Briggs Myers' right arm
Fall 1971	Peter and Betty announce break-up of their marriage and pending divorce
August 24, 1972	Death of Ann Myers Hughes in Boston
Nov. 1972	Malignancy again appears on Isabel Briggs Myers' right arm
Feb. 9, 1973	Peter and Katharine Downing Heisler married in California
Sept. 1975	Isabel Briggs Myers signs contract with Consulting Psychologists Press (CPP), Palo Alto, California, to publish MBTI
Oct. 1975	First national MBTI Conference, Gainsville, Florida; Isabel Briggs Myers keynote speaker
Dec. 31, 1975	Isabel Briggs Myers' contract with Eucational Training Service is terminated

July 1977	Isabel Briggs Myers has exploratory abdominal surgey that reveals cancer of the liver
Fall 1977	Second national MBTI Conference in Lansing, Michigan; Isabel Briggs Myers unable to attend
1978	Form G developed at Consulting Psychologists Press
Feb. 15, 1979	Peter begins employment with National Academy of Science, Washington, DC
Oct. 18, 1979	Celebration of Isabel Briggs Myers' 82nd birthday in Philadelphia at third national MBTI conference; Association for Psychological Type organized
May 5, 1980	Death of Isabel Briggs Myers
August 11, 1984	Death of Clarence Gates Myers

Index